California Studies in Classical Antiquity

Volume 1

CALIFORNIA STUDIES
IN
CLASSICAL ANTIQUITY

Volume 1

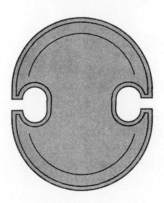

UNIVERSITY OF CALIFORNIA PRESS
BERKELEY AND LOS ANGELES
1968

CALIFORNIA STUDIES IN CLASSICAL ANTIQUITY
Senior Editors: Truesdell S. Brown, W. Kendrick Pritchett
Advisory Board: Darrell A. Amyx, Philip Levine, Thomas G. Rosenmeyer

VOLUME 1

Library of Congress Catalog Card Number: 68–26906

University of California Press
Berkeley and Los Angeles
California

Cambridge University Press
London, England

Printed in Great Britain

Prefatory Note

California Studies in Classical Antiquity will be published annually, or approximately so, and will present papers in Greek and Latin philology, literature, history, and philosophy; in classical archaeology and ancient art; in Greek or Roman science and technology; and in related fields, such as comparative literature, when there is some relation to classical antiquity. Papers will be contributed chiefly by faculty members and graduate students on the various campuses of the University of California, by visiting professors, and, on occasional invitation, by other scholars.

Truesdell S. Brown
W. Kendrick Pritchett
Editors

Darrell A. Amyx
Philip Levine
Thomas G. Rosenmeyer
Associate Editors

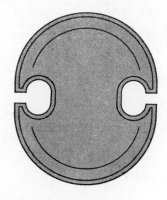

Contents

viii   Contents

THOMAS W. AFRICA

Cleomenes III and the Helots

There are few episodes in Greek history as significant as the Hellenistic revival of Sparta as a major power under the "Lycurgan restoration" of the revolutionary king, Cleomenes III. According to Rostovtzeff, "had it not been for the concessions made by Aratus to Antigonus and for the unwillingness of Cleomenes to carry out the full program of his supporters, a social revolution on a large scale, perhaps throughout Greece, might have been the result of the reforms of Agis and Cleomenes, which they themselves regarded as rather political than economic and social."[1]

In the last few years, valuable studies of Hellenistic Sparta have been made by the Israeli scholar, Binyamin Shimron of Tel Aviv University, and all students of the period are indebted to his work. Recently, Professor Shimron has suggested some "modifications" in the remarks made by Emilio Gabba and myself in our respective books on Phylarchus.[2] In particular, Shimron has questioned my assertion that Cleomenes enfranchised 2,000 ex-helots,[3] because "there is no foundation for this statement in the sources."[4]

It is true that the sources do not specifically make such a statement, but I believe that a case can be made for my contention. The

[1] M. Rostovtzeff, *Social and Economic History of the Hellenistic World* (Oxford: Clarendon Press 1941) I, 209.

[2] B. Shimron, "Some Remarks on Phylarchus and Cleomenes III," *RivFC* 94 (1966) 452–459. Gabba's views on Phylarchus are well presented in *Studi su Filarco* (Pavia 1957), reprinted from *Athenaeum* 35.

[3] T. W. Africa, *Phylarchus and the Spartan Revolution* (Berkeley 1961) 15, 26.

[4] Shimron (supra, n. 2) 458.

ultimate source for Cleomenes' career and policies is "the trustworthy
narrative of Phylarchus,"[5] who was a contemporary partisan of the
Spartan king, but unfortunately his histories have been lost. Polybius
alludes to Cleomenes' redivision of land and his "subversion" of the
patrios politeia,[6] but, as Shimron observes, "the reforms in themselves
were objectionable to him, and . . ., therefore, he ignored the social
aspects of Cleomenes' activities, concerning himself with his military
career only."[7] Pausanias, who was a collector of hostile Achaean calum-
nies,[8] says nothing of Cleomenes' social policies. Trogus Pompeius (via
Justin) preserves some material which is discussed below, but this is only a
brief passage in a digest of a digest.

Happily, the Phylarchan account has been preserved in
part by Plutarch in his lives of Agis, Cleomenes, and Aratus, but Plutarch, alas, was not a careful writer, nor was he concerned with details
of interest to modern historians.[9] The pious Boeotian priest wrote, not
histories or even biographies, but "eidological" studies of famous men,
and he often omitted data which he felt did not reflect the character of his
subject, or perhaps which he had forgotten.[10] Part of the program of the
Spartan reformers was the abolition of debts, and Plutarch vividly
recounted the holocaust of mortgages during the brief reign of Agis IV.[11]

5 Rostovtzeff (supra, n. 1) I 208.

6 Polybius 4.81.2, 14. cf. 2.47.3.

7 B. Shimron, "Polybius and the Reforms of Cleomenes III," *Historia* 13
(1964) 148. Shimron's contention that Polybius considered Cleomenes' reforms a return to the
patrios politeia (pp. 147–155) has been criticized by F. W. Walbank, "The Spartan Ancestral
Constitution in Polybius," in *Ancient Society and Institutions*, Festschrift for V. Ehrenberg
(Oxford: Blackwell, 1966) 303–312.

8 Pausanias 2.9.1 claims that Cleomenes was a wicked stepfather who
poisoned Agis' son, Eurydamidas. Yet, Cleomenes was deeply in love with the boy's mother,
Agiatis—Plutarch *Cleomenes* 1.2; 22.1.

9 Plutarch *Timoleon* 1.1–3; *Solon* 27.1; *Cimon* 2.5; *Alexander* 1; *Galba* 2.3.

10 In the life of Flamininus, Plutarch omits the Roman's complicity in
the murder of Brachylles (Polybius 18.43.10). In the life of Brutus, he omits the affair of
Brutus' financial agents at Cyprian Salamis (Cicero *ad Att.* 5.21). In the life of Coriolanus,
Plutarch ignores Fabius Pictor's version of Coriolanus' non-heroic death in exile (Livy
2.40.10). In the life of Pericles, he omits the ignominious Egyptian expedition (Thucydides
1.104, 110. Diodorus Siculus 11.71.5–6; 74.3–4; 75.4; 77.2–5), but perhaps his sources were
silent on Pericles' involvement in the fiasco (A. W. Gomme, *A Historical Commentary on Thucydides* (Oxford: Clarendon Press, 1956) I 306–307). As for Plutarch's many distortions of fact,
one glaring example may suffice—he represents Caesar's reduction of the recipients of the
grain dole at Rome from 320,000 to 150,000 as a census illustrating the great loss of life in the
civil war (*Caesar* 55.2, cf. Suetonius *Caesar* 41.3).

11 Plutarch *Agis* 13.3.

Cleomenes, too, intended to abolish debts,[12] but Plutarch does not record that he fulfilled his promise. Yet, modern historians agree that the king did abolish debts,[13] because, as Shimron says, "the abolition of debts by Cleomenes, not expressly recorded, can be deduced from *Cleomenes* 16.5 and 18.2."[14] These references are demonstrably Phylarchan passages,[15] and, though they might only refer to slogans and not deeds, I concur that Cleomenes probably abolished debts. Since Plutarch omits such a crucial detail, perhaps the enfranchisement of the ex-helots also escaped his notice.[16]

In 223 B.C., the Spartan revolution was in peril. Antigonus Doson had joined the Achaean League's war against Cleomenes an broken the Spartan hold on the Peloponnesus. Antigonus and the Achaeans had recovered Corinth and Argos, and they sacked the city of Mantineia and enslaved its inhabitants for having supported Sparta. To oppose Antigonus and his allies, Cleomenes had 4,000 citizen soldiers—most of whom were former *perioikoi* who had been enfranchised in the revolution of 227,[17] at least 5,000 mercenaries,[18] and an unspecified number of non-citizen Laconians. To supply his troops and pay the mercenaries was a severe strain on the limited financial resources of Cleomenes, who was always short of money.[19] For additional funds, the Spartan king relied on the subsidies of Ptolemy III, Euergetes, to whom he had even given his own mother and children as hostages.[20] However, the Egyptian king was niggardly and had paid Aratus only six talents a year when the Achaean League had been his pawn against Macedon;[21] it is unlikely that Cleomenes received much more from the parsimonious monarch.

[12] Plutarch *Cleomenes* 10.6.

[13] Rostovtzeff (supra, n. 1) III 1368, n. 34. W. W. Tarn, *CAH* VII 754. F. W. Walbank, *Aratos of Sicyon* (Cambridge: Cambridge University Press, 1933) 86; *A Historical Commentary on Polybius* (Oxford: Clarendon Press, 1957) I 245.

[14] B. Shimron, "The Spartan Polity after the Defeat of Cleomenes III," *CQ* 14 (1964) 232, n. 3.

[15] For a comment on Plutarch *Cleomenes* 16, see Africa (supra, n. 3) 28.

[16] Plutarch was so careless that in *Comparison between Agis and Cleomenes and the Gracchi* 5.1, he states that Cleomenes "freed *all* the slaves," which contradicts his own narrative. Such contradictions are common in his writings.

[17] Plutarch *Cleomenes* 11.2.

[18] Polybius 2.69.3.

[19] Plutarch *Cleomenes* 27.2. See the ironic comments of Robert von Pöhlmann, *Geschichte der Sozialen Frage und des Sozialismus in der Antiken Welt* (Munich: Beck'sche, Ed. 3, 1925) I 390–391.

[20] Plutarch *Cleomenes* 22.3.

[21] Plutarch *Aratus* 41.3. Cleomenes offered to pay Aratus double the sum.

To make matters worse, Cleomenes knew that Antigonus' envoys were in Alexandria, trying to persuade Ptolemy to cease supporting Sparta.[22] Always resourceful, Cleomenes raised 500 talents by selling freedom to 6,000 helots who could each pay five minae for their liberty.[23] Some scholars have doubted that a helot could amass such a sum,[24] and K. M. T. Chrimes is sure that the favored helots must have been *neodamodeis*, who received freedom and land in return for military service.[25] However, Plutarch says "Helots" not *neodamodeis*, and H. Michell has observed: "This figure [5 minae] should be accepted with reserve, although there does not seem to be any particular reason for rejecting it. . . . At a time when the old political and economic system of the Spartans was in decay, it is quite likely that many helots had enriched themselves at the expense of their impoverished masters."[26] For generations, the economic base of the Lycurgan polity had been in shambles,[27] and it would be absurd to assume that all helots were still the plodding paupers whom Tyrtaeus had seen centuries before in conquered Messenia.[28] If (as Phylarchus says through Plutarch) some Spartans flinched at the mere mention of Lycurgus in the time of Agis,[29] many helots must have managed to make a profitable living on the *kleroi* of their masters. To free helots to serve the state in a military capacity was no novelty at Lacedaemon,[30] but the Hellenistic opportunist, Cleomenes III, was the first Spartan king to put a price on liberty.

Not only did Cleomenes raise money by emancipating 6,000 helots, but he strengthened his phalanx by enrolling 2,000 of them as hoplites and arming them "in the Macedonian manner,"[31] that is, with the *sarissa*, helmet, sword, shield, breastplate, and greaves.[32] Such equipment was reserved for the Spartan citizen hoplites,[33] whose number 4,000, was now augmented by 2,000. Thus, I believe, Cleomenes ex-

[22] Plutarch *Cleomenes* 22.7.

[23] Plutarch *Cleomenes* 23.1.

[24] Walbank (supra, n. 13) *Aratos* 108, n. 1. Tarn, *CAH* VII 760.

[25] K. M. T. Chrimes, *Ancient Sparta* (Manchester: Manchester University Press 1949) 40; but elsewhere she calls them citizens. (See infra, n. 34.)

[26] H. Michell, *Sparta* (Cambridge: Cambridge University Press 1952) 78. Cf. Shimron, "Nabis of Sparta and the Helots," *CP* 61 (1966) 7, n. 38.

[27] Plutarch *Agis* 5. Phylarchus in Athenaeus 4.141F–142C (Jacoby, 81 F 44).

[28] Pausanias 4.14.5.

[29] Plutarch *Agis* 6.2.

[30] Michell (supra, n. 26) 251, cites the evidence from 425 to 369 B.C.

[31] Plutarch *Cleomenes* 23.1.

[32] Walbank (supra, n. 13) *Commentary* 275.

[33] Plutarch *Cleomenes* 11.2.

panded the citizenry of Sparta to 6,000 to meet a desperate emergency.[34]

The gear for the new citizens was expensive, and Cleomenes was still in need of money. He tried to acquire more funds by sacking Megalopolis when the inhabitants of that city refused to join him, but, despite Polybius' notorious claim that Phylarchus mentioned 6,000 talents in loot, the Spartan got little booty there.[35] In 222, news came that Antigonus' ambassadors had convinced Ptolemy to stop subsidizing Sparta. Before the mercenaries could learn of his financial straits, Cleomenes sought a decisive engagement with Antigonus and the Achaeans.[36] Within ten days of the ill tidings from Egypt, the battle of Sellasia was fought, but the Spartans were defeated and Cleomenes fled into exile.

According to Plutarch, many of the mercenaries died for Cleomenes at Sellasia, as did "all the Lacedaemonians, six thousand in number, except for two hundred."[37] Admittedly, Greek writers often carelessly described as "Lacedaemonian" a force which included *perioikoi* and even mercenaries as well as Spartan citizens.[38] However, Polybius was quite precise about Cleomenes' contingents at Sellasia: the king commanded the Lacedaemonians and the mercenaries on Olympus, while his brother and colleague, Eucleidas, commanded the *perioikoi* and the allies on Euas.[39] Commenting on this passage, F. W. Walbank states: "The 'Lacedaemonians' are the Spartiate phalanx of 6,000 (Plutarch, *Cleomenes* 28)."[40] One third of the Spartans who died so valiantly for the revolution were ex-helots who had been freed for a price and enfranchised to fight for Cleomenes.

In the aftermath of Sellasia, Cleomenes and a few retainers fled to Egypt, and Antigonus occupied Sparta without much resistance, for the Spartan king had counseled his people to submit to the victor, who had expressly declared war on "the tyrant" Cleomenes and not on Sparta.[41] All the sources agree that Antigonus treated the defeated state

[34] Chrimes (supra, n. 25) 13–14, accepts a citizen body of 6,000, but believes that the original 4,000 had greater privileges.

[35] Plutarch *Cleomenes* 25.1. Polybius 2.55.7, 62–63, on which see Africa (supra, n. 3) 33–34.

[36] Plutarch *Cleomenes* 27.5. Polybius 2.63.1–2.

[37] Plutarch *Cleomenes* 28.5.

[38] At Pallantium before the revolution, Plutarch states that Cleomenes had less than 5,000 "Lacedaemonians" (*Cleomenes* 4.5) which included non-citizen Laconians and mercenaries, such as the Cretans and Tarentines who slew Lydiades at Leuctra (6.3).

[39] Polybius 2.65.9.

[40] Walbank (supra, n. 13) *Commentary* 279.

[41] Justin 28.4.

with moderation and merely "restored the *patrios politeia*."[42] Antigonus was anxious to leave Laconia because Macedon had been invaded by Illyrians, and he was content to restore the ephorate without meddling further in domestic affairs at Lacedaemon.[43]

"Within a few days,"[44] the king departed for Macedon, but he left the Boeotian Brachylles as military governor of the defeated city.[45] The Spartan kingship was left in abeyance, but the victors did not disturb the freeborn citizenry of Cleomenes. As Shimron notes, "in 218 Cheilon tried to rouse the multitude against the ephors . . . by promising *kleroi* and a redistribution of land, but he failed completely, only two hundred men joining him. If the great majority of old and new Spartans had been deprived of their land, there would have been a far greater response to his call, especially as his attempt came after the Cleomenists' reversal of Antigonus' political arrangements."[46] Chrimes believes that the 6,000 ex-helots had been allowed to retain their freedom,[47] but this would require considerable liberalizing of the "Lycurgan" *patrios politeia*. In a passage which has long been recognized as a garbled fragment of Phylarchus, Trogus Pompeius describes the defeated Cleomenes advising 4,000 "survivors of Sellasia" to submit to Antigonus.[48] Since only 200 Spartans had survived the debacle, the 4,000 must mean the families of the Cleomenean citizenry of 227 B.C., and an inference may be made that Antigonus or Brachylles revoked the enfranchisement of the families of the 2,000 ex-helot hoplites. Possibly, the victors returned all the 6,000 former helots to bondage.[49] Surely, the 4,000 Spartans would not have been solicitous over the fate of the 2,000 ex-helots who had fought and died for Sparta. Thucydides reports that in the fifth century, the Spartans callously murdered 2,000 *neodamodeis* who had fought most valiantly for

[42] Polybius 2.70.1. Plutarch *Cleomenes* 30.1. Pausanias 2.9.2.

[43] To anyone except Cleomenes, the *patrios politeia* at Sparta included the ephorate, and ephors are mentioned by Polybius 4.22.5 as active in 220 B.C.

[44] Polybius 2.70.1.

[45] Polybius 20.5.12.

[46] Shimron (supra, n. 14) 236–237. In 219 B.C., Cleomenes' supporters regained control of Sparta (Polybius 4.34.1–35.7), and perhaps they took away the lands of the two hundred disgraced survivors of Sellasia, who might be the disaffected men who rallied to Cheilon.

[47] Chrimes (supra, n. 25) 12.

[48] Justin 28.4. See F. Jacoby, *Kommentar* II-C, p. 141. Cf. Plutarch *Cleomenes* 29.2–3 (Jacoby, 81 F 59), and E. Schwartz, *Fünf Vorträge Über den Griechischen Roman* (Berlin 1896) 114–115.

[49] Compare the policy of Philopoemen in 188 B.C. (Plutarch *Philopoemen* 16.4), which outraged Plutarch's source, the Spartan patriot Aristocrates (16.3–5).

Lacedaemon but who were becoming "uppity."[50] At any rate, Cleomenes had fled the country, and his ex-helots no longer had a royal patron.

There is a probable confirmation of a Cleomenean citizenry of 6,000 in the morass of constitutional fictions surrounding the venerable Lycurgus. It is difficult to share the confidence which some recent authors have placed in the authenticity of "Lycurgan" traditions.[51] Acceptance of the historicity of Lycurgus "the lawgiver" requires faith such as can move mountains. Hellanicus found no place in history for Lycurgus,[52] and even Apollo was not sure whether the Spartan Moses was a god or a man.[53] In all probability, Lycurgus was a religious reformer who at some remote time had abolished human sacrifice at Sparta.[54] When the social structure at Lacedaemon was radically changed to meet the challenge of the Messenian revolt in the seventh century, the authority of the famed reformer of the past was invoked to sanctify the new regime.[55] The Sicilian scholar, Timaeus, realized the essence of the Lycurgan problem when he stated that "there were two Lycurgi at Sparta at different times, and the achievements of both were ascribed to one of them."[56]

Like its Mosaic counterpart, the Lycurgan legislation, which Plutarch reports, was the composite work of many generations and various reformers, who all cast the aura of the deified Lycurgus about their programs. Modern scholars should never forget the grave warning of Plutarch, who had surveyed the vast and contradictory literature on the great lawgiver: "About Lycurgus the lawmaker, there is nothing certain which is beyond dispute, for there are different versions of his birth, his travels, his death, and especially his laws and his polity, and there is even less agreement among historians as to when the man lived."[57] Though Ephorus and a host of lesser authorities helped to confuse the topic, the Lacedaemonians themselves were the worst offenders. Spartan

[50] Thucydides 4.80.

[51] For example, Chrimes (supra, n. 25); N. G. L. Hammond, "The Lycurgean Reform at Sparta," *JHS* 70 (1950) 42–64; and G. L. Huxley, *Early Sparta* (London 1962). I am in general agreement with Chester G. Starr, "The Credibility of Early Spartan History," *Historia* 14 (1965) 257–272.

[52] Strabo 8.5.5.

[53] Herodotus 1.65.

[54] Pausanias 3.16.10.

[55] H. T. Wade-Gery, *CAH* III 557–565, is still convincing. See also W. D. Forrest, "The Date of the Lykourgan Reform in Sparta," *Phoenix* 17 (1963) 157–179.

[56] Plutarch *Lycurgus*, 1.2. Cf. Cicero *Brutus* 40.

[57] Plutarch *Lycurgus* 1.1.

informants told Herodotus of the Cretan inspiration of Lycurgus and gave the historian a contradictory chronology for the lawgiver.[58] At the beginning of the fourth century, King Pausanias was exiled by the ephors and wrote a tract on Lycurgus, damning the ephorate as un-Lycurgan.[59] As a descendant of Pausanias,[60] Cleomenes III probably based his harangue on the usurpation of power by the ephors on his distinguished ancestor's pamphlet.[61]

Agis IV, of course, had a different version of the historical development of the ephorate.[62] Whether the ephorate was "Lycurgan" or (as is more likely) a later institution, is irrelevant—the traditions of its origin were the products of political propaganda and obliterated whatever authentic memories may have survived. Pausanias' contemporary, the wily Lysander, also contributed to the confusion of Spartan constitutional history when he hired a ghost-writer, Cleon of Halicarnassus, to compose a work defending the election of kings at Sparta, doubtless on Lycurgan grounds.[63] The document, which was discovered among Lysander's papers after his death, was apparently most persuasive.[64] Not to be outdone by the political propagandists, the Hellenistic Spartan historian, Aristocrates, claimed that the great Lycurgus had communed with the naked sages of India in his search for wisdom and inspiration.[65] Such was the literary pastiche from which Plutarch drew material for his life of Lycurgus.

In *Lycurgus* 8.3, Plutarch states: "Lycurgus divided . . . the area of the city of Sparta into nine thousand lots for the Spartans. . . . Others say that he made six thousand lots for the Spartans, but that King

---

[58] Herodotus 1.65. See Michell (supra, n. 26) 20, n. 5. The notion that Lycurgus borrowed his laws from Crete is a product of the Pan-Doric propaganda of fifth-century Sparta; it impressed Ephorus a century later—Strabo 10.4.17. However, Xenophon in the early fourth century was told that Lycurgus owed nothing to any foreign inspiration, *Laconian Constitution* 1.1. Apparently, the Spartans changed their minds on this weighty point.

[59] Xenophon *Hellenica* 3.5.25. Strabo 8.5.5. Aristotle *Politics* 5.1.1301b.

[60] Plutarch *Agis* 3.3–5.

[61] Plutarch *Cleomenes* 10.1–3. Note the comparison between the two kings in Pausanias 2.9.1.

[62] Plutarch *Agis* 12.2. See Africa (supra, n. 3) 15.

[63] Plutarch *Lysander* 24.2–25.1. Diodorus Siculus 14.13.2,8. Plutarch *Agesilaus* 8.3.

[64] Plutarch *Lysander* 30.3–4.

[65] Plutarch *Lycurgus* 4.6; cf. 31.5. For examples of comparable historical romanticizing, see Lionel Pearson's excellent paper, "The Pseudo-History of Messenia and its Authors," *Historia* 11 (1962) 396–426.

Polydorus added three thousand later. Still others say that Polydorus simply doubled the forty-five hundred originally instituted by Lycurgus." Plutarch adds that each lot was sufficient to produce 82 medimni of barley for the maintenance of a Spartan and his family, but Plutarch seems to have erred here.[66] Whatever the size and productivity of the "Lycurgan" *kleros*, " there had never been, in historical times, an equal division of land at Sparta, and there had always been rich and poor."[67] This, of course, did not preclude the leveling tendency of the *syssitia* and the Lycurgan discipline. What is most significant in the passage from Plutarch is the variant numbers of the citizenry attributed to the action of Lycurgus. The figure of 9,000 is not implausible for archaic Sparta, for Herodotus states that there were 8,000 Spartans in 480 B.C., and they mustered 5,000 at the battle of Plataea.[68] While one tradition considered 9,000 as the proper number of Lycurgan Spartans, other experts on Spartan antiquity preferred different figures and involved good King Polydorus, the friend of the *demos*,[69] in the change. The identity of one of these sources was surmised over a century ago by George Grote: "The eighth chapter of the life of Lycurgus by Plutarch, in recounting the partition of land, describes the dream of King Agis, whose mind is full of two sentiments—grief and shame for the actual condition of his country—together with reverence for its past glories, as well as for the lawgiver from whose institutions those glories had emanated."[70]

Though he was too sweeping in denying any land division prior to the third-century reformers,[71] Grote aptly recognized in Plutarch's text the 4,500 citizens proposed by Agis IV.[72] Since Sparta no longer held Messenia, Agis had to settle for a smaller citizenry than 9,000, and the Lycurgan canon was adjusted accordingly, just as a convenient oracle from the goddess Pasiphaë was concocted to justify Agis' policies.[73]

[66] Plutarch *Lycurgus* 8.4. See Michell (supra, n. 26) 225–227.

[67] Tarn, *CAH* VII 741. Michell, (supra, n. 26) 207, 219.

[68] Herodotus 7.234; 9.10, 28. Cf. Aristotle *Politics* 2.9. 1270a. Michell, 226, feels that 9,000 is "impossibly high and must be rejected," but Chrimes (supra, n. 25) 287, and Huxley (supra, n. 51) 41, 119, n. 251, accept the figure.

[69] Pausanias 3.3.2–3. See Forrest (supra, n. 55) 170–171.

[70] George Grote, *History of Greece* (London: Murray, Ed. 2 1849) II 543–544. Cf. Hammond (supra, n. 51) 60, n. 108. Unknown to Grote, Lachmann and others had earlier assigned the sources of the passage to the era of Agis and Cleomenes, see Grote, p. 546, n. 1.

[71] Grote (supra, n. 70) 530–538.

[72] Plutarch *Agis* 8.1.–2.

[73] Plutarch *Agis* 9.3. See Africa (supra, n. 3) 53.

Probably, Plutarch discovered the "Lycurgan" number of 4,500 in Phylarchus' vivid account of Agis' "restoration."[74] The third figure, 6,000, was, I contend, Cleomenes' citizen body which included the 2,000 ex-helots. Plutarch likely found it in the writings of the Stoic Sphaerus, who wrote on Lycurgus and Spartan institutions[75] and is cited in the biography of Lycurgus on the number of the Gerousia.[76] In the biography of Cleomenes, Plutarch claims that Sphaerus was Cleomenes' tutor who later aided the king by providing expertise on the Lycurgan discipline for the revolutionary regime.[77] However, these episodes were not reported in Phylarchus' histories, for Diogenes Laertius, who used Phylarchus as a source,[78] makes no mention of trips to Sparta in his life of Sphaerus.[79] Furthermore, Diogenes also used Plutarch's lives,[80] but apparently he was not impressed by the achievements credited there to Sphaerus. Plutarch must have found the claims of influence on Cleomenes in Sphaerus' own writings, but the opportunistic Stoic was equally friendly with Ptolemy III, who betrayed Cleomenes, and with Ptolemy IV, who imprisoned the Spartan king and desecrated his corpse.[81] Though "the extant evidence is slight and the role of Sphaerus in the reform, if any, is obscure,"[82] it is possible that the Stoic served Cleomenes as a propagandist in the halcyon days of the revolution when the king of Sparta could pay for publicists.[83] In this capacity, Sphaerus was an antiquarian attuned to the political needs of his employer, and it is likely he asserted that the original citizenry of Lycurgus was 6,000, later enlarged by Polydorus. The many conflicting policies attributed to Lycurgus may not throw light on the realities of archaic Sparta, but they invariably reflect the needs and notions of later Spartan politicians.

In summary, while not specifically stated (any more than Cleomenes' abolition of debts), it is probable that the Spartan king enfranchised the 2,000 ex-helots who were armed with Macedonian gear.

[74] Africa, 15. See also Alexander Fuks, "The Spartan Citizen-Body in Mid-Third Century B.C. and its Enlargement Proposed by Agis IV," *Athenaeum* 40 (1962) 253.

[75] Diogenes Laertius 7.178.

[76] Plutarch *Lycurgus* 5.8.

[77] Plutarch *Cleomenes* 2.2; 11.2.

[78] Diogenes Laertius 9.115.

[79] Diogenes Laertius 7.177–178.

[80] Diogenes Laertius 4.4; 9.60.

[81] Diogenes Laertius 7.177, 185. Athenaeus 8.345E.

[82] Rostovtzeff (supra, n. 1) III 1367, n. 34.

[83] Africa (supra, n. 3) 17–18.

Even Shimron admits that "it is a plausible conjecture that they were promised some reward after the victory, but not more than that can be said."[84] It may be objected that *kleroi* for the 2,000 new citizens would create a problem, but Cleomenes probably promised them land from the territories of his enemies after the hoped-for defeat of Antigonus and the Achaeans. The king of Sparta was desperate for soldiers, and he was never scrupulous about the traditions of his nation, which he reinterpreted to suit his fancy. A man who was willing to overthrow the ephorate (which was venerable if not Lycurgan) and who sold freedom to helots, would not balk at enfranchising freed men merely because it violated tradition. Despite his pose as the restorer of Lycurgan ways Cleomenes III was a most unconventional Spartan. Under the stress of military necessity, even ex-helots had a role as citizen soldiers in the new order, which, unfortunately for Cleomenes and for them, was extinguished at Sellasia.

University of Southern California
Los Angeles

---

[84] Shimron (supra, n. 2) 458.

DARRELL A. AMYX

2

The Case of the Dunedin Painter*

It is my purpose here to reexamine a well-known group of vases, supposedly Corinthian, that have been thought to be the work of a single hand. The artist who decorated all, or most, of these vases has been called the "Reigenmaler" ("Group-Dance Painter") by Professor J. L. Benson,[1] the "Dunedin Painter" by me.[2] At first there seemed to be no real problem about this Painter, other than that of deciding firmly which of the vases associated with him were actually by him. In recent years, however, I was bothered first by a suspicion, then by a growing conviction that not all of these vases could be ancient, and that exactly those which I took to be by the Dunedin Painter himself must be modern.

* This investigation could not have reached even its present state of partial completion without the willing cooperation of several long-suffering informants. For photographs of, and for information pertaining to, the vases under discussion, I am most particularly indebted to Professor J. L. Benson, Dr. Dietrich von Bothmer, Dr. Giovanna Delli Ponti, Dr. Richard Green, Professor J. Walter Graham, the late Dr. H. Köhn, Professor Elaine P. Loeffler, Dr. F. Mellinghoff, Dr. Stephen E. Ostrow, Dr. H. Sichtermann, Dr. Hermine Speyer, Dr. Mario Torelli, and Mr. Ben F. Williams. In several critical instances, their help amounted to far more than passive acquiescence, and must be counted as active collaboration in the research. Dr. Richard Bronson gave valued assistance on several occasions. Mr. Joseph V. Noble, Vice-Director for Administration, Metropolitan Museum of Art, New York, has very kindly tested the glazes of several specimens, and finally provided the technical proof which made this article possible. Miss Susan Kallemeyn helped with the final stages of preparing this report. Lastly, I must acknowledge the receipt of generous financial support from the Committee on Research at the University of California, Berkeley.

[1] J. L. Benson, *Die Geschichte der korinthischen Vasen* (Basel 1953) 38f, List 59 (hereafter, *GkV*); idem, *AJA* 60 (1956) 226 and 61 (1957) 176.

[2] D. A. Amyx, "Corinthian Vases in the Hearst Collection at San Simeon," *Univ. Calif. Publ. in Classical Archaeology* 1:9 (1943) 231, n. 114 (hereafter, *Cor. Vases*); idem, *Antike Kunst* 5 (1962) 6, n. 18.

Proof was hard to establish, since the vases in question are widely scattered, and several of them have gained a respected place in archaeological literature. Only very recently was it possibe, after years of effort, to obtain conclusive evidence that these vases are forgeries. The present report aspires finally to expose the Dunedin Painter, and briefly to consider the place in Corinthian ware of the small residue of genuinely ancient vases which have been associated with his work.

The detection of forgeries among Greek vases does not generally present serious problems to the specialist. Attic pottery, in particular, has been so thoroughly studied that a forged specimen is not likely to remain undetected for long. The modern "versions" of Attic vases which are sold as souvenirs are perhaps easiest to distinguish from their ancient models, because of clearly recognizable differences of shape, style, and technique. Modern replicas,[3] in our present fuller knowledge of the originals, have become almost equally easy to identify. Another sort of falsification, familiar to students of Attic pottery, arises from the common practice of "restoring" the decoration on fragmentary, mended-up vases, particularly those that were destined for the market. A large proportion of the Attic black-figure and red-figure vases that found their way into European museums in the nineteenth century arrived in such a "repainted" condition.[4] Much of this modern repainting has been removed, but examples of repainted vases are still abundant—left untreated not through ignorance, but through lack of staff time for cleaning them. These specimens, too, are (at least to specialists) usually easy to recognize under direct examination of the vase, and often even from the study of photographs. By now, no competent student of Attic vase-painting is likely to be deceived by any of these kinds of imposture.

The situation as regards Corinthian pottery is different. Corinthian vases have been less intensively studied than Attic vases, and

[3] For example, the replicas of the large kylix by Oltos, Tarquinia RC 6848. See P. Arias, M. Hirmer, and B. Shefton, *A History of 1,000 Years of Greek Vase-Painting* (London, New York 1961) 321f and pls. 100–104, with lit.; Beazley, *ARV*[2] (1963) 60, No. 66, wherein the existence of the modern copies is noted. One of these copies is Berkeley, UCLMA 8/4095, which was made, according to the inventory record of the Museum, by Sig. Antonio Scappini (so spelled: error for "Scapini"?—see Noble in Dietrich von Bothmer and Joseph V. Noble, *An Inquiry into the Forgery of the Etruscan Terracotta Warriors in the Metropolitan Museum of Art, Metr. Mus. Papers*, no. 11 [New York 1961] 21 and 36). There are, in the museum at Berkeley, several other replicas of ancient vases which are said to have been made by Scappini (or Scapini).

[4] When it is said that a vase "needs cleaning," what is usually meant is that there is modern repainting on it which ought to be removed.

the detection of forgeries among them presents a different set of problems. One difficulty arises from the fact that Corinthian ware, which varies widely in quality, was also much imitated in antiquity, especially in Etruria; hence, if there is doubt whether a particular vase is actually Corinthian, one of the questions which must be considered is whether the piece is an Etruscan or other *ancient* imitation of Corinthian ware. Recent advances in the study of Etrusco-Corinthian pottery have done much to alleviate this problem, but there is (even among experts) still room for uncertainty and confusion. The possibility of Etruscan origin has indeed been entertained as a means of explaining certain peculiarities of vases by the Dunedin Painter. But there are other problems, too. A few years ago, in discussing a particular group of ancient Corinthian vases to which modern decoration had been added, I wrote: "There are many repainted Corinthian vases, on which the remains of ancient decoration, fragmentary or worn, have been touched up or completely covered over by a modern restorer. Outright forgeries, which begin with a vase that never had painted figures, are much less common; forged *vases*, although they exist, are very rare."[5] Of these three classes, the first corresponds to that which also includes the hordes of "repainted" Attic vases, and in either case the proper treatment is the same. The second class, that showing gratuitously added decoration, was discussed in the article cited above. Our present concern is with the third class, that of entirely modern vases, which have succeeded in "passing" as ancient works.

The story of the Dunedin Painter begins nearly twenty-five years ago, in a grouping first proposed by me.[6] In this proposal I mentioned, as "also Corinthian (not Italic, as sometimes suggested), four E. C. vases by one hand: olpai *CVA* Providence 1, pl. 6:3 and *Encyclopédie Photographique de l'Art* (*Musée du Louvre*), II, 267 (=Louvre E 438, NC 765?); oinochoai Toronto 189, RHI, pl. 14 and p. 58 (same as Montelius, *Civ. Prim.*, pl. 297, 16?) and *CVA* Scheurleer 1, pl. 3, 1 (different view, Allard Pierson Museum, *Algemeene Gids*, 1937, pl. 56); near, but later: NC 768A (new, Merlin, *Vases grecs*, pl. 15, A), cited for style by Scheurleer." There was as yet no question of authenticity; nor was there in R. J. Hopper's "Addenda to Necrocorinthia" (1949),[7] in which the

---

[5] "A Forged Corinthian Animal Frieze," *Brooklyn Museum Bulletin* 21:2 (1960) 9–13.

[6] Amyx, *Cor. Vases* (supra, n. 2) 231, n. 114.

[7] Hopper, *Annual of the British School at Athens* 44 (1949) 233, Nos. 2 and 4, and 242, Nos. 8 and 10.

four vases are mentioned, and in general accepted as Corinthian (though with note of their peculiarities).

In 1953, J. L. Benson presented a formal list of these vases as works of his "Reigenmaler."[8] His list differed from mine only in that he accepted the olpe NC 768A (with frieze of dancing women) into the main body of attributions, and (inadvertently) omitted the oinochoe in Toronto. In an article of 1956,[9] he added as a new attribution the round aryballos Dunedin, Otago Museum 48.208; and, in the following year,[10] he made good his earlier omission of the Toronto oinochoe, added my unpublished attribution of an oinochoe in Essen, and further remarked: "Still another oinochoe by the Group-Dance Painter (to judge from a not entirely satisfactory photograph) is illustrated on pl. VIII, right, of G. Nicole's *La peinture des vases grecs* (in Corneto: cf. NC 740; also illustrated by P. Romanelli, *Tarquinia*—in the series *Itinerari dei Musei e Monumenti d'Italia*—1940, pl. 63, right)." Since that time, I have been able to identify and study, in the Museum at Tarquinia, the vase last mentioned by Benson, and to satisfy myself that this piece (and not the oinochoe in Toronto) is the one illustrated in Montelius (see above).

Our Painter received his official canonization, so to speak, through Professor Luisa Banti's entry, "Pittore della Carola," in *Enciclopedia dell'Arte Antica*, II (1959), pp. 355f, in which she summarized the situation as of that date, accepting as the Painter's own work the olpe NC 768A (illustrated by her, *ibid.*, fig. 515)—that is, Benson's "name-piece," which I had kept apart from the main list, while at the same time I had withheld from the Painter the name given him by Benson, since there was no chain of women on any of the other pieces. The next mention of the Painter appears in a footnote of mine,[11] published in 1962. Therein I cited, as a work "near the Dunedin Painter" (using the name which I had chosen for him, for reasons given above), the head-pyxis Berlin F 984 (NC 894). At the same time, I felt obliged to issue a warning statement that "there may be forgeries among the vases attributed to this artist," thus finally giving voice to doubts which had in fact been nagging me for some time. These doubts, and the results of my further attempts to resolve them, are the subject of this investigation.

---

[8] Benson, *GkV* (supra, n. 1) 38f, List 59.
[9] Benson, *AJA* 60 (1956) 226.
[10] Benson, *AJA* 61 (1957) 176.
[11] Amyx, *Antike Kunst* 5 (1962) 6, n. 18.

Nine vases have been mentioned above which have thus far been attributed to or brought into association with the Dunedin Painter. Two more examples, both unpublished, may be added as direct attributions: an oinochoe in Raleigh, North Carolina, and a globular aryballos in the Vatican. For reasons which will become clear further on, I divide the lot into two separate lists:

THE DUNEDIN PAINTER

Round Aryballoi

1. Dunedin, N.Z., Otago Museum 48.208. Provenience unknown (ex Coll. A. B. Cook). J. K. Anderson, *Greek Vases in the Otago Museum* (Dunedin 1955) 26, No. 33; J. L. Benson, *AJA* 60 (1956) 226 and pl. 72, fig. 26. In frieze: woman standing to right, between ram and panther; at back, swan. (Benson)

2. Rome, Vatican, Mus. Etr. 802. Plates 1:1 and 1:2. Provenience not given. In frieze: siren to right, with wings spread, panther to right; below, wave pattern.

Oinochoai (with narrow foot)

3. Toronto C.255, from Tarquinia (ex Sturge Coll.). Robinson, D. M., Cornelia G. Harcum, and J. H. Iliffe, *A Catalogue of the Greek Vases in the Royal Ontario Museum of Archaeology, Toronto* (Toronto 1930) (hereafter cited as RHI) No. 189, pl. 14 and p. 58 (ill.); Amyx, *Cor. Vases* 231, n. 114; Benson, *AJA* 61 (1957) 176. Three animal friezes; woman in middle frieze.

4. Raleigh, North Carolina Museum of Art G 57.14.7. Plate 2:1. Provenience unknown (bought in New York by donors). Shape and decoration as last.

5. Amsterdam, Allard Pierson Museum 1285 (ex Scheurleer, Hague). Said to be from Egypt (von Bissing Coll.). *CVA* Scheurleer 1, pl. 3, 1; Snijder, *Gids*, pl. 56; Amyx, *Cor. Vases* 231, n. 114; R. J. Hopper, *BSA* 44 (1949) 233, No. 2; Benson, *GkV* 39, List 59, No. 4. Slender shape, with flattened shoulder and tall neck; decoration as last two.

6. Essen, Folkwang Museum. Plate 2:2. Benson, *AJA* 61 (1957) 176. No stated provenience. Shape and decoration as last.

Olpai

7. Paris, Louvre E 438 (NC 765). Provenience unknown (Italy?). Amyx, *Cor. Vases* 231, n. 114; *Enc. Phot.* II 267; W. Schmalenbach, *Griechische Vasenbilder* (Basel 1948) pl. 23; R. J. Hopper, *BSA* 44 (1949) 242, No. 10; Benson, *GkV* 39, List 59, No. 3. Four animal friezes.

8. Providence, Rhode Island School of Design C-2336. Plate 3:1. Provenience unknown (acquired in 1916). *CVA* Providence 1, pl. 6, 3; Amyx, *Cor. Vases* 231, n. 114; Benson, *GkV* 39, List 59, No. 2. Four animal friezes; woman in third frieze.

OTHER VASES

Oinochoe (with narrow foot)

(a) Tarquinia RC 5145, from Tarquinia. Plate 1:3. O. Montelius, *La civilisation primitive en Italie* (Stockholm 1895–1910) (hereafter cited as *Civ. Prim.*) pl. 297, 16; Benson, *AJA* 61 (1957) 176 (cf. Payne, p. 298, under NC 740); G. Nicole, *La peinture des vases grecs* (Paris 1926), pl. 8, right; P. Romanelli, *Tarquinia (Itinerari,* 1940, 1957, etc.) 115, fig. 63, right (=Photo Anderson 41026); Photo Alinari 26043, right. Three animal friezes; woman in middle frieze.

Olpe

(b) Paris, Louvre E 603 (NC 768A). Provenience unknown (Italy?). Amyx, *Cor. Vases* 231, n. 114; Benson, *GkV* 38, List 59, No. 1 (attributed to the Group-Dance Painter); A. de Longpérier, *Musée Napoleon III: Choix de monuments antiques* (Paris 1867–1874), pl. 15 (sic); G. Perrot and C. Chipiez, *Histoire de l'art dans l'antiquité* IX (Paris 1911) 609, fig. 320; A. Merlin, *Vases grecs* (Paris n.d.), pl. 15, A; L. Banti, *Enc. dell'Arte Antica* II (1959) 355, fig. 515; I. Jucker, *Antike Kunst* 6 (1963) 60 and pl. 21, 3–5. Four friezes, one with bust of woman, another with chain of women; animals.

Head-Pyxis

(c) Berlin F 984 (NC 894). Amyx, *Antike Kunst* 5 (1962) 6, n. 18. On body, two friezes: (1) between handles, chain

of women; (2) frieze of animals. Both friezes are in silhou-
ette technique, with no incision. In upper frieze, filling
ornament of dot-cluster rosettes; in lower frieze, thick
sprinkling of "solid" rosettes, unincised.

   The separation of these vases into two lists accords with my
belief that those in the first list are by the Dunedin Painter, and modern;
whereas those in the second list, *not* by the same hand as the others, are
genuinely ancient, and Corinthian.
   The suspicion that some of the vases in the first list might not
be Corinthian arose because of certain peculiarities in their shape and
decoration. The possibility that some of them might be Etrusco-
Corinthian had in fact been suggested, but no one had doubted that the
vases were ancient. Any such doubts would have been confronted
by Payne's certification of the olpe Louvre E 438 (No. 7, above)
as Corinthian. The oinochoai in Amsterdam (No. 5) and Toronto (No. 3),
and the olpe in Providence (No. 8), had all been published as ancient, and
Corinthian, the only deviation from this opinion being that of Luce,
who (in *CVA* Providence 1, p. 16) had surmised, with a query, that his
olpe might be Italo-Corinthian. The unpublished oinochoe in Essen,
I have been told,[12] had been regarded by some scholars as Etrusco-
Corinthian; Greifenhagen thought it Corinthian, and so likewise (much
earlier) did Furtwängler, who took it to be "echt, aber nicht sonderlich
gut." Hence there seemed at the time no reason to doubt that the
aryballos in Dunedin (No. 1), accepted as Corinthian by Anderson, and
attributed to the Painter by Benson, was another genuinely ancient vase.
Then, when the aryballos in Rome (No. 2) and the oinochoe in Raleigh
(No. 4) first came to my notice, they were so obviously by the same hand
as the rest that no one could seriously have denied them a place in the list.
In fact, repeated scrupulous examination of every element in their decoration has convinced me that, whatever else is to be said of these eight vases,
they were all painted by the same artist.
   Among the vases in the second list, the oinochoe (a),
attributed to the Painter by Benson, is particularly important, and its
stylistic relationship to the oinochoai in the first list will be fully considered further on; but before that is done, it may be well to look at some
of the peculiarities of the vases here attributed to the Dunedin Painter.

12 In a letter from Dr. H. Köhn.

The Dunedin aryballos (No. 1) itself seems very strange for a Corinthian vase of this shape, and the syntax of its decoration cannot be matched in Corinthian ware.[13] Particularly bothersome is the wide and unusually tall neck, in contrast with the normal Corinthian type, which has a shorter, narrower neck and a wide overhanging mouthpiece. For these features there seems to be no good Corinthian parallel. In the decoration, there seems also to be no match in Corinthian ware for the inverted "sawtooth" rays on the edge of the lip, the mere strokes serving as "tongues" on the shoulder, and the absence of any decoration below the two narow bands under the main frieze. The addition of the Vatican aryballos (No. 2) (pls. 1:1 and 1:2) only intensifies the impression that something is amiss. Its shape is like that of the Dunedin aryballos; the hand is manifestly the same; and there is, besides, a wave pattern below the main frieze, a feature unknown to me in archaic Corinthian pottery.[14] Therefore an inconsistency is present: we have aryballoi decorated with animal friezes in a style apparently Corinthian, but of a shape and with subsidiary decoration unlike anything in Corinthian ware.

The olpai, too, look un-Corinthian. Both of them have abnormally long, slender necks and slender lower bodies, showing an inward curve to the base that is far less emphatic than is usual in Corinthian ware, and the handles form a sinuous curve instead of having the expected angular bend. In fact, their shapes look more Etruscan than Corinthian.[15] Furthermore, on both olpai there is a row of dots or short vertical strokes on the raised "collar" between the neck and the body.[16] This feature is commonly found on Etruscan, but is unknown on

[13] Contrast, for example, the Corinthian aryballos, Boston 18.487 (NC 621A; Payne, pl. 23:1). There are of course several subtypes of Corinthian round aryballoi, but none of them comes closer than this example to the shape of the two pieces here in question. Nor have Etruscan aryballoi thus far provided any really close likenesses to our examples. The shape of the mouthpiece and handle seems curiously reminiscent of that of Proto-Corinthian pointed aryballoi.

[14] The aryballos Toronto C. 653 (RHI, 49 and pl. 12, No. 167, "purchased in Rome in 1923") comes closest in shape to our two pieces, and there is a wave pattern like that on the Vatican aryballos beneath its main frieze (hoplites marching to the right); but I feel almost certain that this vase is modern, and possibly also by the Dunedin Painter.

[15] Etruscan olpai display wide variations in their shapes, mainly in proportions which are aberrant from the usual Corinthian types. In the present instance, a good idea of what is meant can be gained from looking at those illustrated in Sieveking-Hackl, pl. 27, especially Nos. 633, 634, and 635a.

[16] This feature is often present on Etruscan olpai, but even there it is not quite the same as what we have on our two olpai. In all Etruscan examples that I have found, the "row of dots" (sometimes rendered as diagonally slanting bars) on the collar is

Corinthian, olpai. But the olpe in Providence (pl. 3:1) exhibits features which prevent us from accepting it even as an Etrusco-Corinthian vase. The form of the rays at the base, which are convex and leaflike, resembles nothing Corinthian *or* Etruscan of the supposed period, reminding us rather of the usual form of rays in later Attic black-figure, from around the time of Exekias, and after.[17] Another oddity which seems hard to justify is the form of one large rosette in the lowest frieze (behind left-side panther of center triad at front of vase): "petals" with rounded tips are incised, daisy-like, wholly within its contours. But, if we have an olpe of a shape which looks Etruscan, decorated with animal friezes which look Corinthian, and embellished further with details which look neither Corinthian nor Etruscan, we are forced to wonder whether it is ancient.

Of the four oinochoai, those in Toronto and Raleigh (pl. 2:1) have a shape very similar to that of ordinary Corinthian (for example, like NC 740 and others mentioned under that entry, especially Tarquinia RC 5145), with bulging body, rounded shoulder, and narrow foot. Those in Amsterdam and Essen (pl. 2:2), however, have a different shape: narrower body, distinctly flattened shoulder, tall narrow neck, and small mouth. I know nothing quite like them in either Corinthian or Etruscan ware. In view of the fact that all four vases were decorated by one hand, this inconsistency is also disturbing.

Consideration of the style and decorative syntax of the Dunedin Painter's vases brings us now to the oinochoe Tarquinia RC 5145 (a), above (pl. 1:3), attributed to the Painter by Benson. This vase *is* ancient Corinthian: the clay is a clear yellow-buff, and the style of decoration is wholly consonant with Corinthian practices. Indeed the

rendered in *black-polychrome* technique; that is, with white dots (or bars) overpainted upon a glazed background. Examples: Munich 633, 634, 635a (S.-H., pl. 27); Würzburg 777a, 777b, 777c, 777d (Langlotz, pl. 225 and p. 137); Toronto C.254 and C.226 (RHI 59 and pl. 14, Nos. 192–193; W. L. Brown, *The Etruscan Lion* [Oxford 1960] 56, Nos. 8–9); Rome, Vatican 136 (Albizzati, pl. 13; Brown, *op. cit.*, 56, No. 7), and others by the Queen's College Painter (on whom see Amyx in *Studi Etruschi*, 35 [1967] 105); Vatican 137 (Albizzati, pl. 13, with slanting bars), and Vatican RG 84 (Beazley in J. D. Beazley and F. Magi, *La raccolta Benedetto Guglielmi nel Museo Gregoriano Etrusco* [Vatican City 1939] 74 and pl. 28, also with slanting bars), both by the Rosoni Painter; Seattle Cs 20.4 (Amyx in *Studi in Onore di Luisa Banti* [Rome 1965] 5 and pl. 4, c); vases by the Mingor Painter (Amyx in *Studi Etruschi*, 35 [1967] 88–97) and many others.

17 E.g., Arias, Hirmer, and Shefton (supra, n. 3) pls. 62–67. Therefore the first appearance of this type of rays, even in Attic black-figure, comes appreciably later than the supposed date of the Providence olpe. The Dunedin Painter's own inconsistency, in that he provides his two olpai with two different types of rays, is also disconcerting.

resemblance of this oinochoe to the others is strikingly close—awkwardly close, even for routine animal-frieze decoration. For the Tarquinia oinochoe has exactly the same figures, in exactly the same arrangement, as the vases in Essen and Amsterdam; and precisely this configuration is found also on the other two vases, except for the omission, in the lowest frieze, of a swan on the oinochoe in Raleigh, and of a goat on that in Toronto. Given the otherwise suspicious character of the vases by the Dunedin Painter, it becomes all but mandatory to conclude that the oinochoe in Tarquinia is the ancient model, of which the other four pieces are modern copies or imitations. Professor Benson's attribution of the Tarquinia vase to the Dunedin Painter (working from inadequate illustrations) is perfectly understandable under these conditions; and its detachment, by me, from the main list of (forged) vases attributed to the Dunedin Painter now finds a logical explanation.

       The two olpai do not show quite the same close agreement in composition and syntax. The figures are differently disposed, and the greater number of friezes, on a vase of a different shape, encourages other minor deviations from the pattern. Nevertheless, the repertory is the same, there are many similar groupings, and the figures tend to show, individually, the same carbon-copy likeness as those which appear on the oinochoai. Much the same thing may be said of the creatures on the two aryballoi.

       Under more detailed inspection, the stylistic likeness between the oinochoe in Tarquinia and the vases here attributed to the Dunedin Painter is less close than it appears at first glance. The surface is different in one telling feature, in that the glaze on the former has the expected smoky look where it is thinly applied, whereas on the Dunedin Painter's vases it has a constantly heavy thickness throughout. The filling ornament, too, produces a different effect. On the Tarquinia oinochoe it shows much greater variations in size and shape; note, for instance, the many small round dots—conspicuously fewer on all the other vases (contrast the oinochoe in Raleigh, pl. 2:1)—and the indented "petal-like" contours of the larger rosettes, in contrast to the blobby rosettes with indistinctly indented contours on the other vases. On the oinochoe in Tarquinia the figures themselves are more freely rendered, with lively contours and rather careless, slap-dash incision born of long practice, whereas those on the other vases are pinched, tightly controlled, and more mechanically rendered. Some consistent differences in details of rendering are also present. Instead of three short arcs for rib-markings of quadrupeds which are usual on the Tarquinia vase, we often find on the others two pairs of short parallel strokes, with red stripes in alternate interstices between pairs of incisions. Other slight but important differences of rendering, too complex to be briefly described but clearly evident on close examination, distinguish the style of the Tarquinia oinochoe from that of the others. Therefore also on stylistic grounds it appears that we have, on the vases decorated by the Dunedin Painter, not the work of the same artist but a close copy of the style of the Tarquinia oinochoe. To carry the argument to its logical conclusion: since the shapes of the olpai and the aryballoi by the Dunedin Painter are not closely matched in Corinthian ware, whereas at least two of the oinochoai (those in Toronto and Raleigh) are very close to that of the *Corinthian* oinochoe Tarquinia RC 5145, and since the style of the Painter agrees with no Etrusco-Corinthian style that is known to me, but closely resembles that of the Tarquinia oinochoe, we must find it increasingly difficult to escape the assumption that the Dunedin Painter is a *modern* practitioner who derived his inspiration from the oinochoe in Tarquinia. We must next consider whether there is any other evidence which contradicts, or fails to support, this hypothesis.

Proveniences are of little help, since most of the vases in question seem to have come to their present locations through private donors who bought them from dealers. The oinochoe in Toronto is said to have come from Tarquinia. The oinochoe in Raleigh was purchased by the donors from a private dealer in New York. The one in Amsterdam, formerly in the Scheurleer Collection, is said to have been "found" in Egypt, and to have been in the collection of von Bissing. There is no stated provenience for the oinochoe in Essen, but it was already in that collection during the lifetime of Furtwängler, who died in 1907. The olpe in Providence is said to be of unknown provenience; it was given to the Museum in 1916 by a private donor. The olpe Louvre E 438, because of its inventory classification, presumably came from Italy. Of the two aryballoi, no provenience was stated for Vatican 802, nor for Dunedin 48.208, which is said (in a letter) to have been in the collection of A. B. Cook. So we have for one vase a stated provenience of Tarquinia; for another (Louvre) a presumption of Italian provenience; for a third, "Egypt"; for the rest, unknown or unreported. One of these vases (Toronto) appears to support the notion that these vases may have been *made* in Tarquinia; another (Louvre) mildly supports it; and all but one of the rest do not dispute it. The single case of alleged Egyptian provenience (Amsterdam), may give us pause, but it is not completely damning to our theory (if it was bought in Egypt from a *dealer*, it could easily have been transported there in modern times). And we may even doubt the certainty of the statement of provenience, because von Bissing was especially noted as a collector of Egyptian antiquities, so that an undocumented assumption of Egyptian provenience might well have become attached to non-Egyptian objects in his collection. It is also significant that none of the vases in question is associated with any known excavation context.

The question of technique must also be considered. The clay varies considerably from one piece to another. That of the Amsterdam vase is said to be "brune pâle," which does not sound exactly Corinthian (I saw the vase once, long ago, but made no record of the color of its clay). The Providence olpe is said (in the publication) to have a "reddish buff" clay, or (in a letter from Dr. Elaine Loeffler) "a curious reddish-brown color." The Toronto oinochoe is described (in the publication) as having a "fine buff" clay, or (in a letter from Professor J. Walter Graham) as "possibly Etruscan." The clay of the Raleigh oinochoe is said to be "tannish." That of the Essen oinochoe is described (in a letter from Dr. Köhn) as "durchwegs von heller Terrakott-Farbe." Of the Dunedin aryballos, it is reported (in a letter from Dr. Richard Green) that the clay is "somewhat darker than the general run [*sc.* of Corinthian ware], although not so much darker as pinker." I have no record or report of the clay of the remaining two examples. Given the assumption that all eight vases were decorated by one hand, and the tenor of the descriptions cited above, which suggests *un*-Corinthian clay, we are again faced with a discrepancy which discourages us from accepting them as Corinthian, or even as ancient vases.

Up to this point in the investigation, it seemed to me that all of the evidence was pointing toward one inescapable end, but then a serious snag was encountered. The informed and perceptive reader will have observed that as yet nothing has been said about the glaze. The glaze of the Raleigh oinochoe (as seen in a color photograph) ranges from a rather dull black through red-brown to orange-brown, in such a way as to suggest that the variation is a result of firing conditions. That of the Toronto oinochoe (as seen in color slides) ranges from dull black to chocolate-brown, in a much narrower range. The oinochoe in Amsterdam, according to the published description, has "peinture en noir brillant." The figure-decoration on the Dunedin aryballos is said to be "of a somewhat thin brown color." (On the olpe in Providence, see

Plate 1   Amyx

3. Tarquinia RC 5145. Corinthian oinochoe. Photo-graph courtesy of Fratelli Alinari (No. 26043, right).

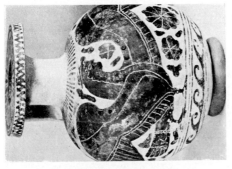

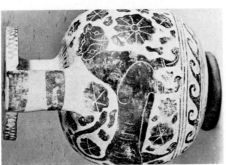

1 and 2. Rome, Vatican 802. Aryballos. Photographs courtesy of Musei Vaticani.

2. Essen, Museum Folkwang. Oinochoe. Photograph courtesy of the Museum.

1. Raleigh, N.C., North Carolina Museum of Art, G.57.14.17. Oinochoe. Photograph courtesy of the Museum.

Plate 3

Amyx

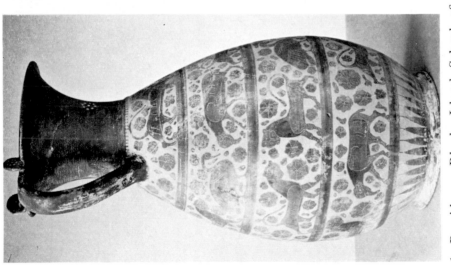

2. Once Lecce, Museo Archeologico Provinciale "Sigismundo Castromediano." Photograph courtesy Deutsches Archäologisches Institut, Rome.

1. Providence Rhode Island School of Design, C-2336. Olpe. Photograph courtesy of the Museum.

below.) Concerning the rest of the vases, I have no useful information. These variations in color, although they seem more Etruscan than Corinthian, would not be unnatural for an *ancient* black glaze. At least they give a strong impression that the glaze was fired, not simply painted on. What does seem unnatural is the evenly thick pasty application, which does not vary in density as ancient Corinthian and Etrusco-Corinthian glazes generally do. Furthermore, the surface "wear," where it appears, seems unnatural. The glazed surface (especially on the olpe in Providence and the oinochoe in Raleigh) looks abraded, as if it had been rubbed with sandpaper. Seeking a solution to this problem, and recalling that modern *paint* (of the kind used in "restoring" ancient Greek vases) will come off readily if rubbed with alcohol or one of several other solvents known to the curatorial profession, I sent out a call for help. This "detergent" test was applied, at my request, to several of the vases (Dunedin, Essen, Providence, Raleigh): the color did not come off. So at least it was evident that the glaze, as its coloring had suggested, was fired.

Still, the fact that the glaze was fired is not conclusive proof that it is ancient, for modern vases with *fired* decoration (like the copies of the big Oltos cup in Tarquinia[18]) are known to exist. Another simple test is available which, according to Mr. Joseph V. Noble, the expert who devised it, should prove conclusively whether the glaze—if the vase was made before the alleged "rediscovery" of the ancient glaze process in 1942—is ancient or modern. This is the test which was used in the technical investigation of the large Etruscan warriors in the Metropolitan Museum of Art,[19] and it furnished a part of the proof that these works are modern. The testing process, which is one of refiring the glaze at different temperatures, is based on the assumption that, before 1942, in modern black glazes imitating the ancient glazes the black color was obtained by the addition of manganese or a similar coloring agent, whereas the ancient glaze, being an "iron-type" glaze, required no such "doctoring." The test is supposed also to identify modern *paints* which imitate ancient glaze. It was found by experimentation that, if refired at 500° Centigrade, genuine ancient black glaze would remain unchanged in color, whereas ordinary paint or coloring material would be burnt out and lost at that temperature. (As we might have been prepared to believe, the glazes of the Dunedin Painter's vases passed this test.) To distinguish between ancient and modern black *glazes*, a refiring at about 1025° Centigrade

18 See supra, n. 3.
19 Noble in Bothmer and Noble (supra, n. 3), 22.

caused the ancient black glaze to reoxidize to red, whereas the spurious glaze made with a mineral pigment, such as lead, cobalt, or manganese, would remain black. By this latter test it should be possible to determine, once and for all, whether the glaze on the vases by the Dunedin Painter is ancient or modern. Mr. Noble very kindly agreed to help me meet this problem. Glaze samples were obtained from the vases in Toronto and Raleigh, which he then subjected to the firing tests described above. The result, in both cases, was to show that the glaze which was tested was "equivalent to the ancient black glaze." Thus we seemed to have reached an impasse.

Discouraged by the apparent impossibility of solving this riddle, which had reached its latest crisis in June, 1963, I had put the whole matter aside to ripen, thinking that chance in the form of new material might one day come to our aid. In the summer of 1966, in Rome, new evidence did appear, in a very strange form. While browsing through the photographic archives of the German Archaeological Institute, I chanced upon a picture of a vase once in Lecce (Germ. Inst. Neg. 59.1185; here, pl. 3:2),[20] which dramatically changed the odds.

This vase is indeed a curious concoction. It purports to be a typical "Tyrrhenian" amphora, of Attic manufacture, but even at first glance it betrays many incongruities. The whole of its decoration, from top to bottom, is a hodgepodge of disparate elements. The palmette-lotus frieze on the neck has separately painted leaves and petals, as in later Attic black-figure, not the solid masses with incised leaf-divisions which are proper to the time of the "Tyrrhenian" amphoras. Furthermore, the lotuses lack the central "sepal" which is the hallmark of Attic conventional lotuses (with but few exceptions, none of which appear on "Tyrrhenian" amphoras), thus agreeing rather with the Corinthian and the Chalcidian types. The fat, leaflike rays at the base of the body, the like of which we have already encountered on the olpe in Providence, are also a later-sixth-century phenomenon, not suited to the first half of the century. As for the figurative decoration, the main scene on the side shown in our illustration, representing the Calydonian boar-hunt, appears to be Attic, but that is because it is a literal transcription

[20] Inquiry as to the present location of the vase produced a reply from Dr. Giovanna Delli Ponti, who reports that it was brought into the Museum in the 1930's as a confiscated object—pursuant upon the "denunciation" of a dealer whose offering price had been refused by the local private owners. It was promptly released by the authorities, who saw that it was modern. Its present whereabouts is unknown.

of the scene on the ovoid neck-amphora Tarquinia RC 5564, by the Camtar Painter.[21] That vase is not a "Tyrrhenian" amphora, as the group is now defined, but its style is close enough to have satisfied a modern copyist.

Below the main scene, there are two animal friezes, as often on "Tyrrhenian" amphoras, but in this case their style is "Corinthian," not Attic, and they are *by the Dunedin Painter*. Here we have the same animals, in the same arrangements, and in the same style, as those on the vases which we have attributed to the Dunedin Painter. The renderings are slightly less careful, but there can be no doubt that the hand is the same.

I have not been able to examine the Lecce amphora at first hand,[22] hence I am not certain whether any of the *potting* is ancient (I am inclined to doubt it), but by now it should be obvious that at least the *painting* on this vase is modern.[23] If that is true, and if the painter of its two animal friezes is modern, then the Dunedin Painter is modern. Furthermore, the time of his activity is becoming clearer. We can state positively that he was active (for some part of his career) in or following 1884, the year in which one model for the Lecce vase (the Camtar Painter's neck-amphora in Tarquinia) was excavated, and that some of his activity antedates 1907 (the year of Furtwängler's death—for Furtwängler had seen the oinochoe in Essen). How long before, and how long after, this date-range he was active we do not know. But it seems very apt, and perhaps significant, that the evidence of his activity spans the turn of the century, and falls at a time when there was apparently a lively trade in copies (not necessarily forgeries) of vases found at Tarquinia.[24] Indeed,

21 J. D. Beazley, *Attic Black-Figure Vase-Painters* (Oxford 1956) 84, No. 1; D. von Bothmer, *Amazons in Greek Art* (Oxford 1957) 6, No. 1 and pl. 2:1. For the boar-hunt scene, see *Monumenti inediti pubblicati dall'Instituto di Corrispondenza Archeologica* (Rome 1829–1891) XII, pl. 10. A drawing of the vase (side A) is also published in Montelius, *Civ. Prim.*, pl. 300:2. Since the amphora in Tarquinia was excavated in 1884 (see Bothmer, *loc. cit.* [supra, n. 3]; and add *NSc* XIII [1883–1884] 227f), the Lecce amphora must date no earlier than that year.

22 See supra, n. 20.

23 Reconsideration is proposed also for the broad-bottomed oinochoe, once in the Hearst Collection at San Simeon, which was published as a "mystery" by H. R. W. Smith, *AJA* 49 (1945) 467–470, figs. 2:8 and 3:2a–2c. Its shape and subsidiary ornament are Etruscan. The animal frieze, though different in several ways from the work here attributed to the Dunedin Painter (for instance, in the scale of the animals, the lavish use of added color, and the absence of filling ornament), shows strong stylistic affinities with that Painter: compare especially the bird, *loc. cit.*, fig. 3:2, b with the Dunedin Painter's birds, e.g., here, pl. 3:1. In this case, the vase *may* be ancient, but it seems likely that the frieze on it is modern, and perhaps by the Dunedin Painter, despite Smith's mention of its "tolerable glaze and paint."

24 See supra, n. 3.

it seems quite possible that, if the Dunedin Painter is ever identified by name, he may prove to be the same person as one of those copyists (such as Scapini) whose names are already known.

Had it not been for the evidence of the "temperature tests" to which the glazes of two of the vases were subjected, according to which the samples tested were "equivalent to ancient black glaze," we might at this stage have regarded the issue as closed. Since, however, the technological evidence was still at variance with our stylistic conclusions, some further investigation was needed, in order to find the source of the disagreement. In the summer of 1967, Mr. Noble again came to my rescue. There had been some talk of getting one of the suspect vases to New York for a complete examination; and now, thanks to the willing cooperation of the Rhode Island School of Design, the olpe in Providence was sent to New York, where, for the first time, Mr. Noble was able to use the entire vase (and not just a sliver of glaze) as a basis for his study. This time, the tests confirmed my stylistic conclusions about the vase.

In a letter dated August 15, 1967, Mr. Noble wrote, in part: "The glaze, while fired, is not of the ancient type, and this confirms your opinion that the piece is a forgery." Among his reasons for this conclusion he stated: "(1) The 'black' glaze is not black, but a uniform brownish tone. (2) Upon firing a sample of the 'black' glaze at a temperature of 1020° C. it did not reoxidize to a red color as an ancient iron base black glaze would do, but remained a dark brownish color." Concerning the earlier tests of small bits of glaze from the oinochoai in Toronto and Raleigh, he stated that the "specks of black glaze sent to me from another Dunedin Painter vase apparently were taken from an area painted with added red, red ocher, and were misleading." So the technical problem is solved, at least for the olpe in Providence, and I believe that if the same test were applied to uncontaminated parts of the black glaze on the other vases by the Dunedin Painter, the results would be the same. That is to say, I believe it is now firmly established that the eight vases attributed above to the Dunedin Painter are modern.

*   *   *

There are still three vases at the end of our list: those which were set apart from the eight (nine, if we now include the Lecce amphora) which I have taken to be by the Dunedin Painter. Most important is the oinochoe in Tarquinia (a), which, it seems obvious to me, is genuinely ancient, and truly Corinthian, and the model for the Dunedin Painter's "Corinthian" style. The large olpe, Louvre E 603 (NC 768A) (b), which I had placed "near" the Dunedin Painter, and which Benson had given to the artist himself, must now be reconsidered in the light of the present state of our investigation. In this case, too, it seems obvious to me that the olpe is manifestly ancient, manifestly Corinthian, and manifestly *not* by the Dunedin Painter. Nevertheless, we may at last find a point at which my long-standing disagreement with Professor Benson over this piece can find a happy ending. As long as the modern, imitative pieces by the Dunedin Painter stood in the way, it was hard to see this vase clearly in its ancient context. But now, if we place it beside the oinochoe in Tarquinia, we can far more easily find our bearings.

There is indeed a close resemblance: the two pieces are strikingly similar in the contours of the animals, in many anatomical markings within the animals, and in the use of filling ornament. Although I could not grant that either of these (ancient) vases is by the Dunedin Painter, I can readily grant the possibility that both might be by the same hand. Between them stand only slight differences in the rendering of details (e.g., in the rendering of belly-stripes of quadrupeds, and in the eyes of panthers), which might possibly be resolved if we could assume the olpe to be slightly later than the oinochoe—that is, that it shows the same style a little further developed. One day, we may hope, a bridge will be found which will more securely connect the two pieces; for the present, I can only say that they are possibly by the same hand. If, eventually, proof should be forthcoming, we could then revive, for the painter of these two vases, the name originally proposed for the whole list by Benson, the "Group-Dance Painter."

The head-pyxis Berlin F 984 (NC 894, sic), the third vase in my second list (c), has only silhouetted decoration. A firm attribution would be unwise, but, now that the list of vases associated with the oinochoe in Tarquinia is so short, we need to collect all the related material that we can find in order to renew the stylistic study of the two surviving pieces. On the pyxis, the contours of the animals (though hastily drawn) are enough like those on the oinochoe and the olpe to suggest a real stylistic connection. The relative lateness of its shape—in odd contrast to the "early" form of its animals—suggests that its decorator was an archaizer, and this idea is consistent with the impression which we gain from the two main pieces. Whether this pyxis can add anything substantial to our knowledge of their style remains uncertain; but, if other works can be found which belong to this stylistic grouping, it may help in a modest way to establish the limits of the style.[25]

We are left, at the end of this study, with two main conclusions, and several open avenues for further investigation. First, we have established that the works here attributed to the Dunedin Painter are the product of a modern hand. Secondly, we have placed in a different group the several ancient vases (including the Dunedin Painter's model in Tarquinia) which have in the past been associated with the first grouping, and have admitted the possibility that the two main pieces may be by a single artist. Open for further study is the more precise identification and location of the Dunedin Painter; and, likewise, the bridging of the stylistic gap between the oinochoe Tarquinia RC 5145 and the olpe Louvre E 603, for which more material is urgently needed. To reach out more broadly from these central problems: the pursuit of the identity of the Dunedin Painter might well be coupled with a general investigation of nineteenth- and early twentieth-century copying of Greek pottery, particularly at Tarquinia; and the further study of the (putative) Group-Dance Painter could be used to fix more firmly the chronological and stylistic placement of all the vases in this area of Corinthian ware. The final answers to these questions must await further evidence, and further study.

University of California
Berkeley

ADDENDUM: THE OINOCHOE IN ESSEN

This paper had to be submitted while a reply was still awaited concerning certain technical tests which were to be applied to paint samples from the oinochoe in Essen. When the report finally arrived, it contained the very surprising conclusion that there was, on the basis of the tests, "no reason to doubt the authenticity" of the vase.

---

[25] Compare also the broad-bottomed oinochoe Athens, N.M. 522 (CC 527), on which the figures have very little incision; and a small olpe in Gela, *NSc* (1956) 312, fig. 29, a, which has only silhouetted decoration. But after the removal of the Dunedin Painter's works from the original corpus, we are left with the need of making a fresh start toward the stylistic reinterpretation of the oinochoe in Tarquinia and the olpe Louvre E 603, and for this purpose we need all the help we can find.

Dr. F. Mellinghoff, Curator of the Folkwang Museum in Essen, who has very kindly been providing information on the vase, arranged for the tests to be made. For this purpose, he sent samples of the red and of the brown/black coloring from the oinochoe to Professor U. Hofmann at the Institute for Inorganic Chemistry in the University of Heidelberg. The results of Professor Hofmann's tests are so important that his letter must be quoted in full:

"5 Februar 1968. *Betr.:* Pulver von schwarzer und roter Malfarbe Ihrer Vase im korinthischen Stil.

Sehr geehrter Herr Doktor Mellinghoff!
        Die geringe Menge des Materials, die Sie mir zusenden konnten, machte natürlich die Untersuchung schwierig. Es war nur möglich, die Röntgeninterferenzanalyse zur Mineranalyse einzusetzen.
        (1) Das Malpulver Rot enthält α-Fe_2O_3 und daneben in geringen Mengen Quarz und Feldspat. Vielleicht sind auch noch Reste von Tonmineralen vorhanden. Das Ergebnis stimmt sehr gut mit der Röntgenuntersuchung der roten Farbe von attischen Vasen überein.
        (2) Das Malpulver Braun bis Schwarz. Es zeigt anhand einer starken Streuschwärzung, dass es zum Teil ein Glas ist. Es zeigt weiter die stärksten Interferenz von Quarz, Feldspat, Tonmineralresten und α-Fe_2O_3. Ausserdem sind die Linien von $(Mn,Fe)_2O_3$ and Mn_3O_4 zu erkennen. Aller Wahrscheinlichkeit nach geben diese Verbindungen die braune Farbe.
        (3) Dies stimmt auch dabei überein, dass Ihr amerikanischer Archäologe beim Erhitzen auf 1020°C. keine Umwandlung der Farbe in Rot erzielte, sondern dass die Farbe dunkelbraun blieb. Schwarze Eisenoxidverbindungen werden beim Glühen auf 1000° C. rot. Braunschwarze Manganverbindungen bleiben braun.
        (4) Mit Manganverbindungen ist oftmals die braunschwarze Bemalung ausgeführt worden. Mir sind viele Stücke aus dem Neolithikum bekannt, deren Braunschwarz mit Manganverbindungen hergestellt worden war.

Auf Grund unserer Untersuchungen besteht kein Anlass, an der antiken Echtheit Ihrer Vase zu zweifeln. Mit vielen Grüssen, Ihr /s/ U. Hofmann."

Dr. Mellinghoff, in his letter to me of February 6, 1968, transmitted a copy of Professor Hofmann's report and indicated that he accepted his conclusions. He also quoted the opinions of dipl.–chem. D. Ankner in the Römisch-Germanisches Zentralmuseum in Mainz, that Mr. Noble's technical findings did not necessarily rule out an ancient origin for the oinochoe in Essen. In closing, Dr. Mellinghoff wrote: "After these aspects we cannot pretend the oinochoe to be proved as a falsification. . . . Personally I think the discussion is not yet finished and I await the publication of the first *California Studies in Classical Antiquity*."

It may seem a poor return for Dr. Mellinghoff's many courtesies to place his remarks at the end of my already completed report, but the timing of the publication made this procedure necessary. Be that as it may, we are both interested in learning the truth, and all of the material is available for further investigation by anyone who wishes to use it.

My case was made primarily on stylistic grounds, using Mr. Noble's technical findings as supporting evidence. For a long time, we had difficulty in reaching an agreement, because of the inadequacy of the samples tested, but his detailed examination of one whole vase (the Providence olpe) finally brought us together.

Now, however, in the case of the Essen oinochoe the argument has been shifted to a different ground. It is not the *results* of the tests (which correspond exactly with Mr. Noble's results for the olpe in Providence), but the *interpretation* of these results that now comes into question, for it is argued specifically on technical grounds that these findings do not preclude the possibility that the vase may be ancient— that is, that Mr. Noble's assumptions about ancient black glaze are wrong. But the evidence thus far accumulated gives every reason to believe that Mr. Noble is right. The use of red ocher (Fe_2O_3) for the red coloring is of course not decisive either way, for, although it was so used in ancient times, it has always been easy to duplicate in modern times. The real difficulty lies in the black glaze (FeO, more often Fe_3O_4), for the production of which a special firing process was used which had, until recently, defied successful duplication.

Professor Hofmann bases his argument for the genuineness of the Essen oinochoe on his knowledge of Neolithic vases on which manganese was used as a coloring agent. This phenomenon is indeed well known (*e.g.*, see Marie Farnsworth and Ivor Simmons, "Coloring Agents for Greek Glazes", *AJA* 67 [1963] 389–396; Joseph V. Noble, *The Technique of Attic Painted Pottery* [New York 1965] 36), but it cannot be extended to refer to the historic period in Greece, for which the situation is summarized by Farnsworth and Simmons (*op. cit.*, p. 396): "As far as the mainland [*sc.* of Greece] is concerned, manganese does not appear to have been used for black glaze after the Middle Helladic period." Hence it becomes apparent that the results of the technical examination of the oinochoe in Essen are *in themselves* an argument against its genuineness.

THE "LECCE" NECK-AMPHORA

An abbreviated version of this paper was read at the 69th General Meeting of the Archaeological Institute of America at Boston on December 28, 1967, and an abstract of that report appeared in *AJA* 72 (1968) 161. As a result of this publicity, further information of considerable interest has come to light concerning the neck-amphora formerly in Lecce (pl. 3.2), and notice has been received of an unpublished companion piece now in the Metropolitan Museum of Art.

Dr. Dietrich von Bothmer has very kindly informed me that he believes the Lecce neck-amphora to be identical with an amphora "in the Lederer Collection" which was mentioned, together with the companion piece, by him in *AJA* 48 (1944) 161, Note 5. The photograph which he sent to me indeed appears to illustrate the other side (with Amazonomachy) of the Lecce neck-amphora, which was accordingly being offered for sale by Lederer in 1932–33. This assumption offers no contradiction with the statement by Dr. Delli Ponti in 1967 (see above, Note 20) that the neck-amphora came briefly into the Provincial Museum of Lecce "in the nineteen-thirties."

Bothmer's second vase, "by the same hand" as the first, is the column-krater New York, M.M.A. 49.101.10, formerly in the Untermeyer Collection, acquired by anonymous gift in 1949 (*Cat. Anderson Galleries 18–20 April 1916*, No. 298; *Cat. Parke-Bernet 10–11 May 1940*, No. 111; Bothmer, *AJA, loc. cit.*). On this vase, the main body frieze is filled with scenes copied from Tarquinia RC 5564; there is *one* lower animal frieze, by the Dunedin Painter; on each handle plate, a bird to left; and, on top of rim, lotus-palmette frieze of peculiar form. Bothmer reports that he had written an article on this column-krater which he submitted "back in the early fifties" for a Festschrift volume honoring the late Paul Jacobsthal, but which was never published. In his most recent letter, Bothmer speaks of other vases, mentioned in that article, which he has associated with the New York column-krater. For our present purposes, we need only observe that the animal frieze clearly establishes it as a work of the Dunedin Painter.

We must give Bothmer the last word on another question which was raised in our discussion of the Dunedin Painter. He says: "Our krater is not the work of Scapini. I have a technical analysis of the glaze which militates against an attribution to that workshop."

—D.A.A. (5-14-68)

WILLIAM S. ANDERSON

3

Two Odes of Horace's Book Two

In his recent book entitled *Latin Explorations*,[1] Kenneth Quinn has proposed a number of new interpretations. I should like to deal with two of his suggestions for Horace's Odes, one of which seems to me to be correct, the other wrong. Normally, there is no need to comment extensively on what appears a correct interpretation, since it suffices to register one's agreement. However, in the case of Quinn's tentative treatment of Mystes in *Carm.* 2.9, I believe that a different and stronger argument can be made to support him.

When one disagrees with an interpretation, one need only justify one's position through the way one handles that interpretation and by the interpretation that one proposes to substitute. I shall, therefore, attempt to demonstrate that Quinn's reading of Ode 2.14 cannot be accepted, but that we are obliged to return, with minor modifications, to the traditional reading of that famous poem.

ademptum Mysten: Horace *Carm.* 2.9

The main lines according to which Horace's Ode 2.9 should apparently be read were well established by the time Porphyrion produced his scholia in the third century A.D. We may assume that he was merely repeating generally accepted ideas when he introduced the ode with the following words: "hac ᾠδῃ Valgium consularem amicum suum solatur morte delicati pueri graviter adfectum." Although Porphyrion fell into a slight anachronism in referring to Valgius as *consularis*

---

[1] *Latin Explorations: Critical Studies in Roman Literature* (London 1963).

perhaps fifteen years before his actual consulship,[2] nevertheless he did define the poem as a *consolatio* written on the occasion of the death of a *puer delicatus*. Commentators have normally started from Porphyrion's definition and devoted their attention either to documenting the consolatory and funereal commonplaces or to establishing the date of the poem's composition.[3]

Quinn deals with the ode in a different manner, arguing that it belongs to a number of poems in which Horace makes an "assault on love elegy."[4] He suggests—I believe correctly—that Mystes is not dead, but that Valgius and his poetry are pursuing a conventional elegiac theme: the loss of a beloved to a rival. He bases his suggestion on two points: (1) that the erotic theme is stock; (2) that Horace's tone would be heartless if in fact Mystes were dead. Although I agree with Quinn's conclusions, I do not think that he has made a cogent enough argument, for the first point carries no necessary force until one shows, by means of the second and additional points, that the traditional interpretation cannot be maintained. To do that, it is obligatory to go back to Porphyrion and to reconsider the categorization of this ode as a *consolatio*. Horace's deliberately improper treatment of consolatory themes, far more than the existence of stock elegiac themes, accounts for the charming irony of this poem and proves that Mystes cannot be dead.

Inasmuch as death constitutes one of the most common phenomena known to mankind, and furthermore it touches the emotions very closely, people from earliest times developed words to deal with this situation, to formalize it and so reduce the emotional stress placed by death on individuals and society. The extant consolatory material, Greek and Latin, is impressively large, not only speeches, letters, and poems or inscriptions composed as *consolationes*, but also rhetorical advice in such handbooks as that of Menander to those eager to compose a *consolatio*.[5] Perfectly aware that each death occurs in a set

---

[2] The consulship of Valgius is securely dated to 12 B.C., more than a decade after the publication of Odes I–III.

[3] Kiessling-Heinze's edition of the Odes (Berlin 1965)[8] represents the height of this tradition. Cf. also G. Pasquali, *Orazio lirico* (Florence 1920), 257ff. for discussion of consolatory themes. E. Fraenkel, *Horace* (Oxford 1957) does not discuss 2.9.

[4] Quinn (supra, n. 1) 158–162.

[5] Orellius, in his commentary on this poem, refers to Statius *Silvae* 2.1 and 6 for poetic *consolationes* in similar situations of a dead *puer delicatus*. For other *consolationes* in Latin, cf. Cicero *Epist. ad fam.* 4.5. and 13, 5.13, 16, 17, and 18; Catullus 96; Horace *C.* 1.24;

of particular circumstances, the rhetorical writers nevertheless also saw the common elements which one could fall back on. And indeed we may say that there is a certain comfort in times of mourning in speaking and hearing commonplaces, for that reinforces the ultimate consolatory topos, that death is common to us all. Roughly speaking, we may divide the usual *consolatio* into two portions: (1) a sympathetic comment on the grief of the person to be consoled, normally by praise of the dead person and the close relationship that existed between the dead and the mourner; (2) a collection of arguments adapted to the circumstances of death, the character of the dead, the person of the mourner, etc. which provide some comfort and attempt to direct the attention realistically back to life.[6] The first part serves more or less to win the ear of the person to be consoled, for it defines the speaker as a sympathizer, one who can be trusted. Then, the second part comes with its properly consolatory topoi.

No rules existed to set the relative proportions of these two parts, for again circumstances vary. When a person has died at an advanced age or after a long sickness, grief is usually less than if a child or a husband or wife has died. Sometimes, the consoler is ignorant of the circumstances and personalities and so must reduce the first portion to vague generalities; sometimes, on the other hand, the consoler knows the facts and people all too well and out of prudence hides behind vague generalities. But if one writes a consolation, one must at least affect to believe that the death is regretted. Often, the reality of the present grief arouses such response on the part of the consoler that he himself seems to lose his sense of proportion and dwell too long on the immeasurable loss sustained by the world and the mourner at the recent death. As he does so, however, his very expressions of sympathy provide an indefinable amount of human comfort which in many cases proves more effective than the formal, expected words of consolation. In any case, for all their variations, *consolationes* work with these two related sections. I know of no true effort to deal with a death that does not both sympathize with the grief and soothe it by persuasive argument.

consolatio ad Liviam; etc. In Greek, pseudo-Plutarch to Apollonios provides a good example. For discussion of the form, see R. Volkmann, *Die Rhetorik der Griechen und Römer* (Leipzig 1885) 358ff and R. Kassell, *Untersuchungen zur griechischen und römanischen Konsolationsliteratur* [*Zetemata 18*] (Munich 1958).

6 Menander, p. 413 Spengel explicitly distinguishes between these two parts.

In Latin literature, the two most elegant poetic *consolationes* are those written by Catullus to his friend Calvus and by Horace to Vergil. Upon examination, the latter proves a paradigm for the balanced treatment of the two themes, while the former exhibits a marvelous blending of the two. In Ode 1.24, which consists of precisely twenty lines, Horace spends exactly ten commiserating with the grief of Vergil for Quintilius and exactly ten consoling him and urging him to face the reality of the death.[7] Thus, Horace recognized and utilized the conventional disposition of the consolatory arguments. The six elegiac lines of Catullus 96 belong essentially to the second or consoling part of the *consolatio*, but Catullus avoids any obvious attempt to persuade Calvus that he must cease lamenting, and the sympathy he implies for the loving grief of the husband amply fulfills the requirements of the first part. Naturally from what the six lines do say—that Quintilia, if her soul can respond, is greatly comforted by the love of Calvus that has continued even after death—it follows that Calvus should be somewhat consoled. Catullus, however, chose to leave the literal meaning of his poem implicit as he combined, in his own artistic way, the two themes of sympathy and consolation.

Having established so much, we may now consider the poem which, according to Porphyrion, consoles Valgius for the death of his beloved boy-favorite. Viewed as a serious *consolatio*, Ode 2.9 seems riddled with defects, surprisingly so for a work of the mature Horace. In the first place, the poet, who addresses Valgius as *amice* (5), shows not the slightest sympathy for his friend's grief. Of the many conventional things that could be said by way of commiseration, some of which he had quite consciously and deftly deployed in 1.24, Horace says not one. We might expect to hear how wonderful Mystes was, not so much virtuous as handsome, a veritable Nireus, a model of attractive ways and quickly responding affection. Or Valgius might be congratulated on the perfect relationship that existed between them. The poet would also lament with Valgius the tragic circumstances of the death that cut off the young Adonis in his prime. For all these conventional points and others, Statius offers verbose parallels in his two poems, *Silvae* 2.1 and 2.6, which he wrote to console Melior and Flavius on the deaths of their respective *pueri delicati*. Far from sympathizing with Valgius, Horace criticizes him consistently for being out of touch with reality. We are

[7] Cf. the able analysis of S. Commager, *The Odes of Horace* (New Haven 1962) 287ff.

left with the impression that Valgius should not be grieving, that his *flebiles modi* (9) and *molles querelae* (17–18) must be considered almost ridiculously inappropriate.

In the second place, Horace does not really console Valgius. We might say that he tries three arguments: (1) Nature does not always mourn, so you should not. (2) Archetypical examples from myth, Nestor, Priam, and the sisters of Troilos, did not eternally lament their young heroes, so you should not. (3) You should instead devote yourself to a panegyric honoring Augustus' triumphs in the East. Of these, the first is not conventional, probably because it starts from a pathetic fallacy and so possesses no genuine consolatory force. In all the long unimaginative letter of pseudo-Plutarch to Apollonius, nothing resembling Horace's first argument appears; and I find no analogue in any of the Latin *consolationes* known to me. You can, of course, appeal to Nature and produce a cogent consolatory point, for example, if you remind the mourner that all Nature is subject to change and that therefore this one death falls into the general scheme of things. But Horace, quite ineptly it would seem, uses his reference to Nature to criticize Valgius' mourning rather than to explain Mystes' death as a natural, hence tolerable, event.

The tragic deaths of Antilochos and Troilos belonged to the conventional *exempla* that one could evoke to console parents and other close relatives upon the occasion of a young man's death. Once again, however, Horace has altered the expected usage. Instead of pointing to Antilochos and Troilos and drawing the conclusion that, if even the great young heroes of epic and tragedy died, we must be prepared to accept the death of our young men, he diverts the argument inappropriately toward the act of mourning. Now, although Nestor and Priam did eventually stop their open lamentations, strong traditions existed and had become commonplaces by Horace's time that both men indulged their grief extravagantly before they did stop. Callimachus originated a saying, which both Cicero and pseudo-Plutarch repeat, that Troilos wept less than his father Priam did.[8] As a consolatory dictum, that meant that, once dead, Troilos had passed beyond this world of tears; but it also made rather pointed reference to Priam's lamentations. As for Nestor, the death of Antilochos affected him so violently that he became an *exemplum* of the man who regrets his long

[8] Fragment 491 in Pfeiffer. Cf. Cicero *Tusc.* 1.93 and [Plutarch] *Apoll.* 24 p. 113 E.

life. This exemplum was used familiarly by Propertius 2.13.45–50 in the same years that Horace was writing our Ode, then again by Juvenal in Satire 10.250–255. Thus, the tradition tended to emphasize the fact that the two fathers also mourned like us, not that they stopped grieving.[9]

The most shocking argument, however, is the third. It cannot be duplicated, I make bold to assert, from any known Classical *consolatio*. Consider what Horace appears to be saying: Valgius, these lamentations are womanish (*molles*) and utterly unworthy of you; so give them up and write a poem instead on the glorious victories of Augustus in the East. I do not see how any words could be more gauche to a man in profound mourning for dead Mystes. Why should he compose a poem about Augustus now? How is that supposed to console him? When a man is plunged in grief, you do try to persuade him to reduce the grief, but you do not unfeelingly prescribe to him an activity that cannot be anything but meaningless in such an emotional crisis. Suppose you knew a writer or scholar who, when his son was killed in an accident or in war, began to mourn deeply and devote his time to developing a somewhat sentimental memoir or biography of the dead boy. Would you or anyone ever have the effrontery to tell that man, either to his face or in a letter, that he should abandon such a foolish scheme and instead exalt the genius of President Johnson in a learned work? I doubt it.

If, as I believe, this has been a fair analysis of the usual interpretation of Ode 2.9 as a poetic consolation on the occasion of Mystes' death, then we are left with our choice of conclusions: either Horace was incredibly and uniquely inept in treating his *consolatio* here or the usual interpretation is incorrect. I prefer the second alternative, and I shall now address myself to it. The main objection to the traditional interpretation lies in the apparent bad taste of the "consolation," its brutal disregard of Valgius' feelings, indifference to Mystes, and impertinent advice to write panegyric; in short, it does not exhibit the appropriate attitude for the occasion of a death. Suppose, as Quinn does, that Mystes is not literally dead; then we need not demand that Horace speak solemnly and sympathetically, since the extravagant grief of Valgius is now what is inappropriate to the occasion. Any "errors"

---

[9] In their comment on the passage of Propertius, H. E. Butler and E. A. Barber, *The Elegies of Propertius* (Oxford 1933) suggest that Callimachus may have originated the exemplum of Nestor in this context.

in the handling of the *consolatio* become now not a sign of Horace's incompetence, but rather an indication of his ironic distance from Valgius' need for any consolation in such trivial circumstances.

There is only one word which can be claimed to refer specifically to Mystes' death in the Ode, and that is the adjective *ademptum*. Nobody would be so foolish as to deny that *ademptum* could mean "dead" Mystes here. The commentators often content themselves by referring to Horace *C*. 2.4.10, where the same form does signify death. They could also cite Catullus 68.20 and 92 or 101.6, where the poet apostrophizes his dead brother as *adempte*; or a passage like Ovid's about Daedalion's grief for his dead daughter, *natam delamentatur ademptam* (*Met*. 11.331). Ovid, however, shows us how versatile the participle can be. In the same story where he tells of Daedalion's daughter, he reports Ceyx' grief for Daedalion as follows: *fratrem lugebat ademptum* (*Met*. 11.273). On the basis of the verb, it would be natural to interpret the participle with the sense "dead," exactly parallel to the participle about Daedalion's daughter. In fact, Daedalion is not dead at all; he has been metamorphosed into a bird. Ceyx grieves because his brother has quite literally been taken away, from him, not from life.

If the participle, then, can refer to a person who has been "taken away" and still remains alive, can we suggest the circumstances in which Mystes, still alive now, might have been taken from Valgius? It is hardly likely that he suffers exile like Ovid, who calls himself *ademptum* while languishing on the Black Sea.[10] On the contrary, he probably suffers not a bit, having been taken away with his own consent, not by some dread force like death, but by an admirer. Here, too, Ovid offers evidence. In *Met*. 13.871ff, Polyphemus has just finished expressing his passionate disappointment with Galatea's rejection of his love, and he has threatened his successful rival Acis. In this context, Ovid resorts to a simile:

> surgit et ut taurus vacca furibundus *adempta*
> stare nequit silvaque et notis saltibus errat.

Neither Galatea nor the cow of the simile is dead: both have been snatched away by rivals in love.[11] In *Heroides* 8, Hermione appeals to

---

10 *Trist*. 3.10.1 and *Pont*. 4.6.49.

11 Ovid uses active *ademit* in *Met* 5.16 to refer to Perseus' taking of Andromeda away from her original fiancé Phineus.

Orestes to save her from Pyrrhus, who has taken her away against her will, and she strengthens her case by using several analogies:

> an, si quis rapiat stabulis armenta reclusis,
>   arma feras? rapta coniuge lentus eris?
> sit socer exemplo, nuptae repetitor *ademptae*. (16–18)

Orestes should act vigorously like his father-in-law Menelaus, for Hermione has suffered a fate like Helen's; *rapta* and *adempta* are synonymous. In each case, it was a passionate male that took away the woman. Livy reports a rather similar situation in connection with Philip V of Macedon, whose lust during his younger years earned him great notoriety: "uni etiam principi Achaeorum Arato *adempta* uxor nomine Polycratia, ac spe regiarum nuptiarum in Macedoniam asportata fuerat" (27.31.8).

If Mystes is very much alive and has been seduced from Valgius by someone else, like Helen from Menelaus or Polycratia from Aratus, then the attitude of the poet towards Valgius becomes understandable. Furthermore, it now seems appropriate to address Valgius as Horace does; for it is significant that the poet says nothing of Valgius' tears, of mourning clothes or funeral arrangements, but concentrates attention exclusively on *flebilibus modis*, *amores*, and *mollium querelarum*. Valgius' grief is couched in a poetic mode, and his theme is love lost, a theme requiring pathetic complaints in tearful measures. Viewed in this circumscribed manner, as a poet working a monotonous elegiac theme, Valgius can then be asked to change his theme by Horace without difficulty, for Horace will not have transgressed against the decorum of funereal occasions.

There are many stock situations in erotic poetry, and just about every one became material for the amatory elegists of Rome. One of the most versatile situations features a triangle of love, in which the poet-speaker poses as the plaintive lover who has lost his girl—or boy—friend to a rival. Neither Catullus, Tibullus, Propertius, nor Ovid ever speaks of his beloved in these instances with the word *ademptus* or *adempta*; but the absence of this word from the vocabulary of surviving Latin love poets does not in any way prove that it could not be or was not so used. The poets tended to use some form of *rapere* or its compounds when they placed the blame largely on the rival; to shift some responsibility to the beloved, they used *capere*, *corrumpere*, and the like. Propertius, for example, in 2.8 starts his poem as though Cynthia has just been snatched from him (obviously by another man, who is not relevant here to the scope of the elegy):

> eripitur nobis iam pridem cara puella:
> et tu me lacrimas fundere, amice, vetas? (1–2)

In the course of his complaint, Propertius characteristically compares himself to an epic hero:

> ille etiam *abrepta* desertus coniuge Achilles
> cessare in tectus pertulit arma sua. (29–30)

And he concludes his examination of the passionate longing of Achilles with the following *sententia*: *tantus in erepto saevit amore dolor* (36).

We can say, then, that the situation of stolen lover, male or female, is a stock one, with its conventional details and vocabulary. Moreover, the few lines from Propertius suggest that the attitude of the elegist towards his predicament was more or less predictable: it was *dolor*, which would be expressed dramatically in tears or, in literary terms, by a formal *querela* and *flebiles modi*. Filled with self-pity and grief, the elegist magnifies his sorrow into the proportions normally found only in times of death; and he comes to treat the loss of his loved one as entirely equivalent in pathos to the loss of a loved one by death.[12] It then becomes the role of the elegist's friends to try to console him; or the elegist himself may possibly review consolatory topoi as he oscillates between sentiment and rational self-control. To return to Propertius 2.8, it should be noticed that the elegist, after stating the dramatic occasion as the loss of his *cara puella*, then addresses a friend who has apparently tried to console him. But Propertius indignantly rejects such friendly advice and so characterizes it in the light of his own grief:

> et tu me lacrimas fundere, amice, vetas? (2.8.2)

Farther on, he reverts to the awkward attempt at consolation made by the friend. As T. A. Suits has recently suggested, lines 7–10 consist of

---

12 Cf. Propertius 1.20.4ff and Horace *C.* 3.20 for situations similar to this; Propertius 2.20 and [Tibullus] 3.2.1–8 for grieving complaints on the loss of a lover.

"arguments which are supposed to have been set forth prior to the opening of the elegy and which the poet now quotes sardonically." [13]

> omnia vertuntur: certe vertuntur amores:
>   vinceris aut vincis, haec in amore rota est.
> magni saepe duces, magni cecidere tyranni,
>   et Thebae steterunt altaque Troia fuit.

These lines are consolatory platitudes applied clumsily to the situation of the *erepta puella*. Everything is subject to change, and so are mortal lives and love. Great men have perished, great cities have fallen, so we all must die—or lose our lovers.

Just as Propertius enlivens the drama of his *dolor* with the rejected arguments of a consoler and thereby justifies his "grief," Horace exposes the triviality of the elegist's "grief" by his artful use of consolatory themes. In 1.33 he playfully consoled Albius (possibly Tibullus) in his moment of violent *dolor* for Glycera. Now, in 2.9 he employs a new method to deal with the elegiac grief of his friend Valgius. He is not consoling Valgius according to the conventional arguments of the *consolatio*, for he does not want his friend to be comforted and so feel that Mystes deserves elegies, nor does he wish Valgius to transfer his affections to another *puer* or *puella* and therewith expose himself to the necessity of composing additional elegies. Horace attacks the basic mood of elegy, its querulous tone, and he implies that its failure to change brings it into conflict with nature and the mythical *exempla* it so lavishly adduces. For reasons which are partly lost to us because of our ignorance of Valgius himself, but are partly controllable because of the way the poem develops, Horace urges the poet to change, to take up the grand theme of Augustus' victories in the East. In the first two stanzas, the poet showed how the order of nature changes, never stays in the condition analogous to human grief for more than a short season. In the last two stanzas, as he urges his Augustan theme on Valgius, Horace describes the achievements of the princeps as alterations and subjections of the natural scenery of the East, Mt. Niphates, the Euphrates, and the somehow constricted plains of Scythia. The implication is, that Augustus has an almost divine power to order nature and that the changes he has effected in the East represent an improvement. To attune his poetic talent with such a theme should challenge and excite

13 *TAPA* 96 (1965) 433.

Valgius, whereas it is sheer folly to continue turning out trivial elegies on the stock theme of worthless Mystes, lost (*ademptum*) to the embraces of someone else.[14]

Finally, we may note that Quinn's reading of the ode in reference to a stock situation of erotic elegy and our insistence that Horace does not attempt to deploy the arguments of the *consolatio* in proper fashion, but in mockery of the false exaggerated *dolor* of Valgius the elegist, both together serve to explain the position of this poem in Book II. It has long been recognized that the first twelve poems of the Book form a group, with 1 and 12 acting as a frame and the five pairs from 2 through 11 carefully arranged so that the reader may find important corresponsions between, say, 2 and 3 or 4 and 5 or 6 and 7.[15] When, however, scholars come to 8 and 9, they have contented themselves with vague corresponsion, for 2.8 clearly takes up a typical woman of the amatory tradition and treats very lightly her amazing impunity in forswearing herself: Barine is the standard fickle, faithless courtesan. Since they treat Mystes in 2.9 as dead and Valgius' mourning as profoundly serious, they must content themselves with saying that both 2.8 and 9 are erotic poems or try to go a little further and define a contrast between all too faithless Barine and all too loyal Valgius.[16] We can now say that both poems treat elegiac loves, both comment lightly on such love affairs, the first presenting such *amor* in terms of the perfidious woman who regularly takes on the role of *domina*, the second looking at it in the person of the stock complaining lover, ridiculous in himself but particularly so in this case because he has been victimized not by a seductive Barine, but by a *puer*, Mystes whose only interest is that he is *ademptus*.

The Occasion of Horace's *Carm.* 2.14

In interpreting 2.14 Quinn starts from an altogether acceptable hypothesis: that the ode, like many superior lyric poems in-

---

[14] As we noted earlier, the encomiastic part of a *consolatio* is standard: the deceased must be praised as supremely worthy of our grief. Horace has refused to give any praise of Mystes himself, and he thereby implies how foolish Valgius is to waste his time eulogizing a *puer* of slight merit. If Valgius wishes to be encomiastic, he should use his talents on a worthy subject, Augustus.

[15] Cf. W. Port, "Die Anordnung in Gedichtbüchern augusteischer Zeit," *Philologus* 81 (1925) 299.

[16] Kiessling-Heinze (supra, n. 3) 194: "Gegenstücke sind übrigens auch die allzu ungetreue Barine des vorigen und der allzu getreue Valgius dieses Gedichts."

cluding those of Horace himself, employs an imaginary situation and a speaker who need not be identified as Horace. The problem he sets himself, then, is to define for us the particular situation and speaker which, as he sees it, Horace imaginatively created within the circumscribed world of this poem. Since any good poem works with great economy to introduce the audience to its private world within the space of a few opening lines, Quinn rightly concentrates first on the initial stanza of this ode. He has this to say about the situation: "The scene implied is a rather different sort of dinner party from those in i, 27 or iv, 13. The reader is once again called upon to fill in the semi-extraneous details for himself, and each reader will naturally fill them in differently. A speaker (whom we should be ingenuous in taking to be Horace himself) breaks in on a conversation to address his host, Postumus, with a gloomy earnestness that comes (we may suspect, taking up a hint in the last stanza) as much from what he has imbibed of his host's liquor as from what he has imbibed of Epicurean philosophy." [17] Once he has distinguished this dramatic scene and the speaker's tone, Quinn contents himself with sweeping over the next four stanzas, enthusiastically described as "pure poetry" and poetry made out of a commonplace, in order to draw all our attention to the final two stanzas.

Perhaps, though, before we go to the sixth stanza, we should look more closely at the first, to see whether we can agree with the inferences which have been drawn about its dramatic scene. The earnest, gloomy speaker is there, I concede, although I see no reason as yet—nor will I when I come to the last stanza—to diagnose this gloom as the result of drink. The dinner party I see nowhere implied in the first stanza. I do not say that the party is excluded, if later portions of the poem seem to bring such a scene to the fore; I do say that the first stanza offers no evidence at all for a party. The earnest, gloomy speaker starts from a background that Horace does not choose to define. And if he implies anything, he does it by the words that he inserts in that stanza, not by ideas drawn from the last stanza. Thus, although *pietas* appears regularly in gloomy poems on the unavoidability of death, to emphasize the absolute inflexibility of the natural order,[18] in this poem Horace stresses the point more than strictly necessary. Not only does the

---

[17] Quinn (supra, n. 1) 100–101.

[18] Orellius cites a fragment from Aeschylus' *Niobe*; cf. also Euripides' *Alcestis* 962ff. Horace refers to *pietas* as a brief topos for similar circumstances in 1.24.11 and 4.7.24.

futile "battle" of *pietas* against the invading forces of age and death
serve to make vivid the first statement of the poem about the "fleeing
years," but also Horace continues the theme into the second stanza with
an apparently hyperbolic reference to extravagant sacrifices designed
vainly to buy off Pluto. Suppose we conclude that this cluster of material
on *pietas* constitutes all that Horace wishes to imply of the dramatic
scene at this point. What should we infer from it? I suggest that
Postumus has been talking with some confidence about his right relations with god and man, possibly even claiming that the gods therefore
will guard him in the future. The earnest, gloomy speaker, then, pitying
the simple-mindedness of Postumus, tries to impress upon him a true
grasp of his mortality. I do not insist on the necessity of my inferences;
I do not believe, on the other hand, that, if we are looking for Horace's
implications as to the dramatic scene, we are entitled to ignore the
details of the opening stanza and rush to the last stanza to grasp a
tenuous hypothesis.

At the end of the second stanza, Horace names two mighty
giants of mythology, Geryon and Tityos, who have been overcome by
death, then expands his net to include in the next three stanzas all mankind as victims, because mortal, of Pluto. It serves his purposes both of
inclusiveness and of consolation to move from the second person singu-
lar (Postumus alone) to the first person plural by means of the relative
clause (*quicumque . . . vescimur* 10) and the attached "universalizing
doublet" (*sive reges / sive inopes erimus coloni* 11–12). The fourth stanza
uses two main verbs in the first person plural, and the fifth stanza, although not specifying the agent of the gerundive *visendus*, presumably
expects the audience to supply *nobis* rather than restrict the action as yet
to *tibi* (Postumus). Only in the sixth stanza, in the inserted relative
clause (*quas colis* 22), does Horace decisively break away from the
generalizing form to concentrate once again on Postumus; in retrospect,
the initial gerundive of that stanza acquires as its agent *tibi*. In its
structure, therefore, this poem is quite typically Horatian. Its first two
stanzas are devoted to sketching as much of the situation involving
Postumus as the poet cares to introduce; the end of the second stanza
fades neatly into the dominant theme of the central stanzas (as the
speaker both warns and consoles Postumus with the vision of all men's
mortality); then the sixth stanza, starting as a mere continuation
of the gerundive construction in stanza five, cleverly transfers all
attention back to Postumus, who obviously is expected to draw,

with us, some conclusions for his personal situation from the generalizations. And Postumus' personal situation, as the final two stanzas reveal, obligate him to live a little more reasonably, to concentrate less on *pietas* and more on the blessings which he already possesses.

For Quinn, "the line of meaning remains relatively unimportant until we get to stanza 6" (p. 103). Then, according to him, the opening line brings us sharply back to Postumus' home.[19] As many commentators have been prone to observe, the phrasing of 20–21 is remarkably like a justly famous passage of Lucretius. In most cases, the editors have confined themselves to this safe observation. A few, however, have dared to draw a comparison between the two passages and remarked on the un-Lucretian qualities of Horace's poem.[20] Quinn makes a striking innovation by arguing that Horace *alludes* to Lucretius and, through that allusion, economically conveys the fact that the speaker in the Ode, like the speaker of the similar lines in Lucretius, utters words which we are not to accept. "Horace, we should repeat, is writing for an audience that knows its Lucretius. An audience that can be relied on to catch the echo of a familiar quotation. And, more than that, to recall the context of a familiar quotation."[21]

Again, the hypothesis is an attractive one. Horace does like to allude to familiar poetry, and he surely referred to Lucretius on more than one occasion in his earlier Satires.[22] However, in my experience one of the most pernicious pursuits of classical philology is the tracking down of supposed reminiscences, whether it be for the purpose of identifying sources or positing allusions, and it is the task of a responsible critic to demonstrate conclusively by fact, not by rhetoric, that a putative allusion exists and functions. Just because Horace's audience "knows its Lucretius" is no reason to assume that the context of Lucretius controls that of Horace. To put it quite brutally, Horace's audience did indeed know its Lucretius, better than Quinn does, and I find it

[19] In fact, we start to supply the opening line of the stanza with the pronoun *nobis* in accordance with the preceding context until in the following line the deictic *harum* and the relative clause *quas colis* make clear, as I have shown above, that the correct agent to understand is *tibi*.

[20] So Munro in his commentary on the passage of Lucretius and Commager (supra, n. 7) 287.

[21] Quinn (supra, n. 1) 105.

[22] E.g., *Serm.* 1.5.101ff and 2.4 passim. Cf. A. Weingärtner, *De Horatio Lucretii imitatore* (Halle 1874).

utterly impossible to believe that it could ever have distorted Lucretius into the shape required by Quinn. If that is so—and I shall demonstrate my assertion—then the supposed allusion vanishes like a bubble. We must return, then, to the safer comments of the traditional editors, that Horace's line is like Lucretius', possibly inspired by the unquestioned poetic power of Lucretius, possibly an affective evocation of another commonplace (like *pietas*) of meditations, poetic and rhetorical, on death. In the second alternative, Lucretius' passage would function merely as a further witness to the existence of this quite likely "commonplace."

At first sight, Horace's passage, *linquenda tellus et domus et placens | uxor*, does have striking affinities with Lucretius' longer passage:

> iam iam non domus accipiet te laeta, neque uxor
> optima nec dulces occurrent oscula nati
> praeripere et tacita pectus dulcedine tangent.
>
> (Lucr. 3.894–896)

Both home and wife are mentioned, and Horace could be said in *placens* to vary the epithet *optima* of Lucretius to fit the Alcaic meter. We may be sorry that Horace has omitted the affective picture of the children and their welcoming kisses, but Latin *variatio* does operate in this free way in other instances. So far, then, Horace might be alluding to Lucretius. If it can be shown that the context of Lucretius fits closely that of Horace, then the possibility of allusion becomes more of a likelihood. As I have argued, the context of Horace is far from clear at this point, not patently the dinner party that Quinn affirms. Nevertheless, in these final two stanzas, Horace, with the help of Lucretian echoes, could intend to work out, in an ironic way not at all unusual for him, a surprising clarification of the dramatic scene. So we may legitimately investigate the context of Lucretius, if only with the hope that it may assist us.

Quinn says: "What is the context of these lines in Lucretius? They are given as typical of the talk of men at dinner parties when among their cups they start to lament the brevity of human life:

> hoc etiam faciunt ubi discubuere tenentque
> pocula saepe homines et inumbrant ora coronis,

ex animo ut dicant 'brevis hic est fructus homullis;
iam fuerit neque post umquam revocare licebit.'"23

To summarize the remainder of his argument, because Lucretius satir-
izes this dinner talk and because Horace's context seems to be another
dinner with talk of a similar vein, it follows that Horace is also satirizing
the speaker. But is Quinn right in his construction of the context in
Lucretius 3.894–896; is the context in fact defined by a passage which
in all manuscripts appears nearly twenty lines later, which seems not to
refer back to 3.894 but forward to a *new* context and quite different
statements?

Quinn reports that J. P. Postgate saw reason to transpose
3.912–918 to a point immediately before 894–899, but he does not
explain why Postgate did so and whether in fact he agrees with that
dubious authority. Having obscured the issue, though, he conveys the
impression that his view of the context of 894–899 is certain. But no
recent edition that I can discover even deigns to mention Postgate's
transposition, let alone follow it. Editors and translators regularly agree
that the manuscript order makes good logical and poetic sense, and they
would willingly assent to the summary of the Lucretian scholar Cyril
Bailey, who, introducing comments on 3.912–930, wrote: "Lucr. passes
from the solemn mourners at the graveside"—he refers to 3.894–911—
"to the ordinary pleasure-loving man (the Epicurean in the popular
sense) who cries 'let us eat, drink, and be merry, for to-morrow we
die.'"24 If Quinn had not made the mistake, I should have said that it
was impossible to confuse Lucretius' meaning, for after moaning the
three lines quoted by Quinn (3.894–896), the unidentified friends continue unambiguously: *misero misere . . . omnia ademit una dies infesta tibi
tot praemia vitae* (898–899). In other words, the future tense of Lucretius'
passage is not a warning uttered by a maudlin, half-drunk guest, but a
lament voiced by a friend at the tomb or bier of the dead man who, now
that he has died, will no longer enjoy life's blessings. A second speech is
then assigned to mourners (904ff), again making clear the condition of

23 Quinn (supra, n. 1) 104–105. He appends a note fixing the passage as
Lucr. 3.912–915. Then, without directly facing the question of the remoteness of 3.894 from
3.912 or the apparently disjunctive use of *etiam* in 912, he seems to sweep away any objections
with these two laconic sentences: "The order of the lines in this passage of Lucretius is
disputed. Some editors follow Postgate in putting 912–918 immediately before 894–899."
See my discussion infra.

24 Bailey, *Lucretius* (Oxford 1947) II 1146.

the person being apostrophized (*leto sopitus* 904, *horrifico cinefactum te prope busto* 906): he is dead, they have been weeping (*deflevimus* 907) at his funeral rites. Therefore, when in 912 Lucretius starts with *hoc etiam faciunt*, we have every right to expect some additional details about the attitude toward death, but we certainly will not let the relative clause (*ubi discubuere* etc.) that qualifies this new group of people cancel the details which Lucretius has carefully introduced to define the previous group as mourners. The banqueters of 912ff have absolutely nothing to do with the statements of 3.894ff.[25]

Once the context of Lucretius is demonstrated to be other than what Quinn has argued, the particular Lucretian allusion which he finds in this Ode vanishes. Whatever the dramatic situation of Postumus, he surely is not dead, as is the person being addressed in the Lucretian passage supposedly echoed by Horace; nor is the speaker a mourner as in Lucretius. We must then inspect more closely the final two stanzas of Horace's Ode to see whether any of the conjectures of Quinn are in fact supported by the Latin. Horace tells us that Postumus possesses land (*tellus*), a presumably fine home (*domus*), and a charming wife (*placens uxor*). Without Lucretius to lean upon, we cannot draw any safe conclusions as to the location of these items. One certainly can have a *domus* either in the city or country; one's wife can be in either home at a set time; and *tellus*, a poetic word, although I suspect that it here refers to agricultural land, might merely denote the earth which all men must leave at death. When the speaker continues the list of Postumus' possessions by mentioning and pointing to some cultivated trees (*harum quas colis arborum* 22), Quinn infers crucial details for the hypothetical scene of the poem: "Not a rural scene, but a scene in a wealthy Roman's house in the city. The speaker is looking out from the *triclinium* into his host's formal garden in the *peristylium*."[26]

Now, most readers of this poem have inferred the opposite from these same trees: a rural scene, not an urban one. Without the Lucretian allusion, it is possible to determine the relative strength of each inference on its own merits. Does the speaker point to a formal garden in a peristyle, or does his gesture embrace a group of trees

---

[25] The same introductory words, *hoc etiam*, occur in 3.1024 and serve a similar purpose. There, Lucretius has completed one argument about death with 1023; he then announces that he is proceeding, as he indeed does, to a new way of consoling oneself for the inevitable extinction of death. The word *etiam* is clearly disjunctive in such usage.

[26] Quinn (supra, n. 1) 106.

cultivated on a country estate? Horace did know of gardens within a peristyle, gardens which included some kinds of trees or shrubbery which could be qualified by the terms *silva* or *nemus*. In *Epist*. 1.10.22, he refers to such a garden, not without a certain irony that may well affect his choice of the word *silva*: *nempe inter varias nutritur silva columnas*. It is generally assumed that a similar garden is evoked by a passage in *Carm*. 3.10.5–6: *nemus / inter pulchra satum tecta*.[27] A *nemus*, however, does not suggest to the Roman mind a profusion of trees; it defines rather something like a forest glade, a grove. I take it that, in fact, there were few, if any, true trees in the garden of the usual peristyle, for the simple reason that they would be of the wrong scale. The *nemus* in such a case was the variegated growth of the clearing seen through the columns (which represented to the pastoral imagination the trees of the woods). Now, Horace goes to great pains to specify what he means when he is referring to the garden of the peristyle: he mentions *silva inter columnas* or *nemus inter tecta*. He does no such thing here. In a context not otherwise defined, cultivated trees would not, I believe, suggest to a sophisticated Roman audience, any more than it has to most readers of Horace today, a formal garden in the peristyle. Too many Romans of Horace's generation were familiar with Vergil's *Georgics* and the agricultural writings of Varro and the great Cato to interpret these trees as anything but the various kinds of useful *arbores*, for fruit, timber, shade, and the like, to be seen on a rural estate.

The decisive detail, it seems to me, is the set of cypress. The cypress is not a tree for a garden, and the Romans knew it well. Cato regarded it as an imported item, but attributed to it enough practical value to give careful directions as to its cultivation on the farm.[28] Varro described its use for supporting shoots and for marking off farm-boundaries.[29] Pliny, assimilating this and other information from his many sources, allowed little aesthetic merit to the cypress, except where it was allowed to grow in stands and then cut to represent a variety of forms, like the yew hedge of English country houses.[30] But the cut cypress hedge was a tall hedge, not suitable for the enclosed space of the peristyle but eminently appropriate to define a portion of a large estate under the open sky. The cypress itself is a tall tree, to which Catullus

[27] Cf. [Tibullus] 3.3.15, *nemora in domibus sacros imitantia lucos*.
[28] Cato *R.R.* 151.1.
[29] Varro *R.R.* 1.15 and 26.
[30] *N.H.* 16.60.139ff.

assigns the poetic epithet *aerea*;[31] and Vergil, comparing mighty Rome among the lesser cities of the world, thinks of cypress towering into the air among mere shrubs.[32] It is because of its height that Varro used the cypress to mark off the boundaries of his farm, visible to everyone from a great distance. Therefore, if Postumus is the master of cypress trees, we are entitled to assume that these trees, notoriously tall, devoid of shade, unappealing to the eye, but useful for wood and providing supporting stakes for plants, formed part of a plantation in the country, not a formal garden in a peristyle.

The final stanza must also be approached without prejudice. We have found no evidence in any preceding line for a dinner scene or the conversation that usually accompanied Roman *convivia*. On the contrary, the details from which legitimate inferences may be drawn seem to point to a rural setting, probably a stroll among the trees of Postumus' plantation. When the speaker concludes his monologue by predicting the wasteful behavior of Postumus' heir with the hoarded wine in his cellar, there is no reason to follow Quinn and assume that a sly comparison is being made between two kinds of dinner, the present one with its lack of wine and various future ones where precious Caecuban is spilled on the *pavimentum*. The speaker does intend an implicit comparison, undoubtedly, between Postumus and his heir, but not in the sense Quinn suggests. On the one hand, we consider Postumus here and now; he has locked up his choice Caecuban, that is, cut himself and his friends off from the pleasures of the dinner party. The very last thing that Horace wants us to picture is a Postumus acting as host. On the other hand, the speaker invites us to imagine Postumus' heir who, once he becomes master of that cellar, will make extravagant use of the wine, probably in dinner parties. All the abstemious self-denial of Postumus will ironically result in the drunken spilling of his treasured bottles.

In rejecting Quinn's hypothesis of the dinner scene and the somewhat inebriated speaker spouting his maudlin commonplaces, I wish also to raise questions about the way Quinn presented the poem in general: as a dramatic monologue in which the focus of Horace, the sophisticated Roman audience, and intelligent modern readers rests upon the speaker. For Quinn, Postumus functions only as a host of the speaker; otherwise, we concentrate on the slowly revealed foolishness of the speaker, his guest. In order to establish this thesis, though, Quinn

[31] See 64.291.
[32] *Ecl.* 1.25.

limits his careful reading to three stanzas only, as if the central portion of the ode could be eliminated from consideration. He is very flattering to Horace, of course, in that he praises those more or less ignored stanzas as "pure poetry." But if those stanzas are good poetry, unqualified in any way to awaken suspicions about their speaker; if their picture of death is to stir some kind of assent in our imaginations, how can we be expected suddenly to reject this impression and scorn the speaker as a drunken fool? By all the standards of poetic economy, we should have expected Horace to plant here and there words that occasioned doubts as to the speaker's reliability, precisely where Quinn senses "pure poetry." The result of Quinn's reading is a speaker who produces line after line of excellent poetry, then surprises us by his folly, and a Postumus who is virtually a cipher, in short a poem whose "meaning" resides in a highly original interpretation of three out of seven stanzas.

      The traditional interpretation of this ode has devoted itself almost exclusively to Postumus. Whether or not the speaker is to be identified with Horace, nevertheless it has been assumed that the words he utters have authority and serve to reveal to the Roman and modern audience of Horace not the character of this speaker, but the true nature of Postumus' existence. I find this interpretation, *pace* Quinn, essentially unassailable. In what follows, then, I should like to bring out, perhaps a little more elaborately than is customary, the poetic art by which this ode operates. After all, it should be self-evident that with Horace we are far less interested in *what* he says than in *how* it is said. We should have little difficulty in locating a multitude of verbal and thematic parallels, to prove how trite—if that is what we seek to demonstrate—the idea of the ode is. Particularly in Book II Horace devoted attention to aging Roman nobles and politicians who miss the true enjoyments of existence. Postumus differs somewhat from Dellius of 2.3 and Quintius Hirpinus of 2.11, but there is little appreciable difference among the speakers of the three poems either in attitude or arguments. When we compare the three poems as to the manner in which the speaker makes his argument, it is immediately obvious that 2.3 and 11 consist of direct advice whereas 2.14 works obliquely, or, to use Heinze's terms, as indirect paraenesis.[33] Through this indirection, we gradually acquire an impression of Postumus and apply the details used to describe him to the familiar scheme of counsel utilized in such odes as 2.3 and 11.

33 Kiessling-Heinze (supra, n. 3) 216.

As part of their direct method, both 2.3 and 2.11 start concretely from the present situation. In 2.3 the speaker uses an imperative *memento* that looks to the future (supported by the future perfects *vixeris* 5 and *bearis* 7), but it is quite evident that the advice being given applies to both present and future. Then, by pointing to the natural beauty surrounding Dellius, by the present imperative *iube* 14, and by the clause *dum . . . patiuntur* 15–16, the speaker makes it clear that he contrasts the future with the present, the only temporal period which Dellius can in any positive way affect. The following stanza fixes attention on the future (17ff), to warn Dellius that he will leave all his accumulated possessions; it is then reinforced by a generalization about all men and their mortality (*omnes eodem cogimur* 24). The whole poem has been explicitly constructed around the present, and the interrelation of tenses and moods helps to reinforce the imperative of the speaker: enjoy these things *now*. In 2.11 the speaker fuses present and future in a different manner, still concentrating on the imperative of *now*. Having revealed what Quintius is doing, anxiously inquiring into the intentions (for the future) of the distant Spaniard and Scyth, the speaker gives his advice (the subjunctive serving as a substitute for the imperative): *remittas quaerere* 3–4. Time flies (*fugit* 5); nature does not remain lovely forever, he warns. Then, he advances his positive alternative to the negative advice with which he began: with a series of questions and an imperative (*dic age . . . maturet* 22–23), he indicates the natural setting of trees (*hac pinu* 13–14) and the physical blessings available to Quintius, but inserts the admonitory *dum licet* 16 to keep Quintius attentive to the transitory aspect of even those advantages which he can be said to control. Thus, 2.11 works explicitly in the present, implicitly in terms of the future's threat. Not one future tense occurs.

By contrast, 2.14 elaborates its themes almost exclusively in relation to the future. After the initial *labuntur* 2, every main clause employs either a future active verb or, what amounts to the same effect, a future passive participle. One relative clause, *quicumque . . . vescimur* 10, in the present tense functions primarily to reinforce *omnibus* and the thought: "We all *shall* die." The second relative clause in the present tense, *quas colis* 22, possesses, as we have seen, major importance, for it restores our attention to Postumus and his present circumstances and encourages us to supply the personal pronoun *tibi* for the gerundive *linquenda* 21. Otherwise, the only verbal form which might be construed to refer to the present is the participle *servata* 26. In the future, the heir will waste the wine which has been locked up carefully; that implies that Postumus *now* locks up his Caecuban, that Postumus owns some wonderful wine and foolishly leaves it untasted. All this explicit emphasis on the future, a consistent aspect of the poem from first to last stanza, surely suggests less about the speaker than about Postumus. If he will open his eyes to a realistic picture of the future (in sharp contrast to his pious expectations), he may at least acquire an appreciation of the present and accept its implicit imperatives. By avoiding the present tense, though, by refraining from all imperatives, by sketching in the scene only through a seemingly incidental relative clause and a participial clause, the speaker keeps his advice indirect, and the poem becomes one of the most artful of these typically Horatian hortatory odes.

A regular element of these odes, as noted in 2.3 and 2.11, is the *dum*-clause. "Gather ye rosebuds *while* ye may," for the roses do not remain in their bloom forever; they are short-lived, and our span of life is short. Horace employs no *dum*-clause to interrupt the oblique methods of 2.14, and he handles the equally conventional appeal to *brevitas* (cf. 2.3.13, 1.4.25, 1.11.6) with great restraint. Of all the trees which Postumus cultivates on his estate, only the cypress will attend their short-lived master (*brevem dominum* 24) when he departs from life. Another common topic of these odes is the heir, regularly represented as an implicit enemy to the present owner of the estate, a warning to use what one has now (cf. 2.3.19–20, 4.7.19; *Epist.* 1.5.13, 2.2.190–191). Here, too, Horace employs the theme with much oblique economy, for he attaches to this unknown inheritor details which apply implicitly to the present condition of Postumus. From the perspective of the speaker, the heir earns the adjective *dignior*, because by comparison with Postumus' tenacious hoarding the younger man's wasteful spilling of choice vintages constitutes a more worthy occupation.[34] So the heir serves as a veiled threat in a specific sense: he reminds Postumus of all the wine which he is vainly leaving behind him untasted.

The artistry which Horace exhibits in this indirect para-

---

[34] It is probably significant that Horace does not include among the affective details in 21ff, where he lists what Postumus will lose by death, any son or children. In this, he differs markedly from Lucretius, who devoted two memorable lines to *dulces nati* running to snatch kisses from their beloved father. We do not, then, have to imagine the heir as a renegade son who frustrates the affection of his late father. On the contrary, Horace suggests that Postumus, childless, has left all his hoarded riches and wines to a dissolute nephew, a youth who never appreciated the uncle except for his money. Postumus has thus failed to enjoy the pleasures of marriage, his *placens uxor*, or the parent's pride in children.

enesis makes it intrinsically unlikely, it seems to me, that Franz Buecheler correctly appreciated this poem in pointing out a series of "infelicities" and assigning it to an early period of Horace's productivity.[35] On the contrary, I should assume that 2.14 was written after both 2.3 and 2.11, just as it is placed after them in the Book, because Horace knew he could rely on the audience's familiarity with the poem's implicit argument and so devoted his attention to his indirect presentation. Buecheler levels his attack in general at "the grossly mythological tone, the extensive reminiscences from Greek, the inclination toward exaggeration," and in particular at verbal awkwardness. Little need be said to counteract his criticism on the three general points. The references to the Underworld are not crude; they have been selected carefully. For example, Geryon (8) was chosen probably because his name connotes great herds of cattle. Postumus, who seems to think that huge sacrifices of bulls might save him from death, can well take that gigantic owner of bulls and cows as a pattern. Tityos also was a giant, but his name, juxtaposed to *tristi*, suggests the pain of death, the permanent *tristitia* which Postumus will be unable to alter. The Danaides and Sisyphus (18–20) emphasize another crucial aspect about the Afterlife to which Postumus is destined: it consists of protracted toil (*longi laboris* 20).[36] The allusions to Greek literature do not stand out in opposition to the rest of the poem. Thus, the supposed echo of Homer in 10, *quicumque terrae munere vescimur*, by its very Homeric associations would serve to validate the generalization about *omnibus*; it also acts as an implicit reminder to Postumus that he should enjoy the bounty of the earth while he can. Finally, if Buecheler meant by hyperbolical such numbers as *trecenis* 5 and *centum* 26, we may concede the fact of exaggeration without also condemning it; for the exaggeration serves rhetorically to bring home the unwise, excessive commitments of Postumus.

In his list of verbal awkwardnesses, Buecheler specified *inlacrimabilem* (6), *enaviganda* (11), *carebimus* (13), and *mero . . . potiore cenis* (26–28). I do not share his judgment about Horace's innovation, *inlacrimabilem*, nor did Horace; for he reused the word in another late Alcaic poem, 4.9.26. Moreover, a little study will reveal how skillfully Horace fitted the sonorous word to the other vowels and consonants of

---

35 *RhM* 37 (1882) 234.

36 I suggest, too, that Horace resorted to the patronymic *Aeolides* 20 in part to enhance the alliteration of those carefully separated, pointedly disposed words *longi . . . laboris*.

the context. With *enaviganda*, Horace also behaved boldly, for he took what had been an intransitive verb of motion and made it transitive: this gerundive construction is particularly striking, in that Horace delays *enaviganda* and separates it from *unda* by a line and a half. But look at what this single word helps the poet to achieve. In the first place, he supports the grammar by a rhyme (*unda . . . -anda*). He also inserts between the related words the Homeric reference, and thereby he juxtaposes the pictures of grim water and bounteous earth; *enaviganda* picks up the water image and insists on the absolute divorce between the two elements. Once dead, we all sail irredeemably across the Styx away from this lovely earth of ours. Finally, the gerundive initiates a procession of such constructions, whose cumulative effect in representing the unavoidable constraints of Postumus' future is undeniable. As for *carebimus*, Horace uses this word freely in his Odes, and here its choice is partially suggested by the sound-patterns of the context.

The last of Horace's supposed infelicities deserves special study, and it will bring us back to the question from which Quinn started: what is the situation of the poem in the first stanza? Buecheler considered juvenile the suppressed comparison in *mero . . . pontificum potiore cenis*, a comparison which all editors agree should be expanded and translated as follows: "wine better than that served at the banquets of the pontifices." I do not deny that such *might* be the correct translation. I suggest, however, that those who are tempted to belittle Horace's poetic maturity on the basis of such a translation might investigate the alternative rendering: "wine better than the banquets of the pontifices." It seems relatively obvious that Horace could easily have avoided "infelicity" by using *vinis* as his last word. If he indeed meant us to compare Caecuban with pontifical wine, the right word was at hand. Inasmuch as he chose *cenis*, not *vinis*, he invited his audience at least to try comparing Postumus' Caecuban wine, locked in his cellar originally but destined at last to be drunk, with proverbially lavish banquets of the pontifical colleges. Does this comparison make any sense? I think it does. Proverbial though such banquets were, they are also to be interpreted closely with the implied personality of Postumus. Buecheler inferred at this point that Postumus was a pontifex, but that is neither provable nor necessary. Banquets of pontifices do, however, represent what Postumus regards as important, for the lavish extravagance of such meals belongs to the same kind of superficial *pietas* as the munificent sacrifices referred to in the second stanza. The comparison, then, serves to remind us of the unwise scale of values cherished by Postumus, for that Caecuban wine, when properly enjoyed, symbolizes a way of life that is indeed better than formal paraphernalia of *pietas* like Postumus'. Indeed, it is no accident that the sound-patterns of 28 echo parts of the opening line. The repeated initial *po-* sound should remind us of the rare and affective anadiplosis: *Postume, Postume*; and of the letters of *fugaces* (1) only *g* and *a* fail to recur in 28. It seems as though Horace encourages us to link sound and sense of the opening and close of 2.14, to interpret the unwise Postumus as a man who puts all his confidence in formal religious *pietas* to guarantee his future, but completely fails to grasp the practical wisdom of his ultimate heir who will prefer the wine at hand to all that is symbolized by *cenae pontificum*, banquets of priests.

One final point needs to be made about the mature conception behind this poem. Although we can hardly be so presumptuous as to date its composition, it should be noted that Horace carefully placed it in immediate juxtaposition to an ode that deals in a strikingly different manner with many of the same themes, including the *pietas* which, I have argued, is so important in 2.14. The interaction of 2.13 and 2.14 is possibly more significant than that of any other pair in a Book which is, as is well known, almost entirely arranged according to paired poems.[37] *Carm.* 2.13 is a recognized masterpiece, and I have no doubt that Horace knew it in 23 B.C. If so, he would hardly have juxtaposed to it an effort that he knew was juvenile, knew that his audience would feel inartistic. He planned that two good poems should interact.

In 2.13, the speaker is Horace, and the poem deals with his own experiences and the manner in which he personally applies them. A tree, or perhaps only a branch, has just fallen near him, almost killing him. Very much alive, but feeling the closeness of death, he now interprets the accident. First, he solemnly speaks of man's inevitable fate: try as we may to avoid particular dangers, sudden death will sooner or later sweep us away (13ff). The speaker in 2.14 made the same point, but in a significantly different context, for, whereas Horace, breathing a sigh of relief, is commenting on his recent near-death by accident, the speaker to Postumus is warning him that death *will* seize him, *pietas* notwithstanding. How did Horace escape this "tragic" demise? In line 12 he modestly calls himself *immerentis*; in line 23 he states that, had he died, he would have been assigned to a place

---

[37] Cf. W. Port (supra, n. 15) 300.

among the *pii*, together with Sappho and Alcaeus. The implication, sufficiently clear in this clever poem, is confirmed by 2.17.27ff and 3.4.27: Horace's special *pietas* earned the miraculous protection of the gods.[38] Thus, a poem, honoring with playful seriousness the beneficent aspects of Horatian *pietas* is placed in immediate juxtaposition to 2.14, where *pietas* of a more formal type, associated with vain sacrifices of bulls and lavish pontifical banquets, is treated as pathetically futile, not only to save Postumus from death, but also to gain him any happiness after death.

Both poems devote considerable attention to the Afterlife, each in its special manner. In 2.13 Horace professes to be speculating or imagining what might have happened to him, had the tree killed him; in 2.14 the speaker confidently predicts what *will* happen to Postumus. Thus, in addition to the contrast between certain future for Postumus and avoided present (but probable future) of Horace, we feel the playfulness of Horace's situation and the quite different destiny of Postumus. It is here in part that Buecheler and others go wrong when they fix on the "crass mythological" elements of 2.14, for the traditional, commonplace elements of the Underworld serve the purposes of the poem as nicely as the patently untraditional, personal mythology of 2.13 contributes to its effects. If he had died, Horace "modestly" claims, he would have experienced an Underworld defined by the exquisite poetry of Sappho and Alcaeus. As they sing among the dead and the monsters of that usually grim world, they transform everyone and everything. Not only are the shades of ordinary people affected, as they gather around in hushed and marvelling silence, but Cerberus also abandons his threatening stance (33ff), Prometheus and Tantalus under the spell of the poetry can ignore their toil (*laborem* 38), and Orion abandons his wild *cura* to pursue lions and lynxes. Compare that picture of Death, in which the "pious poets" transform everything for the better, with the Death to be experienced by Postumus: all is unrelieved wretchedness. Postumus will have only a sense of *tristitia* (with Tityos 8), blackness

---

[38] On Horace's development of a private mythology on the basis of the traditional theme of *pius poeta*, cf. Commager (supra, n. 7) 126ff.

This article was submitted in May 1967, before the publication of the study by A. J. Woodman, "Eheu Fugaces," *Latomus* 26 (1967) 377–400, and hence it could not take note of his useful work. In brief, he also rejects Quinn's hypothesis on 2.14, gives a careful reading of the whole poem, and offers a special interpretation of the last stanza (with which I cannot fully agree), including an analysis of the comparison, *mero . . . potiore cenis* (28) that resembles mine.

(*ater* 17), and permanent, unchanging toil (*longi laboris* 19–20). Postumus, the speaker implies, has damned himself by the unwise way he has chosen to live on earth and so will be among the Damned, utterly barred from the Elysian Fields and the toil-relieving songs of an Alcaeus. But perhaps if he reverses his ways, begins to enjoy his immediate blessings, he may attenuate both the *tristitia* and *laborem* of this life and that which otherwise surely lies in store for him after death. Thus, the ode on the *pius poeta* helps to comment on *pius Postumus* of 2.14 and to confirm, I think, the traditional interpretation vis-à-vis the clever hypothesis of Quinn.

University of California
Berkeley

THEODORE F. BRUNNER

4

A Note on Persius 5.179ff

> ... at cum
> Herodis venere dies unctaque fenestra
> dispositae pinguem nebulam vomuere lucernae
> portantes violas rubrumque amplexa catinum
> cauda natat thynni, tumet alba fidelia vino,
> labra moves tacitus recutitaque sabbata palles.

Conington-Nettleship[1] see in *Herodis dies* a reference to "Herod's birthday," and Ramsay follows suit in his translation as well as in a note *ad loc*. Lewis and Short's *Dictionary*, on the other hand, in citing *Herodis dies* from this passage, gives the definition "the Sabbath." Which explanation is correct?

Conington-Nettleship's suggestion that Herod's birthday "would naturally be celebrated by the Herodians" does not sound convincing. The Jews of Persius' time could well be expected to share the common Jewish aversion to birthday celebrations and feasts which found its origin in a serious offense suffered on such a feast: according to II Macc. vi. 7, the Jews of Antiochus' time were forced to eat of the sacrifices which were offered on the King's birthday.

Furthermore, Persius' description of the practices characterizing *Herodis dies* seems to point toward the weekly sabbath, not an occasional birthday celebration. Even the use of the plural *Herodis venere dies* implies frequent repetition. Standing within the context of a

---

[1] John Conington and H. Nettleship, *The Satires of A. Persius Flaccus* (Hildesheim 1967) 119.

discussion of what Persius considers superstitious behavior, the passage virtually itemizes the most obvious sabbath practices. The obligation of lighting lamps at the onset of the sabbath is reflected in the *dispositae . . . lucernae* of line 181. *Lucernae* would be appropriate, since the seven-branched sabbath lamp, which has its origin in the sanctity attached to the number seven by the cabalists, did not come into household use until the middle ages. The fish diet of the sabbath evening is clearly indicated by the *rubrumque amplexa catinum cauda natat thynni* (182f), where the *natat* probably defines the meal as the *garum*, fish pickled in sauce, a dish which was very popular among the Jews of Persius' time and which is called by Pliny *garum castimoniale*, i.e., "kosher garum" (*Hist. Nat.* 31.95). *Tumet alba fidelia vino* (183): In accordance with the admonition "Remember the Sabbath day, to keep it holy" (Exod. xx.8), a Kiddush service recited by the Rabbi holding a cup of wine had to play an important part in the sabbath celebration even in Persius' time.

In general, wine was preferred for religious ceremonies over any other beverage in keeping with the injunction that wine "cheereth God" (Judges ix.13). The *labra moves tacitus* of line 184 would be an obvious reference to the recitation of Kiddush prayers over the wine, and the *palles* in the same line would refer to the intense involvement of the participants in the service (cf. *vigilandum, nitendum, pallendum est*, Quint. 7, 10, 14), rather than to the supposed gloominess of all Jewish observances, as Conington-Nettleship seem to think (cf. note *ad loc.*). The sabbath is by no means a gloomy, but rather a festive observance, and the festive nature of the celebration is undoubtedly indicated by Persius' *lucernae portantes violas* (cf. also Cicero *Tusc.* 5.73, where pillows filled with roses and violets are used at a festive dinner).

The *sabbata* (184), incidentally, would seem to add final support to the argument that *Herodis dies* is indeed a reference to the sabbath, and that Herod's name is used merely to characterize the holiday as Jewish, just as the Jews are referred to as "of Herod's party" or as "Herodians" in Matt. xxii.16.

University of California
Irvine

5

Theodulus' *Ecloga* and *Mythographus Vaticanus 1*

Theodulus' *Ecloga* is a medieval Latin poem of 344 lines in leonine hexameters (type of the one-syllabled rhyme). Its subject is a contest between shepherds in the manner of Virgil's *Eclogues*. A short introduction tells how two persons, Pseustis (Ψεύστης) and Alithia ('Αλήθεια), met and how an altercation led to a singing competition. This, the kernel of the poem, consists of a sequence of four-line strophes, sung alternately. Every time, Pseustis first presents a pagan myth and Alithia answers with a somehow similar subject from the Old Testament. The arrangement of the whole follows that of the biblical events, though it is the pagan myths that precede. The poem ends with Pseustis' admission of his inferiority, some concluding lines being spoken by Fronesis (Φρόνησις).

The *Ecloga* was very popular throughout the Middle Ages. It was read in schools, imitated by poets, and even commented upon. The number of manuscripts in which it is preserved exceeds 120. About the author nothing is known but his name. The identification with the poet Godescalc (ninth century), favored by Manitius,[1] is now given up. The *terminus ante quem* for the composition is the earliest MS, dating from the eleventh century.[2] For general reasons, a date prior to the ninth century is unlikely.

Particularly interesting among the many questions con-

---

[1] M. Manitius, *Geschichte der lateinischen Literatur des Mittelalters* I, Handb. d klass. Altertumswissenschaft 9, 2, 1 (München 1911) 570.

[2] See K. Strecker, *Neues Archiv der Gesellschaft für ältere deutsche Geschichtskunde* 45 (1924) 20.

nected with this poem is that of the sources of the pagan myths. J. Osternacher, to whom we owe also the best critical edition,[3] published in 1907 a commentary in which he collected a vast mass of parallels.[4] His assumption that Theodulus knew most of the quoted authors was corrected by Manitius (*op. cit.*, supra, n.1, 573) who limited the number of direct sources to six: Virgil (especially the *Eclogues*), Ovid's *Metamorphoses*, Prudentius, Sedulius, Martianus Capella, and—most important for the subject matter—the mythological sections in Servius.[5] That the latter is Theodulus' principal mythological source is certain and had, by the way, already been pointed out before Osternacher and Manitius by J. Frey.[6] It is the purpose of the present paper to draw the attention to three cases of striking coincidence between Theodulus and a second mythological compendium, not mentioned hitherto (as far as I see) among the sources of the *Ecloga*: the medieval handbook known under the name of *Mythographus Vaticanus 1*.[7]

Pseustis:
herbarum succos tractans Cillenius heros
exortes lucis virga revocavit ab umbris,
arte potens tali, credas ut cuncta fateri,
quod natum Maiae l a c t a v i t m a m m a novercae.

Ecl. 197–200

Osternacher has no parallel for Mercurius' being suckled by Juno. This is indeed a rare version. In ancient literature, it occurs

---

[3] *Theoduli eclogam recensuit et prolegomenis instruxit Joannes Osternacher*, program (also separate print) Urfahr 1902.

[4] J. Osternacher, *Quos auctores Latinos et sacrorum Bibliorum locos Theodulus imitatus esse videatur*, program Urfahr 1907.

[5] Manitius speaks of "the mythological handbook used by Servius." But it is most unlikely, to say the least, that this (lost) source of Servius was still available in the ninth or tenth centuries. See also *Philologus* 105 (1961) 135.

[6] Josef Frey, *Über das mittelalterliche Gedicht 'Theoduli ecloga' und den Kommentar des Bernhardus Ultraiectensis*, program Münster 1904, 13: "Als Hauptquelle für die Sagen hat der Serviuskommentar zu Vergil gedient. Nur in wenigen Fällen reicht das dort Gebotene nicht aus, wie in den Sagen von Cecrops, Kadmus, Niobe; aber was hier aus Servius nicht zu entnehmen war, stand wohl leicht aus anderen Quellen zu Gebote, und bei der Beschaffenheit der Serviushandschriften dürfte es nicht ausgeschlossen sein, dass das von Theodul benutzte Exemplar mehr bot."

[7] Edition: *Scriptores rerum mythicarum Latini tres . . .*, ed. G. H. Bode (Celle 1834) 2 vols. Ample information about MS tradition, date, sources, etc. is given by Kathleen O. Elliott and J. P. Elder, "A Critical Edition of the Vatican Mythographers," *TAPA* 78 (1947) 189–207.

only as an *aition* of the origin of the Milky Way: Mercurius—usually it is Hercules[8]—was after his birth brought to Juno who nursed him without knowing who the baby was. When she discovered it, she pushed the sucking baby away. Thus the milk poured out. The testimonies are: Achilles *Isag.* 24, *Commentariorum in Aratum Reliquiae* (ed. Maass, 1898) p. 55, 14; anon., *Isag. in Aratum*, p. 95, 23 Maass; Hyginus *Astr.* 2.43, p. 80, 12 Bunte. Achilles and Hyginus attest the story for Eratosthenes (fr. 2 Powell [probably from the poem *Hermes*]; cf. also *Eratosthenis catasterismorum reliquiae*, rec. C. Robert, 1878, 198). It can be ruled out that Theodulus knew any one of these authors.

But what if the same story is found in a much used medieval mythological handbook? *Mythographus Vaticanus 1*, 119 begins: *Juppiter jacuit in Cyllene monte cum Maja, et habuit filium Mercurium, quem Juno ita dilexit, quod[9] propria mamma eum lactavit, et artem medicam insinuavit.*[10] Both the verbal coincidence of *mamma*[11] *lactavit* and the—otherwise unattested—idea of Juno imparting to Mercurius, along with her milk, the art of healing, suggest a close relationship. For general reasons, it is more likely that the poet depends on the mythographer than vice versa. It may be added that the mythographer narrates the transmission of the medical art as a fact, whereas Theodulus relates it less directly (*credas ut cuncta fateri*)—which, if anything in the delicate matter of priority can be said, seems to be secondary.

> Pseustis:
> Idaeos lepores puer exagitat Ganimedes;
> quem J o v i s arreptum devexit in aethera sursum
> a r m i g e r; ablato divum concesserat ordo
> nomen   p i n c e r n a e,   q u o d   p o s s e d i t   p r i u s
> H e b e.
> *Ecl.* 77–80

This is, of course, a *fabula notissima* for which Theodulus did not need any source. And yet, there is again one striking coincidence with *Mythographus Vaticanus 1*. Chapter 184 runs: *Ganymedes, filius Troili,*

---

[8] See, e.g., Gundel, art. Γαλαξίας in *RE* 7, 566, 59–567, 36.

[9] Bode (supra, n. 7) rightly remarks "*constructio plane nova*," i.e., for *ita . . . ut*.

[10] Remigius of Auxerre (ninth century) seems to depend on this passage, *Commentum in Martianum Capellam* (ed. C. Lutz, 1962) 22.11: *Cyllenius filius fuit Jovis et Maiae quem mox natum Juno suis uberibus applicavit eumque, sicut fingunt fabulae, divino lacte fovit ut fieret immortalis.* Remigius' text was, in turn, copied by *Mythographus Vaticanus 3* (twelfth century), 9.2.

[11] The case does not matter.

filii Priami, quum prima forma ceteris Trojanis praeferretur, et assiduis venationibus in Idae silva exerceretur, ab a r m i g e r o J o v i s, scilicet aquila, quae quondam illi fulmina offerebat, in caelum raptus est, et factus est p i n c e r n a deorum; quod officium prius occupaverat Hebe. ... [12] I do not insist on *armiger Jovis* since this phrase occurs, as Osternacher rightly points out, in Virgil *Aen.* 5.255 and may have been taken over by Theodulus from there. But looking at the end, I cannot help taking 1.80 as a versification of the last sentence of the passage quoted from *Mythographus Vaticanus 1.* When Servius touches on the subject—Ganymedes' replacement of Hebe—he says (*Aen.* 1.28) ... *ministerium poculorum quod exhibuit diis remota Hebe,* and there may be many other ways of expressing this idea. On the other hand, what Theodulus' 1.80 has in common with the mythographer's last sentence, are not only single words (including the prosaic *pincerna*) but the whole structure of the relative clause. It looks also as if Theodulus got into difficulties with the tenses. Should all this be pure accident?

> Pseustis:
> Tithonum thalamis dignans Aurora superbis
> augendo vitam m u t a v i t i n usque c i c a d a m;
> e x t i n c t u m   T r o i a e   s e p e l i v i t   Mennona
>   longac,
> annua cuius aves venerantur festa frequentes.
>
> *Ecl.* 221–24

    Tithonus' transformation into a cicada, a rather rare version,[13] is mentioned in Theodulus' principal mythological source, Servius, on *Aen.* 4.585: *Tithonus frater Laeomedontis fuit: hunc Aurora amatum in caelum levavit, quem longinquitas vitae in c i c a d a m convertit* (similarly on *Georg.* 3.328). But for the Memnon myth, Servius has only a short note in another place, on *Aen.* 1.489: *NIGRI MEMNONIS ARMA quia Tithonus, frater Laeomedontis, raptus ab Aurora, filium suum*

[12] I do not deal here with the sources of *Mythographus Vaticanus 1* (for these, see R. Schulz, *de mythographi Vaticani primi fontibus,* Diss. Halle 1905, especially for ch. 184: pp. 47 and 66). No source is known for the words *pincerna ... Hebe* with which we are primarily concerned. The chapter on Ganymedes in *Mythographus Vaticanus 2* (198) depends either on *Myth. Vat. 1* or the same sources (see F. Keseling, *de mythographi Vaticani secundi fontibus,* Diss. Halle 1908, 97), but does not exhibit the relative clause *quod ... Hebe* either. For a possible relationship between *Myth. Vat. 1,* 184 and schol. λφψ Hor. 3.20.16 see *Philologus* 105 (1961) 133, n. 3.

[13] The instances are listed in Roscher, *Ausführliches Lexikon der griechischen und römischen Mythologie,* 5 (1916–1924) 1025, 22–28.

Memnonem ex ipsa progenitum, ad Troiae misit auxilia. nigri autem dixit Aethiopis, unde prima consurgit Aurora. Mythographus Vaticanus 1,139 has not only both stories connected, but the second much fuller: *Tithonus fuit frater Laemedontis, regis Trojanorum. qui quum adamatus fuisset ab Aurora, petiit ab ea longitudinem vitae. unde tamdiu vixit, donec prae nimia senectute versus est in cicadam. hic filium Memnonem, ex ipsa progenitum, ad Trojae misit auxilia. niger autem dictus* †et†[14] *Aethiops, quia, ubi prima surgit aurora, dubia lux est. hujus apud Trojam extincti et sepulti tumulum aves annuo volatu conventu*[15] *officiose celebrant.* There can be no doubt that the mythographer draws largely from Servius. But the last sentence with the verbs *extinguere* and *sepelire* which recur in Theodulus are not found in Servius—at least not in the extant manuscripts. If Schulz' assumption, *op. cit.* (supra, n. 12) 50, were right that once the full story about Memnon's grave stood in Servius on *Aen.* 1.489, Servius might have a better claim for being Theodulus' source than the mythographer. But this hypothesis is far from being certain. Why should Servius have interrupted the sequence of the story by a comment on the lemma? Servius Danielis who adds some words about Memnon's death does this before the remark on *nigri Aethiopis*. It is therefore rather unlikely that the last sentence ever stood in Servius.[16] But could Theodulus not write the two last lines without a mythographical source? (The story of the Memnon's birds was, e.g., told by Ovid in his *Metamorphoses*.[17]) Here again, I think the verbal repetitions, as well as the connection of both myths, favor the assumption of a dependence of the poet on the mythographer.

We have examined three mythological passages of Theodulus' *Ecloga*. A comparison with the mythographical tradition produced evidence of a close relationship with corresponding sections of *Mythographus Vaticanus 1*. The relationship consisted in all three cases of striking verbal coincidences and, in addition to that, in one case (the first) of a striking coincidence in the subject-matter. In no case was there any other known text coming as close to Theodulus' lines as the

[14] In the light of Servius' *nigri autem dixit Aethiopis*, I think we should read *est* instead of *et*. For a different solution see Schulz, (supra, n. 12) 50 adn. 1.

[15] The juxtaposition of *volatu conventu* is a little awkward. I wonder whether they are not variants and whether in the original text there was more than one substantive.

[16] A further argument is that *Myth. Vat. 2*, 194, which seems to be an excerpt from the same Servius passages (see Keseling, supra, n. 12, 97), does not exhibit the last sentence either.

[17] 13.617ff; see also Osternacher *ad. loc.*

first Vatican mythographer. The question of how these coincidences are to be explained has already been tentatively answered by supposing a dependence of Theodulus on the mythographer. We have to discuss it now again. Unless the coincidences are pure accident (which, I think, can be ruled out if we consider all three cases together), there are, theoretically, three possibilities: either, as already supposed, the poet uses the mythographer, or vice versa, or both have a common source.

To begin with the third, there is, of course, always the chance of some lost or unpublished medieval text (be it a commentary or whatever) containing mythographical information. Moreover, the general character of the mythographer as a mere compilation presupposes a source even where we are unable to detect it. (That means, of course, a source similar to the text of the mythographer, i.e., a prose text, and is therefore an important objection to the second hypothesis.) But the mythographer seems to have combined different sources—one of them being Servius—, whereas Theodulus has the same combination as the mythographer (see the third passage). In short: Theodulus' source, if it was not the mythographer, must have been similar to, not to say identical with, the mythographer. If, instead of playing with unknowns, we keep to what we have and if we take also into consideration that for someone looking for mythographical information, a handbook like *Mythographus Vaticanus 1* must have been a natural resource, the first hypothesis seems to be by far the most likely.[18]

This has also some consequences for the date of *Mythographus Vaticanus 1*. Whereas Elliott-Elder, *op. cit.* (supra, n. 7) 198, incline to assume pre-Carolingian origin, B. Bischoff,[19] basing his judgement on the late date of the *codex unicus* and the (alleged) absence of traces of an earlier utilization, proposed a date as late as the twelfth

---

[18] As for the verbal repetitions, the same procedure can be observed in Theodulus' using Servius (and this may be considered as a further argument in favor of the first, and against the second, hypothesis). Compare, e.g., Theod. *Ecl.* 111 *ille* (*sc.* Demophon) *reversus eo truncum rigat ore supino* with Serv. *Buc.* 5.10 *postea reversus Demophoon, cognita re, eius amplexus est truncum*, or Theod. *Ecl.* 93–96 *fulmina Ciclopes Jovis imperio fabricantes | . . . morti decrevit Apollo; | mox deitate sua . . . spoliatus . . . | Admeti curam pecoris suscepit agendam* with Serv. *Aen.* 7.761 *. . . Apollo . . . Cyclopas fabricatores fulminum confixit sagittis: ob quam rem a Jove iussus est Admeti regis novem annis armenta pascere divinitate deposita.* Incidentally, both Servius passages have been copied verbatim by the first mythographer (chs. 46 and 159)—which leads to the further question (not to be discussed here) whether Theodulus used in this case Servius directly or through the mythographer.

[19] See *Philologus* 105 (1961) 134, n. 3.

century. If my conclusion is right, at least any date later than the eleventh century[20] is excluded.

APPENDIX

Among the myths related by Theodulus and not found in Servius, J. Frey (supra, n. 6) mentioned also that of Cecrops. Theodulus' lines run (53–56):

> egregio Cecropi debetur causa litandi:
> ille bovis primo rimatus viscera ferro
> sacra Jovi statuit, quae posteritas celebravit;
> condidit Athenas; adiuvit nomine Pallas.

Osternacher has no parallels for Cecrops' alleged invention of sacrificing bulls to Jupiter. He would have had difficulties finding any in classical authors, for Pausanias states explicitly 8.2.3: ὁ μὲν γὰρ (*sc.* Cecrops) Δία τε ὠνόμασεν Ὕπατον πρῶτος, καὶ ὁπόσα ἔχει ψυχήν, τούτων μὲν ἠξίωσεν οὐδὲν θῦσαι, πέμματα δὲ ἐπιχώρια ἐπὶ τοῦ βωμοῦ καθήγισεν, ἃ πελάνους καλοῦσιν ἔτι καὶ ἐς ἡμᾶς Ἀθηναῖοι.

There is nothing in the *mythographi* either, but I think the tradition can be traced back to (1) Isidorus *etym.* 8.11.9–10: ... *Cecrops, sub quo primum* ... *Atheniensium urbs ex Minervae appellatione nomen sortita est. hic primus omnium Jovem appellavit,*[21] *simulacra repperit, aras statuit, v i c t i m a s i n m o l a v i t, nequaquam istiusmodi rebus in Graecia umquam visis*, and further down to (2) Hieronymus, *Chron. Eus.* ann. 1551 B.C./1546 B.C. (p. 41[b] 17/24 Helm)[22]: *Cecrope regnante primum* ... *ex Minervae nomine, quae Graece Athena, Athenae nuncupatae* ... / *primus Cecrops b o v e m i m m o l a n s Jovem appellavit.* Theodulus might have known Isidorus.

Hamburg

---

[20] See above, p. 65. But we have probably to put the *terminus ante quem* into the ninth century, for C. Lutz, in the introduction of her recent edition of Remigius' commentary on Martianus Capella, I (Leiden 1962) 23 reckons also with a dependence of Remigius on *Mythographus Vaticanus 1* (see also supra, n. 10).

[21] Another simplification (or misunderstanding). In Pausanias, *loc. cit.*, it is the name Ὕπατος which was first given to Zeus by Cecrops.

[22] Cf. also the Byzantine testimonies collected by Helm *ad loc.* (p. 292 on i).

6

The Hero as Athlete

In the sixth book of his *Descriptio Graeciae* Pausanias lists the statues of Olympic victors that he saw in the Altis of Olympia. His notice of most is brief, confined to what the inscription on the base told him: the name and city of the athlete, the kind of athlete that he was (pugilist, wrestler, etc.), and the name of the sculptor. To this minimum notice he sometimes adds the name of the dedicator, information on victories won, or a brief description of the statue. But occasionally he has more to say about the victors represented. Some were extraordinary persons, if the stories told about them are true. Whatever the truth about their deeds, several of these athletes received worship as heroes or even as deities, reputedly on order of the Delphic oracle. We shall review all hero-athletes that Pausanias mentions and a few others that he does not (and a few heroes who were not primarily athletes, but had similar experiences); but first I call attention to four: Kleomedes, Euthykles, Oibotas, and Theagenes, of whom Euthykles does not appear in Pausanias' list (and although Pausanias tells the story of Kleomedes he does not mention a statue of him).

1. In the Olympic games of 496 Kleomedes of Astypalaia, a pugilist, killed his opponent, Ikkos of Epidauros, in an unnecessarily brutal way. For this reason the Hellanodikai denied him the victor's crown and also fined him four talents. Their decision caused him such great grief and so preyed upon his mind that he went mad. Returning to Astypalaia he smote and broke the pillar that supported the schoolhouse roof, which fell and killed sixty boys at their lessons. The irate Astypalaeans began to stone him. To escape them he ran into a temple

of Athena, got into a chest, and closed the lid on himself. His fellow-citizens, after trying to raise the lid without success, broke the box open and found nothing inside: Kleomedes had vanished. The Astypalaeans consulted the Delphic Apollo on the meaning of this strange event and received the response:

"Υστατος ("Εσχατος Plut.) ἡρώων Κλεομήδης 'Αστυπαλαιεὺς
ὃν θυσίαις τιμᾶθ' ἅτε μηκέτι θνητὸν ἐόντα.
Most recent of heroes is Kleomedes of Astypalaia.
Honor him with sacrifices; for he is no longer a mortal.[1]

2. Euthykles of Locri was a famous pentathlon victor. Once he went on an embassy for his *polis* and came back to the city with some mules that a foreign friend had given him. His fellow-citizens accused him of having taken a bribe to betray his city, convicted him on the charge, and threw him into prison. There he died, probably executed as a convicted criminal (although this is not said in the two sources). Not satisfied, the Locrians voted to mutilate the statue of Euthykles which stood in the marketplace. Apparently the gods took more offense at the mistreatment of the statue than at the wrongful conviction of the man himself, for a blight came upon the land, bringing famine to Locri. So the Locrians consulted Apollo at Delphi, and received from the god a cryptic verse: 'Εν τιμῇ τὸν ἄτιμον ἔχων τότε γαῖαν ἀρώσεις. The unhonored Euthykles' statue thereafter received honor equal to that which Zeus's image received, and the Locrians made an altar (*bōmos*) for the worship of Euthykles.[2]

3. Oibotas of Dyme was a sprinter who (if a real person) lived in the eighth century and entered early Olympic contests. In 756 he won the stadium race, the first Achaean to win an Olympic victory. Yet the Achaeans did not properly recognize his achievement and gave him no special reward (*geras*). In consequence he put a curse upon his people, so that no Achaean won an Olympic victory for nearly three

---

[1] On Kleomedes see Paus. 6.9.6–8; Oinomaos *ap.* Eus. *PE* 5.34, pp. 230b–231b; Plut. *Rom.* 28.5; Origen *Cels.* 3.25, p. 462 Migne; Socrates *Hist. eccl.* 3.23, p. 448 Migne; Theodoretos *Gr. aff. cur.* 8, p. 1018; 10, pp. 1072–1073 Migne; Suda *E* 1724. The first words, *Υστατος ἡρώων*, should be taken as translated here, not as "last of heroes," as if the Pythia were saying that there would never be another (many new heroes were established after 496). See H. W. Parke, *The Delphic Oracle* I (Oxford 1956) 354.

[2] Callim. frags. 84–85 Pf. with *diēgēsis*; Oinomaos *ap.* Eus. *PE* 5.34, p. 232bc. Euthykles apparently had no statue at Olympia.

centuries. Finally, always losing, the Achaeans consulted the Delphic Apollo, who told them the reason for their failures. So they set up an image of Oibotas at Olympia and immediately thereafter an Achaean won the boys' stadium race (460 B.C.). After that Achaean athletes sacrificed to Oibotas at his tomb in Dyme before going to compete at Olympia, and those who won victor's crowns put them on Oibotas' statue in the Altis.[3]

4. Theagenes of Thasos was an all-around athlete, winning over a thousand victories in boxing, pankration, and the long-course footrace (*dolichos*). According to a Thasian story he was a son of Herakles, who had entered his mother's bed in the form of Timosthenes, her husband, just as Herakles' father Zeus had entered Alkmene's bed in the guise of her husband Amphitryon. Theagenes was as mighty as his divine father. When but nine years old he was so pleased with a bronze image of a god, which he saw in the Thasian agora on his way home from school, that he lifted it from its base and carried it home. The Thasians, irate at what they considered a sacrilege, were about to kill the boy; but a prominent citizen succeeded in calming them and had Theagenes carry the image back to the agora. Thus did Theagenes acquire a reputation for tremendous strength among his countrymen and abroad. He performed many other feats of strength thereafter and as a true son of Herakles ate a whole ox in a single day. He became a great athlete, winning many crowns, but like Kleomedes he incurred an adverse judgment of the Hellanodikai. In 480 he entered himself for both boxing and pankration. In the boxing match he defeated Euthymos and was then too much exhausted to participate in the pankration. The Hellanodikai fined him a talent for his failure to compete after announcing his entry; they also fined him another talent for *blabē* of Euthymos, that is, for having entered the boxing match merely to cheat him of victory; and in addition they ordered him to pay damages to Euthymos. Theagenes paid his fines and apparently had no further trouble either with his city or with the Hellanodikai, but ended his days full of fame and honors. Yet he had some enemies in Thasos, one of whom (ἀνὴρ τῶν τις ἀπηχθημένων ζῶντι αὐτῷ, Paus. 6.11.6), after Theagenes' death, went every night to the agora and flogged his dead enemy's bronze statue. One night the image fell upon him and killed him. At the suit of the flogger's kinsmen the Thasians threw Theagenes' statue into the sea. Then blight and consequent famine came upon Thasos. The

3 Paus. 6.3.8, 7.17.6–7, 13–14.

Thasians consulted Apollo at Delphi, who told them to recall exiles: Εἰς πάτρην φυγάδας κατάγων Δήμητρ' ἀπαμήσεις (Δήμητραν ἀμήσεις: codd. Eus. 5.34). So they recalled all exiles, but the land remained barren. Again they sent envoys to Delphi to find out Apollo's meaning, and the god informed them that he meant Theagenes, whose image they had banished. They recovered it and restored it to its place in the agora. Thereafter the Thasians sacrificed to Theagenes as a god (the verb is *thyein*). The cult of Theagenes spread to other cities, Greek and non-Greek. He was especially valued as a healing deity like Amphiaraos or Asklepios.[4]

The four stories obviously have much in common. Themes and features recur among them, and beneath the specific differences of each a common pattern is perceptible.[5] The tale of Kleomedes, and less clearly that of Oibotas, show the whole pattern as outlined below in features A to I. The tales of Euthykles and Theagenes skip over episode CD, although there is a hint of D in the latter. But there is an apparent hiatus at this point in the extant versions of these tales. In the following analysis the numbers in parentheses indicate the stories in the order presented: (1) Kleomedes, (2) Euthykles, (3) Oibotas, (4) Theagenes. When a statement (or clause) is true of all four, the parenthesis is omitted.

A. The athlete performed superhuman feats of strength (1, 4) and won remarkable victories at agonistic festivals.

B. The authorities at Olympia (1, 4) or of the athlete's own city (2, 3) refused to reward him for his victory (1, 3) or punished him (1, 2, 4), either charging him, justly or unjustly, with an offense (1, 2, 4) or simply slighting him (3). This is the initial injury or disappointment that the hero suffers.

The Hellanodikai denied the victor's crown to the boxer Kleomedes for his cruel killing of his opponent. They fined Theagenes

[4] Paus. 6.11, also 6.6.5–6; Oinomaos *ap.* Eus. *PE* 5.34, pp. 231b–232b; Dion Chrys. 31.95–97; Suda *N*410 (who calls the athlete Nikon, but obviously depends on Paus.). The hero's name was spelled *Theogenes* on Thasos, as Thasian inscriptions show. See R. Martin, "Un nouveau règlement de culte Thasien," *BCH* 64–65 (1940–1941) 163–200; M. Launey, "L'athlète Théogène et le ἱερὸς γάμος d'Hérakles Thasien," *RA* 18 (1941) 22–49 and pl. viii; Jean Pouilloux, *Recherches sur l'histoire et les cultes de Thasos* (Paris 1954) ch. ii. I retain the form *Theagenes*, established in the literary sources.

[5] F. Deneken briefly notices the common likeness of the athlete stories in *LM* 1.2527–2528; cf. E. Rohde, *Psyche* (London, New York 1925) 129–130, 135–136.

two talents and also forced him to pay damages for the offenses with which they charged him.[6] The Locrians wrongly convicted the sprinter Euthykles of having taken a bribe to betray his city and threw him into prison, where he died. The Achaeans failed to give Oibotas his proper *geras* for his victory in the stadium race.

C. This initial injury or disappointment brought grief or anger to the athlete, and even madness to Kleomedes. For Euthykles and Theagenes this feature is merged with feature F. Theagenes was undoubtedly angry at the judgment against him, but we are told only that he paid the fines.

D. In revenge the athlete brought destruction (1) or loss (3) upon his fellow-citizens. Theagenes (4) did something that brought the hatred of several citizens, and of one in particular, upon himself.[7] In the Euthykles story (2) this feature is merged with G.

E. For his destructive act his fellow-citizens punished him (1) or his statue (2, 4). This is the final injury that the athlete suffered. For Oibotas (3) we see only the Achaeans' continued neglect of him for three centuries.

F. The athlete vanished (1), or his statue was nowhere visible (3 ,4) or was cast out (2, 4). Euthykles' death in prison (though it follows directly on B) seems to represent his disappearance obscurely (2); and although the sources (see supra, n. 2) mention only maltreatment of his statue, we may understand that the Locrians cast it down (and perhaps outside the city). The Thasians could not recover Theagenes' statue from the sea, until by accident fishermen happened to haul it up in their nets. Oibotas, we observe, lacked a statue for three centuries; this was obviously his complaint against the Achaeans, that the inadequate *geras* (οὐδὲν ἐξαίρετον) given him as first Achaean victor at Olympia was

6 According to Athenagoras *Suppl. pro. Christ.* 14.57, Theagenes killed some-one in an Olympic contest, probably in boxing; but nothing is said about this event anywhere else, whether or not it led to a penalty. The notice may arise from a misunderstanding of the bout with Euthymos, as told by Pausanias. Feature B is partly represented in the Thasians' desire to kill the boy Theagenes for sacrilege.

7 Apparently Theagenes took a leading part in Thasian politics after he retired from athletics. As Pouilloux interprets the evidence (supra, n. 4, 72–75, 90–93, 97–105), he led the pro-Athenian faction and so aroused the animosity of the opposing party. The local legend probably told of some offense that he committed; thus sometimes does reality give occasion for legendary elaboration. But we should not accept the tale of the image's revenge and the consequent oracles as historically true, as Pouilloux does.

something less than a statue; for the Achaeans finally made amends with a statue at Olympia.

G. The gods punished the athlete's fellow-citizens for their treatment of him or of his statue. To avenge Euthykles (2) and Theagenes (4) they blighted the land, causing famine. A god made Oibotas' curse (3) on Achaean athletes effective, so that they lost in all contests (ἦν γάρ τις θεῶν ᾧ τοῦ Οἰβώτα τελεῖσθαι τὰς κατάρας οὐκ ἀμελὲς ἦν, Paus. 7.17.13). This feature appears to be missing in the Kleomedes tale (1); yet the miracle of the vanishing body as a sign of the gods' grace on Kleomedes apparently caused the Astypalaeans to fear punishment from the gods.

H. Calamity or prodigy caused the athlete's city to consult Apollo at Delphi on causes or remedy.

I. Apollo's response in one manner or another informed the fellow-citizens of their wrongful conduct and either ordained or led to a cult of the athlete as god or hero.

Such is the plot of the tale-type that underlies these stories. To the nine features (A to I) listed I must add five others which appear in two or three of the tales, since they will recur in other legends of the type which will also engage our attention in this study.

J. A god was the hero-athlete's father (4) or patron (1, 3). Since Kleomedes took refuge in Athena's temple and vanished there, Athena appears to be his protectress.

K. The athlete had something to do with rock and stone. He was a stone-bearer in either life or death: either he was a victim of stoning (1) or he could carry huge rocks (see Euthymos, below), for which the story may substitute a metal statue, as the bronze image that Theagenes carried (4).

L. After death he had an avenger: a deity who made his curse operative (3), his own statue (4, cf. 2), or his own ghost or revenant, as in several tales below.

M. His statue was powerful or extraordinary (2, 3, 4).

N. A miracle of vanishing or epiphany occurred at the end of his life or after his death. Kleomedes' body vanished from the chest which he had entered (1). Oibotas (3) appears to have fought in the Greek ranks at Plataia more than 200 years after his death—a phantom hero like Phylakos, Autonoos, Pyrros, Echetlaios, and others who returned from the dead to help their countrymen in battle against the Persians and the Gauls.[8] Pausanias' question, how Oibotas could have fought at Plataia so long after the date of his Olympic victory, points to a belief in his presence as a phantom in the battle.

Of the four athletes, Kleomedes and Theagenes lived in the early fifth century (and were born in the late sixth), Oibotas reputedly lived in the eighth century, and Euthykles is undatable. The pugilist Euthymos of Locri, who won many victories down to 476, lost only to Theagenes in 480. That defeat we may look upon as his initial injury or loss (B), not however imposed on him by authorities. The Hellanodikai, in fact, awarded him recompense; yet we must observe that they allowed Theagenes the victor's crown. Like Theagenes, Euthymos had remarkable strength; as a youth he had carried a huge stone to the place where in later times the Locrians showed it to visitors (A, K). He was reputed to be not the son of Astykles, his mother's husband, but of the river-god Kaikinos (J). Euthymos, however, was more fortunate in his relations with fellow-citizens than were the four athletes above. He seems never to have aroused their ire; quite the contrary, they honored him in his lifetime with two statues, one in Locri, the other at Olympia. It happened that both were struck with lightning on the same day (M), a prodigy that caused the Locrians to consult Apollo at Delphi (H); and Apollo decreed sacrifices to Euthymos while he still lived, apparently as a god rather than a hero (I). As Pliny, citing Callimachus, puts it:

> Consecratus est vivus sentiensque eiusdem oraculi iussu et Jovis deorum summi adstipulatu Euthymus pycta, semper Olympiae victor et semel victus. patria ei Locri in Italia. ibi imaginem eius et Olympiae alteram eodem die tactam fulmine Callimachum ut nihil aliud miratum video deumque iussisse sacrificari, quod et vivo factitatum

---

8 Paus. 6.3.8 for Oibotas at Plataia. For other phantom heroes see Herod. 8.38–39; Paus. 1.4.4, 1.32.5, 10.23.2; see my *The Cult and Myth of Pyrros at Delphi* (Berkeley, Los Angeles 1960) 198–205. Perhaps Oibotas' supposed presence at Plataia is the real reason for his statue at Olympia in 460—in that interval the story of his appearance at Plataia had arisen.

et mortuo, nihilque de eo mirum aliud quam hoc placuisse dis.[9]

Euthymos' life-story thus appears to begin and end as a hero-athlete tale, but lacks the middle part: the hero's wrath or madness that brings injury to his fellow-citizens and punishment to himself. But though Euthymos never had to become an avenger himself (except that as receiver of damages from Theagenes he dimly reflects this role), the great exploit of his legend was his victory in combat over an avenging ghost, the Heros of Temesa. The Heros had in life been one of Odysseus' crew, whom Strabo calls Polites. As Pausanias tells the story, this man when very drunk violated a maiden of the town, and the Temesians stoned him to death (B, K). Thereafter his ghost (*daimōn*, Paus.) went about killing everyone he met (C, D, L), until the Temesians decided to move elsewhere (E, since this move would deprive the demon of his needed victims) and consulted the Delphic oracle on where to settle (H). The Pythia told them not to leave, but to appease the ghost, now called Heros, by sacrificing to him every year the fairest Temesian maid (G, I). They did so every year for seven centuries until 472 or later, when Euthymos returned to Italy and came to Temesa on the very day of the sacrifice. He saw the chosen maid, fell in love with her, and decided to save her. He fought Heros when the demon came for her, defeated him, and chased him into the sea, where Heros vanished (F, N).[10] It appears, therefore, that Euthymos' opponent shares with Euthymos the traits and deeds of the hero-athlete, as if the role had been divided between them.

Aelian's testimony is significant. He represents Heros as exacting tribute from the Temesians; no maiden sacrifice is mentioned. Euthymos, defeating Heros, forced him to repay them more than he had taken from them. For verb of combat Aelian uses $\delta\iota\eta\gamma\omega\nu\acute{\iota}\sigma\alpha\tau o$, which suggests an athletic contest. The pugilist Euthymos had a match with Heros, whom nobody else could defeat, as Theagenes with Euthymos himself, whom nobody else could defeat. Heros as opponent of Euthymos plays the role of Euthymos as opponent of Theagenes. In both tales it was Euthymos' opponent who was forced to pay huge sums of money to the community in which the contest took place.

[9] Callim. frag. 99 Pf., *ap*. Plin. *NH* 7.47.152; Paus. 6.6.4–6; Ael. *VH* 8.18.
[10] For the story see Callim. frag. 98 Pf.; Paus. 6.6.7–11; Strabo 6.1.5, p. 255; Ael. *VH* 8.18; Suda *E* 3510. Cf. my *Python* (Berkeley, Los Angeles 1959) 101–103, 119–120.

It is also Aelian who tells us that at the end of his life Euthymos went down to the Kaikinos River and vanished in the stream, as Heros vanished into the sea, where the Kaikinos empties into it—and as Kleomedes vanished at his life's end. Thus feature F appears to have been shared by both hero-athlete and his opponent in the compound myth.

A tradition which Pausanias reports, that Euthymos was still alive in Locri after six centuries, means that he was immortal as a deity. One Delphic oracle established the worship of Euthymos as a deity in Locri while he still lived; another, much earlier in time, according to the story, established the worship of Polites as a deity (*daimōn*) in Temesa. Euthymos, *hērōs* of Locri, complements Heros of Temesa and takes on identical traits. At some point the Temesians, in response to constitutional or institutional changes that allied them with Locri, identified their ancient hero-*daimōn* with Euthymos: he became the Heros of Temesa (see *Python*, supra n. 10, 103). A hero-*daimōn* may change his name, and this change may be mythically represented as his expulsion; but in fact, as an object of cult, he remains the same—a deity that must be honored or placated, powerful to help or to harm.[11] In the cult myth (or hero legend so employed) he takes on diverse characters, champion or villain or ambiguous figure, according to the affections or fears of his worshipers and the nature of the myth. So, as Euthymos, the hero has the role of Herakles in a combat myth, defeating a death demon (=Thanatos) in order to rescue a maiden in distress. As Polites-Heros he has the role of the avenging and marauding demon (L) —a role congenial to heroes (lords), that is, to powerful ghosts so called; and the hero-athlete is as likely to take on this character as the other.

In *Python* (supra, n. 10, 101–105) I have demonstrated the close similarity of the Euthymos-Heros tale in both episode and pattern to that of the Lamia called Sybaris, whom the hero Eurybatos killed in a Delphian tale, and (not quite so close) to that of the Poine-Ker of Argos, whom the hero Koroibos killed. These tales have a female demon and

---

11 We should observe that hard and fast distinctions cannot be drawn between hero and deity. Pausanias calls Heros of Temesa *daimôn*, and Pliny (*NH* 7.47.152) says that Euthymos *Consecratus est vivens sentiensque*, which appears to mean as a god, since hero-worship in the strict sense occurs at the tomb as worship of a powerful ghost. On this question see my *Cult and Myth of Pyrros* (supra, n. 8) 209–211 with n. 32, 255; *The Ritual Theory of Myth* (Berkeley, Los Angeles 1966) 45–46. Giulio Giannelli attempts to find an historical foundation for the Heros legend and fails to notice the mythic parallels: *Culti e miti della Magna Grecia* (Florence 1963) 225–231.

male victim; this reversal of sex and locale are all that distinguish the Temesian tale from the Delphian.[12] In each of the three tales the champion has the name of an Olympic victor. Koroibos of Elis won the footrace (*dromos*) in the first Olympiad, according to the tradition of the games, and in 708 Eurybatos of Sparta was the first victor in wrestling (Paus. 5.8.6–7). The Koroibos who killed Poine-Ker was connected with both Argos and Megara, but was not a native of either: Pausanias implies that he came from elsewhere to help the Argives. He had a tomb in Megara; the tomb of the Olympic victor was situated on the border of Elis and Arcadia (Paus. 8.26.3–4). In spite of this discrepancy G. H. Förster and O. Crusius have considered hero and Olympic victor to be originally identical.[13] The early Olympic victors whom tradition reported are of doubtful historicity; there were certainly no written records of contests and victors kept for the first century of Olympic games, since it was only during that century that alphabetic writing came to Greece, and its use was very much restricted at first. The victor Eurybatos was Spartan, according to Pausanias, who names no father. The vanquisher of Sybaris came from Kuretis, presumably Akarnania, and was a descendant of the river-god Axios (J; compare Euthymos as reputed son of the river-god Kaikinos). The victor Eurybatos won in wrestling, exactly the skill which Sybaris' opponent needed; for the hero mastered her with his arms, carried her out of her cave, and threw her over a precipice, where her body disappeared (F) and became a well (N). At any rate the homonymity of the champion in each of these three stories and an Olympic victor is remarkable.

This homonymity may be coincidence with respect to Eurybatos and Koroibos, who are not labeled athletes in the sources; and it is the opponents of the three heroes rather than themselves that more closely resemble the hero-athlete. These three tales belong to a subtype of the widespread combat myth (*Python*, supra, n. 10, 101–107), and in fact combine the combat pattern with another which resembles that of the hero-athlete tale. This subtype appears to antedate the

---

[12] For Sybaris see Nic. *ap*. Ant. Lib. 8; for Koroibos and Poine-Ker see Paus. 1.43.7–8; Stat. *Theb*. 1.557–668; Conon 19; all dependent on Callim. *Aitia* (see frags. 26–31 Pf.).

[13] Gustav Hugo Förster, *Die olympische Sieger bis zum Ende des. 4. Jahrhunderts v. Chr.* (Zwickau 1891) 3; O. Crusius, *LM* 2.1154, note; see Eitrem, *RE* 11.1420–1421; Luigi Moretti, *Olympionikai* (Rome 1957) 59. That the Elean Koroibos' tomb was a prominent boundary-marker for the people of Elis indicates an old hero's tomb rather than an ordinary mortal's grave.

hero-athlete pattern as outlined above, which was necessarily developed after 776 B.C. We may now perceive that the latter grew out of an earlier type of hero legend, in which the hero was not primarily an athlete, though he usually possessed some athletic prowess. In other words the hero-athlete tale is an old hero legend historicized by the substitution of an athletic victor, an historical person or supposedly so, for the ancient hero in the central role. For the older hero tale certain features of the pattern must be stated more broadly. In B others than Olympic or city authorities may cause injury or loss to the hero; in E it may be others than his fellow-citizens who punish or hurt hm. Other seers than the Delphic Apollo may speak the oracle of H–I.

The four hero-athletes—Kleomedes, Euthykles, Oibotas, Theagenes—are in truth more like Heros than like Euthymos. They are guilty of offenses, spite, and destructive anger. The berserk and destructive athlete Kleomedes, the avenging images of Theagenes and Euthykles, and Oibotas' curse correspond closely to the avenging spirits—Heros, Sybaris, and Poine-Ker (L, D).[14] They are much like Aktaion's ghost (eidōlon) that went about devastating the land and carrying a rock, apparently his means of destruction (Paus. 9.38.5). The Orchomenians consulted the Delphic oracle and were told to find whatever was left of Aktaion's body and bury it; also to fashion a bronze image of the phantom and chain it to a rock with iron. Thereafter the people made offerings (ἐναγίζουσιν) to Aktaion every year.

In this brief notice we observe features of the hero-athlete legend: D, Aktaion's destruction of the land; F, disappearance of the ghost when the remains of Aktaion's body were buried; H, consultation of the Delphic oracle; I, worship of Aktaion as hero or daimōn; K, the ghost carried a rock and the image was fastened to one; L, avenging and marauding ghost; M, an extraordinary image. We can fill out the rest from the whole legend of Aktaion. He was son of Aristaios, grandson of Apollo and Kyrene (J); he offended Artemis by seeing her naked, and his own hounds tore him to pieces after she had turned him into a deer (B, N).[15] This misfortune made burial of his body difficult for his people, it seems (the Delphic oracle told the Orchomenians to bury whatever pieces they could find); and they had not buried him. For this

---

[14] Sybaris is called Lamia, who lost her children through Hera's wrath and so destroyed others' children. Poine-Ker was the avenging spirit of the wronged Psamathe. See *Python* (supra, n. 10) 100–119.

[15] Apollod. 3.4.4; Ovid, *Metam.* 3.138–252.

reason Aktaion, or rather his ghost, was angry (C) and spread destruction (D).

But possibly Aktaion's wrath had more cause than that. We know that the myth of Aktaion was told in rather different ways; and there may have been an Orchomenian version that resembled the Corinthian tale in which Aktaion was torn apart by two parties of men. Archias loved the youthful Aktaion and with a party of Bacchiads (his *genos*) tried to take the boy forcibly from his house. Aktaion's kinsmen tried to wrest him from the abductors; and the boy, pulled in two directions, was torn apart. Melissos, his father, cursed the Corinthians, if they should not avenge his son's death; then he hurled himself from a cliff. Famine and plague came upon Corinth; the city consulted an unspecified oracle and was told to expel the Bacchiads.[16] Here we perceive features B, C, D, F (as consequence of B), G (following on B = E), H.[17] It was Aktaion's father who put a curse on the Corinthians; in a Boeotian version perhaps Aktaion himself (i.e., his ghost) cursed and plagued fellow-citizens for having torn him apart and scattered the pieces. Aktaion's dogs in the familiar myth came from his own house; in the Corinthian tale the renders were his own kinsmen and fellow-townsmen.

The Corinthian tale shows a minor athletic feature. According to pseudo-Plutarch, Melissos committed suicide at the Isthmian games; having mounted to the roof of Poseidon's temple he called for punishment of the murderers of his son, and Poseidon sent drought and pestilence on the Corinthians. Thus the Corinthian Aktaion's death has a connection with the games, and like the hero-athlete he had a divine avenger. In such a story as this we may have a transitional step between the ancient legend of the hero-avenger and the pseudo-historical tale of Olympian victors.

Boeotian Aktaion would appear to lack the divine sympathy that Poseidon showed to the Corinthian, since Artemis herself caused his death; yet we notice that the phantom Aktaion suffered no hindrance from heaven, but, like Heros of Temesa, was allowed to terrorize the inhabitants as an avenging ghost or revenant. So far as the

---

[16] Plut. *Mor.* 773a; Diod. Sic. 8.10; Schol. on Apollon. *Arg.* 4.1212.

[17] In several variants of the type, B is merged with E, the first injury or punishment of the hero with the second. Likewise D may be merged with G, the hero's vengeance with the gods' punishment of the offending citizens. And occasional displacements of features should be expected, a common enough occurrence in the diffusion of traditional tales.

sources inform us (though we must bear in mind the incompleteness of evidence and the brevity of many notices when we deal with Greek myths), the Corinthian Aktaion did not return as avenging ghost: rather, this feature takes the form of his father's curse which brought plague and famine. In the earliest stories the curse is personified as an avenging spirit; historicized or rationalized, the spirit takes the form of impersonal calamity. But there was another Corinthian myth which plainly shows an avenging spirit, the story of Jason's sons, who are two in most sources, Mermeros and Pheres. In Pausanias' story (2.3.6–7) not Medea but the Corinthians killed them, stoning them to death for having carried Medea's deadly gifts to Jason's bride (E). In punishment of the Corinthians' violent and unjust deed the boys (presumably as ghosts) caused all Corinthian infants to perish (G). On being consulted (H) the Delphic oracle ordered annual sacrifices for Jason's sons (I) and an image of Deima. Pausanias saw this image: γυναικὸς ἐς τὸ φοβερώτερον εἰκὼν πεποιημένη (M). Deima is personified Terror, the boys' avenging spirit (L), either their agent or cooperating with their ghosts, much as in the Koroibos myth the demoness Poine-Ker represents the avenging spirit of Psamathe, whom her father, King Krotopos, had wrongfully put to death.[18]

The hero-athlete who wreaks vengeance in person or through his image is a rationalized or historicized version of the avenging demon. The demonic character of the athlete is clearest in the tale of Kleomedes. The mad Kleomedes spread destruction like the avenging ghosts of Aktaion, Polites, and Jason's sons. He destroyed lives by breaking a stone pillar, as Aktaion's ghost carried a rock. The citizens stoned him, as they stoned Polites and Jason's sons.[19] He fled for refuge to Athena's temple, as Jason's sons to Hera's. There his body disappeared as Heros vanished into the sea and the Lamia Sybaris into the earth. The gods favored him and ordained worship of him as a hero.

[18] According to Parmeniskos *ap.* Schol. vet. *in* Eur. *Med.* 264, Jason and Medea had seven sons and seven daughters, whom the Corinthians killed in the sanctuary of Hera Akraia, whither they had fled for refuge. In consequence seven youths and seven maids of distinguished Corinthian families were chosen annually to serve the goddess for a year. According to Paus. 2.3.11, Medea concealed each of her children immediately after birth in the sanctuary of Hera, believing that they would become immortal, but she was disappointed in her hopes. This may mean that they had disappeared (F) when she went to look for them.

[19] When the Thasians wanted to kill Theagenes for removing a god's statue, we can be sure that they were going to stone him, the usual way of collectively executing an offender on the spot.

Whether the athlete was a real person or not makes little difference. If he was real, like Euthymos or Theagenes, a hero-role was superimposed on him. The hero, as we have seen, is ambiguous in character: he might be benevolent, a destroyer of persecutors, or he might be malevolent, a persecutor himself. Equally ambiguous was the very archetype of hero, Herakles, who was also an athlete skilled in every manly art. Above all, he was a legendary founder of the Olympic games, the first Olympic victor, winning in three contests. He was Zeus's son (J) and performed prodigious feats of valor, strength, and appetite (A), including the eating of a whole ox (like Theagenes); he won numerous contests and combats; he went berserk (C) as a result of the madness which Hera unjustly put upon him (B), and killed his own children (D). In fact the several features of the hero-athlete legend are scattered throughout the Herakles cycle (Apollod. 2.4–7); but perhaps the tale of his dealings with Eurytos, the final legend of the cycle, best illustrates the type in the regular narrative order that we have outlined. It is the more apposite in that it begins with an *agōn*. Herakles wanted to marry Iole, daughter of King Eurytos of Oichalia. To win her hand he had to defeat Eurytos and the king's sons in an archery contest. He did so, but they refused to let him marry Iole, much as Kleomedes was denied the victor's crown after defeating Ikkos (B). Then in wrath (C) Herakles drove off Eurytos' horses or cattle (Apollodoros says that Autolykos was the rustler); and he treacherously killed Eurytos' son Iphitos, hurling him from the walls of Tiryns (D). The gods punished Herakles by sentencing him to a period of servitude under Queen Omphale of Lydia (E). Thereafter Herakles took Oichalia, sacked the city, and killed Eurytos and his sons (G). As a direct result of his victory, which meant his winning of Iole, Deianeira gave him the poisoned robe which so tortured him that he burned himself on the pyre at Oita's summit. Hence he was translated bodily to the company of the gods (N). His kinsmen and friends found no bones among the ashes (F) and immediately worshiped him as a hero (διόπερ ὡς ἥρωι ποιήσαντες ἁγισμοὺς καὶ χώματα κατασκευάσαντες, Diodoros); his friend Menoitios sacrificed a boar, goat, and ram to him as hero and established his cult in Opus (I). Oracles, including the Delphic, proclaimed him a god and ordained his worship (H), and Athens was the first city to honor him as a god.[20]

[20] Apollod. 2.6.1–3, 7.7; Diod. 4.31, 37.5–39.4. For Delphic oracles on worship of Herakles see H. W. Parke and D. E. W. Wormell, *The Delphic Oracle* II: *The Oracular Responses* (Oxford 1956) no. 560; cf. nos. 442, 450. This corpus of responses is here-

The hero-athlete tale, therefore, belongs to a wider type of hero legend, and the athlete is a special case of the legendary hero who was warrior, hunter, and athlete in one. The legend type tended to attach itself to famous athletes and shape them into legendary heroes; and then the subtype of hero-athlete tale, once it had been formed, sometimes converted legendary heroes into early Olympic athletes (Koroibos, Eurybatos, Oibotas, Euthykles).[21]

The movement from history to legend may be illustrated from fragments of legend which gathered about the certainly historical athletes Polydamas and Milon. Polydamas (or Pulydamas) of Skotussa was tallest of all men after the ancient heroes. Barehanded he fought and killed a lion (A), as Herakles had done on two occasions. In fact, it was Polydamas' intention to emulate Herakles. A number of stories about his extraordinary strength were told, for example, that with one hand he kept a chariot from moving forward. Of course, he won many victories in the games. And once at Susa in the reign of Darius Nothus (so that Polydamas lived in the late fourth century) he fought and killed, singlehanded, three of the crack Persian warriors called Immortals in an exhibition before the king. Little more is told about his deeds in life; but he had an interesting death. On a hot summer day he and some

after designated PW followed by the number of the response. Feature M occurs at Apollod. 2.6.3; Daidalos made a statue of Herakles at Pisa (Olympia) so lifelike that when Herakles came upon it at night he threw a stone at it, believing it to be a living person. On Herakles as founder of Olympic games see Pind. *Ol.* 2.3–4, 6.67–70, 10.27–85; Diod. 4.14.1–2, 5.64.6; Paus. 5.7.9–8.4; Apollod. 2.7.2.

21 History may be converted into legend, and myth and legend into pseudo-history. There is no need to suppose that there is only one direction in the formation of traditional tales. Either a myth may be retold as an historical event in which a deity is represented as a former great man of the nation, or the tale-type may be imposed upon an actual person or event and recolor the historical facts (often to unrecognizability). The historical person steps into the shoes of a traditional hero and either his actual deeds are reshaped on legendary models or he is credited with wholly imaginary deeds of the sort that occur in traditional tales. That the process may move either way is what W. den Boer fails to see (review in *Mnemosyne* 16 [1963] 435–437), when he asks "how to know whether a story belongs to the series represented by the Pylos war or to that of the Phlegyan war," the latter being an actual event converted to legend. If one takes the event to be historical (one may be mistaken but has grounds for taking it so), one obviously must suppose the movement to be from history to legend; if one supposes it unhistorical to begin with, then one assumes the opposite movement. Furthermore development of the Phlegyan legend has nothing to do with the conjectured development of the original combat myth in the ancient Near East as outlined in *Python* (supra, n. 10) 218, nor does that represent the "scheme of development" of the work, as den Boer mistakenly assumes. Obviously if I suppose a single origin for the type, I do not suppose that each variant develops independently in the manner of the original myth which initiated the type. On this question see my *Ritual Theory* (supra, n. 11) 18–23, 57, 59.

friends went into a cave to drink wine together. When the roof of the cave began to fall in, he tried to hold it up while the others escaped; but great as is strength was, it did not suffice to hold up a hillside, and so he was crushed to death under rock (F, K). His statue at Olympia was powerful for healing fevers (I, M); in fact, the hero in general and the hero-athlete in particular is likely to become a healing deity; Theagenes, for example, had great fame as a healer at his several shrines. The story of Polydamas is fragmentary; but the fragments show that it conformed to the hero-athlete type.[22]

The legend also began to attach itself to the renowned wrestler, Milon of Croton, an undoubtedly historical figure who won victories in seven Olympiads (540–516), although probably not all parts of the legend were ever told about him. His tremendous strength was bound to make him another Herakles, and many tall tales were told about his marvelous feats of strength (A). For example, he could carry an ox on his back and eat a whole ox in a single day like Herakles and Theagenes. And like Theagenes he carried a statue on his shoulder, his own, which he bore to its place in the Altis (K). In fact, he took Herakles for his model, according to report: dressed in lionskin and armed with a club he fought in battle against Sybarites (in this we may perceive feature J, the protector god). Unlike most athletes he was not anti-intellectual, if it is true that he belonged to the Pythagorean community of Croton. Once as he sat with the brothers at dinner a pillar that supported the roof began to totter. Milon not only held it up so that the others could escape, but also succeeded in extricating himself (K). Thus we observe three treatments of the falling-roof theme. Kleomedes, like Samson, pulled a sound roof down, bringing destruction to all beneath it. Polydamas could not support an unsound roof and was crushed beneath it, while his companions escaped. Milon could hold up an unsound roof and save himself along with his companions. The storyteller shapes the traditional episode to suit his purpose. The Kleomedes tale follows the traditional pattern: a supernatural madness comes upon the hero. Polydamas is depreciated as the stupid giant who does not know the limits of his strength. Milon is magnified in a tall tale.

---

[22] Paus. 6.5; Diod. 9.14–5; see Lucian *Deor. conc.* 12, *Quomodo hist. conscr.* 35, on the healing virtues of his statue. In both passages Lucian couples Polydamas with Theagenes. He competed in 408 B.C.; see Förster (supra, n. 13) 21; Moretti (supra, n. 13) 110. Perhaps a trace of feature B may be seen in Promachos' reputed defeat of Polydamas in that year, denied by the Thessalians, who considered him always undefeated.

Like other athletes Milon had an extraordinary death, and his own strength was at last his undoing. Alone in the forest he came upon a log partly split open with wedges. Putting his hands into the cleft and exerting his strength he caused the wedges to fall out, whereupon the log closed on his hands. Unable to free himself, he was eaten by wolves (F).[23]

The athletes of other fragmentary tales look more like historicized heroes or deities. Glaukos of Karystos, a pugilist, was descended from the sea-god Glaukos (J). He was prodigiously tall (close to seven feet) and strong. When he was a mere boy plowing his father's field, the share fell from the plowbeam, and he drove it back in place with his fist (A). On seeing this feat his father entered him in the boxing contest at Olympia. The boy's opponents cut him badly, and as he faced his final opponent he was suffering from so many wounds that he was ready to give up (B). Then his father shouted Ὦ παῖ τὴν ἀπ'ἀρότρου. The boy struck his opponent as he had the plowshare and at once had the victory, his first of many. He was buried on the island called *Glaukou*; that is, he was a hero eponym (I), probably the sea-god Glaukos humanized and historicized.[24]

According to Simonides, not even Polydeukes or Herakles could match Glaukos. Nor could Herakles defeat Diognetos, a Cretan pugilist who killed his opponent, unfortunately named Herakles (ὁμωνυμῶν τῷ ἥρωι), and was therefore denied the victor's crown (B); after that he was sent into exile (E, F). The Cretans honored Diognetos as a hero (I).[25] In the same section of his work Ptolemy Hephaestion mentioned a wrestling match between Herakles and Theseus in which Theseus held his own, so that the spectators said Ἄλλος οὗτος Ἡρακλῆς. Diognetos was clearly another Herakles too and could surpass the hero.

Damarchos, an Arcadian pugilist, turned into a wolf at the *thysia* of Zeus Lykaios, and returned to human form after ten years, according to the tradition of lycanthropy in that cult—a story told by *alazones*, says Pausanias (6.8.2), since the epigram on the base of Damarchos' statue at Olympia made no mention of this marvel. But this

---

[23] Paus. 6.14.5–8; Diod. 12.9.5–6; Strabo 6.1.12, p. 263. The manner of his death resembles that of Aktaion's.

[24] Paus. 6.10.1–3; Philostr. *Gym.* 20; Suda Γ 280, 281. See Appendix I, infra, pp. 99–103.

[25] Ptol. Heph. 5 *ap.* Phot. *Bibl.* 190, p. 151.

4—C.S.C.A.

story is nearly all that we are told about Damarchos. His ten years as a wolf are a lycanthropic expression of feature C, the madness of the hero, and represent the hero as marauding spirit. It is also an expression of feature F, the disappearance of the hero; and as a wolf he represented the Wolf Zeus (I).

Of the wrestler Taurosthenes we are told only that a *phasma* in his shape appeared in Aigina and reported his victory at Olympia on the very day that he won it (Paus. 6.9.3). This was strictly a *doppelgänger*, but may be taken as a form of the ghost, an obscure expression of feature L. This feat of bilocation is also the miracle of epiphany (N) which marks the athlete as superhuman (I). It also resembles the disappearance of Kleomedes' body (F), or the simultaneously lightning-struck images of Euthymos, another telepathic prodigy.[26] Epiphany and vanishing are habits of heroes.

A certain Mitys, not represented as an athlete in the scanty evidence which we have, was killed by a political opponent while engaged in *stasis* (D, E). One day when the slayer was looking at the bronze statue of Mitys which stood in the agora of Argos (evidence of I), it fell on him and killed him (G, M), another evidence of the avenging image (L) as in the story of Theagenes, who was also a victim of political opponents (compare Euthykles).[27]

The hero in general was likely to be bad-tempered and quick to exact vengeance for any slight (not so different from gods in this respect, e.g., Artemis and Poseidon).[28] There was Anagyros, hero of the Attic deme of that name (*Anagyrasios daimōn*, I), who punished the neighbours of his *hērōon* for cutting down trees in the sacred grove (B or E) by throwing their houses from their foundations (C, D, or G), a good example of avenging ghost (L). Or in a variant tradition he caused the offender's mistress (*pallakē*) to fall in love with his son; there follows a Potiphar's-wife tale which ends in the death of all three characters.[29]

[26] Ael. *VH* 9.2 reports a second version which rationalizes the story. Taurosthenes used a homing pigeon to send news of victory to his father, and the bird reached Aigina on the day of victory, flying a distance of approximately 100 miles over hawk-infested mountains. We can hardly suppose that this is a record of an actual occurrence which Aelian's first version distorts.

[27] Aristotle *Poet.* 9.12, p. 1542a, *Mir. Ausc.* 156, p. 846a; Plut. *Mor.* 553d.

[28] See Athen. 11.461c; Fontenrose, *Cult and Myth of Pyrros* (supra, n. 8) 231.

[29] Zenob. 2.55, Diogen. 1.25, Suda *A* 1842, where Hieronymos is cited for the variant tradition. Much better in temper was Drimakos, the slave hero, worshiped on Chios as Heros Eumenes, friendly to both slaves and masters, if they were righteous men. See Nymphodoros *ap.* Athen. 6.265d–266e.

In its variant forms the tale was told of historical athletes
—Euthymos, Kleomedes, Theagenes; but Euthymos' defeat of Heros,
Kleomedes' vanishing body, and Theagenes' avenging statue are
obviously unacceptable as historical events. Almost every feature of
these narratives expresses a recurring motif of traditional story; and
the tales conform to a recognizable story type, usually told of demonstrably unhistorical persons. The athletes dated to the eighth
century or early seventh, to the first century of Olympics, are of very
dubious historicity—Oibotas, Glaukos, probably Euthykles. Most if not
all of these tales were told in Callimachus' *Aitia*, probable source of
Pausanias' and Oinomaos' testimony. The *Aitia* contained poetic
narratives of Euthymos and Euthykles alongside the tale of Koroibos.[30]

The *Aitia* was a collection of myths and legends. We may
expect the tales of Euthymos and Euthykles to have the same character
as the rest, and Callimachus' tale of Euthymos included the incident of
the lightning-struck statues, as Pliny informs us.[31] Therefore we can put
no trust in the Delphic oracular responses included in these tales. That
given to Temesa on the sacrifice of a maiden to Heros is obviously
legendary (PW 392); but those on Kleomedes, Theagenes (two), and
Euthymos' statues are generally if not unanimously accepted as genuine.[32] We must, I believe, reject them; at best their authenticity is
highly questionable. We have no text, not even indirect (or the barest
suggestion of it), for the oracles on Oibotas and Euthymos' statues; but
they seem to have had a content similar to that of the oracle on Kleomedes, in essence to worship or give honor to the athlete. Those on

[30] Euthymos: frags. 98–99 Pf. Euthykles: frags. 84–85 Pf. Koroibos: frags.
26–31 Pf. The Theiogenes of frag. 607 may be the athlete Theagenes, according to R.
Pfeiffer (edition of Callimachus I [Oxford 1949]) pp. 92, 415–416; see Leandros J492.15 *ap.*
Schol. vet. *in* Aristoph. *Pac.* 363. Milon of Croton is mentioned in frag. 758 Pf.

[31] Pliny *NH* 7.47.152 (Callim. frag. 99 Pf.). This is the only source. Of
course, that lightning should strike two statues of the same person in widely distant places,
Olympia and Locri, on the same day is a possible coincidence, although the chances against
its happening are astronomical. But under ancient means of communication how and when
would the event become known and how would it be verified? The incident looks much more
like the hearsay of a later time, for folklore has always been full of reported marvels of that
sort. Callimachus then attached it to his story of Euthymos, perhaps as the final episode, the
hero's apotheosis.

[32] PW accept those on Kleomedes (88), Euthymos (117), and Oibotas
(118), but list those on Euthykles (388) and Theagenes (389, 390) under "Mythical Oracles,"
in a subsection, *Oracles connected with Myths handled by Callimachus*. Yet in the first volume
(supra n. 1) Parke defends the authenticity of the Theagenes oracles (pp. 356–357). He does
not explain the discrepancy in either volume.

Euthykles and Theagenes are a single hexameter line each (there is a variant distich version of the second: PW 391). The Euthykles and first Theagenes responses are quoted above, and the reader will notice that they have the same meaning: if the Locrians or Thasians restore rights to him (the Theagenes response has a generalizing plural) who has been deprived of them, they will then have crops. Each is the deceptively phrased oracle of legend: the consultant either does not understand it or misundertands (*avertissement incompris*). No certainly historical response of Delphi or any other oracular shrine is like that. But this is a subject that I shall deal with elsewhere.

An oracular response, most often Delphic, appears in most of the stories dealt with so far. There are three other responses which concern athletes in one way or another, and though the evidence about the surrounding circumstances is scanty, it points in the direction of the hero-athlete legend. Two of these responses are commonly accepted as genuine; the other is admittedly fictitious, though its dramatic date is Alexander's time.

About Orsippos (or Orrippos) of Megara we have an epigram of three elegiac distichs that was inscribed on the athlete's tomb in Megara. The stone was found in 1769, built into a Megarian's wall (*IG* 7.52), but the first and third distichs had previously been known, since the Scholiast on Thucydides (1.6.5) quotes them. The inscription was made in the second century A.D., and is that which Pausanias appears to have seen (1.44.1), but did not quote. The epigram may be much older, but probably does not go back to the fifth century. The tomb of Orsippos and the response, if genuine, are undatable, but Parke and Wormell conjecture around 500 B.C., apparently because this was the period of heroizing athletes and close to the dates of Kleomedes, Euthymos, and Theagenes.[33]

The epigram on the tomb informed the reader that the Megarians had erected the tomb (and statue?) of Orsippos in obedience to a Delphic oracle (*phama*), because he had recovered Megarian territory that the city's enemies had previously taken away, and had been the first of Hellenes to win an Olympic crown as a naked runner in the stadium race. He was an eighth-century athlete; according to the Scholiasts and Eustathios on Iliad 23.683, he competed in the fourteenth Olympiad (724). Dionysios of Halikarnassos, however, gives the

---

[33] PW 89; but they do not explain why they suppose Athens to have been the consulting city.

honor of being the first naked victor to Akanthos, a Lacedaemonian, in the fifteenth Olympiad (720). Obviously Megara was making a counter-claim to Lakedaimon's and wanted to prove a Megarian to be the first naked victor. Both claims were dubious, since the institution of contests of naked athletes was probably not nearly so early as 720. For according to Thucydides (1.6.5) and Plato (*Rep.* 452c) the change to naked contestants had taken place not long before their time. The Lacedaemonians, however, could assert with truth that they (and the Cretans) were the first Greeks to allow nudity in local games.

Therefore the tradition of Orsippos' victory, as reported in the epigram, is dubious indeed. There was, in fact, quite a different story about his performance in the stadium race. According to the Homeric Scholiasts mentioned, far from winning the race that day, he came to an humiliating end in it. He became entangled in his *perizōma*, fell, and died (or, according to other anonymous authorities, was defeated). Thereafter an unspecified oracle ordained nakedness for the contestants to prevent such accidents in the future.

We are told nothing else about Orsippos, but the fragmentary tradition is enough to indicate that Orsippos is another hero-athlete. Like Oibotas and Glaukos—and perhaps Euthykles—Orsippos belongs to the dim days of the early Olympics. He performed great deeds as warrior and athlete (A). His mishap in the race cost him the victory (B) and his life (F). Beside the anonymous oracle that altered Olympic rules, a Delphic oracle (H) ordered the Megarians to erect a tomb of Orsippos in their agora (I), and according to Pausanias Orsippos' tomb was next to the tomb of the hero Koroibos, slayer of the demoness Poine-Ker. In fact, Megara was renowned for tombs within the city walls (Paus. 1.43.3). Others were those of Alkmene, Hyllos, Pandion, Hippolyta, Tereus, Timalkos, Kallipolis, Ino, Iphigeneia, Adrastos, Megarians killed in Persian Wars, Aisymnos, Alkathoos, Pyrgo, Iphinoe, Astykrateia, and Manto (Paus. 1.41–44). All are legendary heroes, either generally Hellenic or locally Megarian, excepting only the Persian War dead; and they, like the Athenian dead at Marathon, were buried in one tomb and honored as heroes (Paus. 1.32.3–4). Orsippos is quite like the other single heroes: he is named and his tomb stands among theirs. It is likely that his tomb was an ancient structure, equally as old as the others mentioned, which date back to prehistoric Megara. At some point the hero supposedly within was identified as Orsippos, an athlete. He appears to be the hero-athlete in his Megarian form.

The seer Teisamenos was certainly an historical person, and Herodotos tells us about him. Nevertheless we need not accept the whole story that Herodotos tells nor the oracle spoken in it. Teisamenos as an Iamid belonged to a great family of seers in Elis; in this we may see a trace of divine origin (J). The Delphic oracle predicted victory for him in the five greatest contests. He understood from this that he would become a pentathlon victor and entered the contest at Olympia. He failed only in wrestling, in which Hieronymos of Andros defeated him; in this we may perceive the athlete's initial disappointment (B). The Spartans saw the true meaning of the response, that Teisamenos would be a great *mantis* (H, I), in that as *mantis*, and therefore an *hēgēmōn*, he would be victorious in five great battles. So the Spartans invited him to become mantis of their armies. He asked for Spartan citizenship as a condition of accepting, but they, looking on his demand as monstrous (substitute for D), refused to grant it to him (E), and lost him as leader and helper (F). Then the Persian invasion came upon Hellas (G); the Spartans renewed their invitation to Teisamenos and agreed to his terms. Now he demanded citizenship for his brother Hagias too, and the Spartans were forced to grant this additional request. Thus Teisamenos became mantis of Spartan armies, and made the sacrifices before five great battles, the first being Plataia. He established in Sparta a family of Iamid seers, whose prominent tomb indicates heroic honors.[34] In the consultation of a seer, which resulted in his becoming *mantis* of a state and a hero after death, we may see a second expression of features H and I in this story.

The oracle is another example of *avertissement incompris*, the ambiguous, misleading prophecy of folklore. We notice too that Teisamenos consulted Delphi about progeny (περὶ γόνου), presumably his lack of any, but received a response irrelevant to his question, a feature of legendary oracles. Yet it is in Sparta that he had a son (time of birth not indicated: Paus. 3.11.5) and grandson. The story is *aition* of a Spartan Iamid family who were the official *manteis* of the state, and who had a collective tomb on the Aphetais road that went off from the Spartan agora (Paus. 3.12.8).

The historical nearness of Teisamenos and the reality of

---

[34] On Teisamenos see Herod. 9.33–35; Paus. 3.11.5–8. Several historicized myths and legends have entered Herodotos' text as history; e.g., the story of Croesus' son Atys is constructed on the myth of Attis; see J. Wells, *A Commentary on Herodotus* I (Oxford 1912) 70–71.

his position as mantis at five Spartan battles necessarily circumscribed the form which the hero-athlete legend could take in one generation after being attached to him. Apart from the indications of that legend and of the folkloristic nature of the response, the Teisamenos story shows other recurring motifs of Greek tales. Herodotos (9.34) points out that Teisamenos followed the example of Melampus, another Elean seer, when he doubled his demands at a second offer. When the Argives asked Melampus to come to Argos and heal the daughters of Proitos, who had gone mad, he asked for a third (or half) of the kingdom. The Argives refused, but the madness spread to other Argive women. When the Argives again appealed to Melampus, he demanded another third of the kingdom for his brother Bias; and they were forced to grant his terms (see Apollod. 2.2.2). A similar tale of the Cumaean Sibyl is familiar: how after twice refusing her prophetic books Tarquinius Priscus bought the remainder, three hundred, at four times the price at which he could have bought nine hundred, a twelvefold increase for each book (Dion. Hal. *Ant. Rom.* 4.62). Teisamenos was fast slipping into the role of legendary seer; his story combines price-raising seer with hero-athlete. Strangely, a wholly different seer theme enters the Teisamenos tale, as Crahay points out. He is not only a great seer like Melampus and the Sibyl, but also a very poor seer like the mantis of Aesop's fable 170, who had to learn about the burglary of his own house from another man. Likewise, Teisamenos, an Iamid, could not interpret Apollo's words; whereas the Spartans, not famous for intellectual perspicacity, saw its meaning before he did. It is also a suspicious feature of the tale that the Spartans were well aware of a response given to an individual of a distant land. However that may be, Crahay perceives a touch of Delphic propaganda which downgraded the rival oracle of the Iamids at Olympia.[35] In sum, the story and oracle appear to have been composed after the fact, after Tanagra (the fifth battle for which Teisamenos was mantis) and probably after the seer's death.

Since the third oracular story of an athlete appears in pseudo-Kallisthenes' *Life of Alexander*, only a very credulous person could accept it as historical truth. After Alexander sacked Thebes, the Thebans asked Delphi whether they would ever rebuild the city. The god replied that Hermes, Alkeides (Herakles), and wall-stormer (or defender, τειχόμαχος) Polydeukes, contending together (οἱ τρεῖς

---

35 Roland Crahay, *La littérature oraculaire chez Hérodote* (Paris 1956) 102–104.

ἀθλήσαντες) would reestablish Thebes. This appeared to be an impossible prediction: it would never happen. However, when Alexander presided over the Isthmian games, a Theban athlete, Kleitomachos (Renowned Fighter), entered himself for wrestling, pankration, and boxing. He won the wrestling match gloriously and came before Alexander to receive the crown. Alexander told him that if he should also win the pankration and boxing contests, he should be granted anything that he wished. On winning them too he came again before Alexander, and when the herald asked him his name and city for proclamation of his victories, he gave his name, but said that he had no city, because King Alexander had destroyed it. So the king granted his wish that Thebes be rebuilt, and did so in honor of the three gods—Hermes, Herakles, and Polydeukes.[36]

Here is an athlete of great prowess (A), who lost his city (which the king destroyed), so that he had none to be proclaimed at the games (B). The athlete's city rather than his person disappeared in this story—as a stateless man something of his person had vanished (F). There is a Delphic oracle (H), which equates Kleitomachos with Hermes in wrestling, Herakles in pankration, and Polydeukes in boxing (I); this oracle indicates that divine favor made Kleitomachos invincible in all contests (J and substitute for G). The oracle feature (H) reappears in the decree of King Alexander, another son of Zeus, which restored Thebes as a cult act, a dedication of the city to the three gods (I).

In essentials the stories of Kleitomachos and Teisamenos are similar. Both begin with an obscure Delphic oracle which is an *avertissement incompris*. One response plainly predicts victory in five contests, but uses the word *agōnes* equivocally; the other obscurely predicts victory in three contests and means athletic victories. The rulers of Sparta understood the one response and thereby saved their city; King Alexander understood the other (see supra, n. 36) and saved the athlete's city in consequence. Both athletes were clever in their dealings with rulers, gaining a city for themselves and the advantage of their people; and both won rewards, victories, and fame. In these tales we perceive two members of a subclass; and, as often happens, certain

---

[36] Pseudo-Kallisthenes 133–134 Raabe; Tzetzes *Chil.* 400–440. The Syriac version of pseudo-Kallisthenes and Tzetzes' paraphrase have Kleitomachos refuse to name his city after each of the first two contests. Alexander then realized that he was a Theban and promised restoration of Thebes if he should win the third contest. The Greek version has the theme of the wish grant: god or king will grant whatever one chooses (Thompson motif Q115).

themes are given an antithetical expression in a later variant (the Kleitomachos tale in this instance).

The athlete, Kleitomachos, is an historical person whom pseudo-Kallisthenes' fanciful tale places about 120 years too early transferring him from Ptolemy Philopator's reign to Alexander the Great's. The real Kleitomachos won victories at Olympia in 216 and 212 B.C. and at other agonistic festivals around the same time. He was a Theban and victor in wrestling, pankration, and boxing, so that there can be no doubt that he is the original of pseudo-Kallisthenes' Kleitomachos, who represents Hermes, Herakles, and Polydeukes as invincible champion in the three contests. In a tale that Polybios tells, Ptolemy Philopator patronized the boxer Aristonikos and sent him to fight Kleitomachos at Olympia.[37] The spectators, prone to favor challengers against a champion, cheered Aristonikos, until Kleitomachos stopped the bout for a moment and rebuked the crowd. He was contesting, he said, for the glory of the Hellenes, and Aristonikos for that of King Ptolemy; would they rather see an Egyptian carry off the Olympic crown for victory over Hellenes or hear a Theban and Boeotian proclaimed victor? The crowd, chastened by his rebuke, cheered Kleitomachos thereafter, and he won the bout. Although Kleitomachos really fought a bout with Aristonikos in 212, Polybios' narrative shows a legend in process of formation (since the boxing matches had no rounds, and therefore no intervals between, we may doubt whether a pugilist could cease fighting for a space and expect his opponent to stand idle too). The words on proclaiming a Theban as victor (... ἢ Θηβαῖον καὶ Βοιώτιον κηρύττεσθαι νικῶντα τῇ πυγμῇ τοὺς ἄνδρας), attributed to Kleitomachos, are the germ of the proclamation scene in the Alexander tale. In Polybios' story a Theban could not be proclaimed victor, if Aristonikos should defeat Kleitomachos; in the Alexander tale a Theban could not be proclaimed victor, because there was no Thebes. Polybios' story shows feature B more clearly in the Olympic crowd's unjust treatment of Kleitomachos, and C more clearly in Kleitomachos' angry rebuke, when he plainly asserted that the crowd's bad behavior could cause his defeat and bring dishonor to Hellas (D).

Another Delphic oracle cited by Herodotos does not concern athletes, and yet is very like that spoken on Kleomedes. It occurs in Herodotos' story of the Phocaean refugees (1.165–167). The Phocaeans

---

[37] Polyb. 9.7–13. On the historical Kleitomachos see also Paus. 6.15.3–5; Alkaios of Messene ap. Anth. Pal. 9.588. For his date see Moretti (supra, n. 13) 141.

lost their city to the Persians (B) and moved to Corsica. From their city of Alalia they raided and plundered their neighbors (D). The Carthaginians and Etruscans sent a combined fleet against them, destroyed a large part of the Phocaean fleet, and took prisoners from the wrecked ships. The Etruscans of Agylla (Caere) stoned their prisoners on the mainland in or near their city (E, F, K). Thereafter all creatures that passed the spot where the bodies lay became twisted, crippled, or paralysed (G). So Agylla consulted Delphi (H), and was told to make sacrifices to the slain Phocaeans (I), and to establish athletic games, including a chariot race, in their honor—so that athletics have something to do with the tale.

History provides the first steps of the narrative: the fall of Phokaia, the Phocaeans' consequent distress (C), the naval battle, and possibly the killing of prisoners at Agylla. On these facts was imposed the avenging-hero tale; the stoned Phocaeans are very like Jason's sons at Corinth. One may rationalize the tale, as Parke does ("One may explain the miraculous plague as some contagious epidemic, possibly caused by the presence of unburied bodies"); but we may well doubt the historicity of a narrative which conforms in detail and pattern to a recurring type of traditional tale, and which is unsupported by any contemporary or other reliable evidence.[38]

For the last four oracular tales we must realize that we have scanty information, as is also true for the preceding group—Polydamas, Milon, Glaukos, Diognetos, Damarchos, Mitys, Anagyros—which are non-oracular tales, in so far as we know their content. Yet the fragments that we have are sufficient to establish their relation to the group of five (including Euthymos) hero-athlete legends which are our original and

---

[38] See Parke (supra, n. 1) 142–143; PW 64; Crahay (supra, n. 35) 80–81. We have no text for this response, nothing more than Herodotos' ἡ δὲ Πυθίη σφέας ἐκέλευσε ποιέειν τὰ καὶ νῦν οἱ Ἀγυλλαῖοι ἔτι ἐπιτελέουσι; then Herodotos mentions the actual rites and games at Agylla. A common kind of Delphic oracle established cults of gods and heroes. Still we must question the authenticity of this response. Would Etruscans have consulted Delphi in the sixth century? There is no other case. It is true that Strabo (5.2.3, p. 220) mentions an Agyllaean treasury at Delphi, but he gives no date, and nobody else mentions it. In any case would Agylla have sent envoys on the long journey to Delphi in a dire emergency rather than to a nearby Italian oracle or rather than resort to the very Etruscan extispicy? It seems unlikely. And may we suppose that an Etruscan cult, celebrated with annual sacrifices (ἐναγίζουσι) and games, began about 535 as a cult of executed Greeks? Probably this was an ancient and native Etruscan cult, and it was western Greeks who identified the heroes or deities with the slain Phocaeans and devised the story, perhaps to illustrate divine punishment of cruel deeds.

central object of study. Further evidence, if we could ever have it—the versions and episodes that circulated in oral and written tradition—would surely fill in the gaps and complete the story.[39]

In this study my principal purpose has been to establish the presence in Greece of a widespread type of legend which we may call the avenging-hero type, the variants of which tended to represent the hero as an athlete (usually Olympic) and which attached itself to several historical athletes. In the course of study I have had to give special attention to the oracular responses, which represent feature H of the type. They were probably anonymous at first, but they became Delphic in most of the stories considered. Once the Delphic oracle acquired prominence, either story-tellers attributed the untagged prophecies of tales to Delphi, or Delphi claimed the oracles of legend for itself. The oracles on the hero-athletes, in so far as the tales supply their texts, do not conform to certainly historical Delphic responses in content or form. Therefore a second conclusion of this study must be that these oracles are not genuine; they belong to the story-type.

APPENDIX I

Glaukos of Karystos: Bekker *Anecd.* 1.232 and Suda *Γ* 280 give the date Olymp. 25 (680 B.C.) for a victory of Glaukos of Karystos, that is, within the first Olympic century. Scholars have taken this to be an error for 65 (520) or 75 (480), preferably the former (see Förster, *op. cit.* (supra, n. 13) 10; Moretti, *op. cit.* (supra, n. 13) 75–76). The argument for a later date is based upon the following considerations. (1) The sculptor Glaukias, who fashioned the statue of Glaukos that Glaukos' son dedicated at Olympia (Paus. 6.10.3) lived around 480. (2) Glaukos had Pythian, Isthmian, and Nemean victories (Paus. 6.10.3). (3) According to a rhetorical lexicon (s.v. *Glaukos*, Bekker

---

[39] In saying this I am *not* making an argument *ex silentio*. I am making the same kind of statement as in *Python* (supra, n. 10) 68, where, after showing the common plot of the Python myth and several others, I say, "The fact that eight stories show only from eight to twelve of the nineteen features is mainly due to the scanty information that we have about them." W. den Boer calls this a "curious *argumentum e silentio*" (review cited supra, n. 21). It is not. It would be if I were using the statement as support for a conclusion; that is, if it were an *argument*. In fact, both there and here my conclusion is based entirely on the positive evidence which we have. It is the scanty information which furnishes the whole argument. I merely point out in addition that the notices of these stories are few and generally brief, which is true. The positive evidence indicates pretty well the nature of the missing parts.

Anecd. 1.232), Gelon of Syracuse successfully plotted Glaukos' murder (ἀπέθανε δὲ ἐξ ἐπιβουλῆς Γέλωνος. . .). (4) Lucian (*Imagg.* 19) indirectly quotes a poet who placed Glaukos above Polydeukes and Herakles as pugilist; and scholars identify the poet with Simonides (8 Bergk).

All the evidence except Glaukos' date ultimately hinges on Paus. 6.9–12, directly or indirectly. Glaukias was the sculptor of Gelon's chariot, which Pausanias discusses at 6.9.4–5. In sections 6–8 he digresses to the tale of Kleomedes. Then (sect. 9), returning to Gelon's chariot, he informs us that the statue of the pugilist Philon of Korkyra, Glaukos' son, stood beside it, a work of Glaukias, on the base of which was an epigram of Simonides (152 Bergk), which Pausanias quotes. It is a very simple distich: "My country is Korkyra, my name Philon; I am Glaukos' son and have won two Olympic victories in boxing." There follows a very short sentence (seven words) indicating the statue of Agametor of Mantinea. Then in 10.1–3 Pausanias tells about Glaukos of Karystos and his statue, fashioned by Glaukias, which stood next to Gelon's chariot and Philon's statue; Glaukos' statue, therefore, was one of a group that Glaukias did. The son who dedicated Glaukos' statue is presumably Philon: father and son, both boxers, stood together; this appears to be what Pausanias means, and he says nothing to the contrary. Yet it is strange that the son should be a citizen of Korkyra, the father a citizen of Karystos. It looks very much as if Pausanias (and contemporary Olympians) confused one Glaukos with another, the father of Philon, a Corcyrean pugilist of the early fifth century, with the legendary or semi-legendary Glaukos of Karystos, supposed to have competed in the early seventh century. Inscribed on the base were the names *Glaukos* as the represented boxer, *Glaukias* as the sculptor, and Philon as dedicator (or perhaps just *huios*). Either the city was not mentioned, since it was made known in Simonides' epigram on Philon's base, or *Korkyraios* (*Ker-*) had become partly illegible and was taken by Pausanias to be *Karystios* (in which 6/9 letters are in common), because of confusion that had already arisen. We may infer that it was the Corcyraean Glaukos who won victories at other pan-Hellenic festivals.

If Gelon killed a boxer named Glaukos, he could be Corcyraean Glaukos. It is strange that a powerful tyrant should plot the murder of an athlete, especially when he was not a Sicilian. But no confidence should be placed in this information at all. The rhetorical lexicon in which the statement appears drew erratically on earlier lexica. If in the original lexicon the entry *Glaukos* stood next to *Glaukias* and *Gelon* (alphabetical order was not strictly observed in ancient lexica), then careless extracting, mingling of two or more entries, and bad copying easily account for what we find in *Anecd.* 1.232. The original lexicographer had drawn on Paus. 6.9–12, so that we can account for the association of Gelon with Glaukos. But how do we explain an error in which Gelon plots Glaukos' death? There is obviously some confusion somewhere.

If we continue reading on from Paus. 6.10.1–3 we soon reach ch. 12, where Gelon is mentioned again—and a sculptured chariot, that of Hieron, Gelon's brother (12.1). Next to this stood the statue of Hieron II of Syracuse (270–216), who had a son Gelon, whom Pausanias mentions (12.2–3). This Hieron, Pausanias tells us, was assassinated by a Deinomenes who was hostile to the tyranny. Pausanias was wrong: it was the king's grandson, Hieronymos, whom conspirators, including Deinomenes, killed. In any case here is the plot, which occurs in a context in which the name Gelon is prominent and also a sculptured chariot beside which stood the statue of Hieron II, said here to be victim of an assassin who had the same name as Gelon's father. This passage occurs shortly after mention of Gelon's chariot, beside which stood the statue of Glaukos. Here was a plentiful source of confusion for careless extractors. Somewhere in the lexicographical tradition *Gelon* replaced *Deinomenes* and *Glaukos* replaced *Hieron*; then the sentence moved into the Glaukos entry.

There remain the anonymous verses quoted by Lucian, which scholars attribute to Simonides. The poet definitely refers to Glaukos of Karystos, though we need not suppose that the poem was addressed to him, since encomiasts commonly introduced heroes and great athletes of the past in order to enhance the glory of the present victor. The ascription to Simonides is based on Quintilian *Inst.* 11.2.11–16, who tells the story (also told in Cic. *de Orat.* 2.86.352–353) in which a princely victor who hired Simonides told him to collect half of the promised reward from Kastor and Polydeukes, to whom the poet had apparently given too much attention in the victory ode. At the victory banquet Simonides was called outside by a message that two young men wanted to see him. He found nobody, but in his absence the dining hall caved in and killed everyone present. According to Quintilian (sect. 14), authorities disagreed whether the victor in question was Glaukos of Karystos, Leokrates, Agatharchos, or Skopas, and whether the scene was Pharsalos or Krannon. In Cicero's version it was Skopas of Krannon.

The argument, then, for identifying the anonymous author of the verses on Glaukos with Simonides demands that Glaukos of Karystos be the victor in one version of the story and that they be part of the ode. But does the story suit Lucian *Imagg*, 19? There Glaukos was extolled above Polydeukes and Herakles, not underplayed in relation to Polydeukes and Kastor, as the story demands. Lucian says that Glaukos did not boggle at this praise; the story demands that the victor be offended at underpraise. The scene of the story is a Thessalian city, not Karystos or Korkyra (the confusion was well established by Quintilian's time, and Glaukos of Korkyra, as a contemporary, could have hired Simonides), and we may expect the victory banquet to be held in the victor's home town. So the anonymous poet may not be Simonides at all; if he is, then Lucian and the story refer to quite different odes.

We should notice too that the victor was killed under a falling roof, not by Gelon's treachery, so that *Anecd.* 1.232 and the tale cannot both be true of the same Glaukos. And in conclusion we should also notice Simonides' role in the tale, which belongs to our type: Simonides (who won great fame as a poet, A) takes the role of the wronged athlete (B), and the victor that of the city authority; for he was the dynast Skopas II of a noble Thessalian family (and perhaps *tagos* of Thessaly). Simonides had his ghostly avengers, the Dioskuroi (G, J, L), who appeared to the messenger (N). Here too we have the falling-roof theme, and it is developed in a still different manner (see supra, p. 88): the victor, like Polydamas, is crushed beneath the fallen roof; but, unlike Polydamas, he is not the hero and this is his punishment as wrongdoer.

In summary my conclusions are: (1) 680 was in fact the traditional date of Glaukos of Karystos' first victory; (2) it was Glaukos of Korkyra of whom Glaukias made a statue at Olympia; (3) one Glaukos was confused with the other, both being pugilists; (4) the statement that Gelon killed Glaukos is a garbling of Pausanias' statement that Deinomenes killed Hieron II; (5) the anonymous poet of Lucian *Imagg*. 19 may not be Simonides, and the verses do not belong to the ode mentioned in Quint. *Inst*. 11.2.11–16, which was probably addressed to Skopas II (in the story-teller's intention, if not in fact; we need not suppose an identifiable ode; and it is surely not meant to be the ode addressed to Skopas that is a subject of discussion in the *Protagoras*

[5 Bergk.]). The passages from Lucian and Quintilian (cf. Demosth. 18.319) show that Glaukos of Karystos was frequently cited as a traditional example of superhuman pugilistic skill and numbered among the legendary and semi-legendary athletes of the distant past. In Cramer *Anecd*. 2.154 he is associated with Kleomedes and Euthymos.

APPENDIX II

Theme Tabulations: In the following two tabulations the legends are numbered as follows: 1, Kleomedes; 2, Euthykles; 3, Oibotas; 4, Theagenes; 5, Euthymos; 6, Eurybatos; 7, Koroibos; 8, Aktaion; 9, Jason's sons; 10, Herakles; 11, Polydamas; 12, Milon; 13, Glaukos; 14, Diognetos; 15, Damarchos; 16, Taurosthenes; 17, Mitys; 18, Anagyros; 19, Orsippos; 20, Teisamenos; 21, Kleitomachos; 22, Phocaeans at Agylla; 23, Simonides. Parentheses indicate that the feature appears obscurely or doubtfully in the extant sources.

The first tabulation indicates the distribution of the features A to N (see supra, pp. 76–78) among the three legends. The second tabulation shows the legends in which the listed motifs appear. The motif numbers are those of Stith Thompson's *Motif-Index of Folk-Literature*, 2nd ed. (Bloomington: Indiana University Press, 1955–1958).

1. A: 1, 2, 3, 4, 5, 6, (7), 10, 11, 12, 13, 14, 19, 21, (23)
   B: 1, 2, 3, 4, 5, (6), 7, 8, (9), 10, 13, 14, 18, 19, 20, 21, 22, 23
   C: 1, 3, 5, (6), 7, 8, (9), 10, (15), 18, (22)
   D: 1, 2, 3, (4), 5, (6), 7, (8), (9), 10, (17), 18, 22
   E: 1, 2, (3), 4, 5, 6, 7, (8), 9, 10, 14, (17), (18), 20, 22
   F: 1, 2, 3, 4, 5, 6, 7, 8, (9), 10, 11, 12, 14, 15, (16), 19, (20), (21), 22
   G: 2, 3, 4, 5, 6, 7, (8), 9, (10), 17, (18), (20), (21), 22, 23
   H: 1, 2, 3, 4, 5, 6, 7, 8, 9, 10, 19, 20, 21, 22
   I: 1, 2, 3, 4, 5, (6), 7, 8, 9, 10, 11, 13, 14, (15), (16), (17), 18, 19, (20), (21), 22
   J: 1, 3, 4, 5, 6, 8, (9), 10, (12), 13, (15), (20), (21), 23
   K: 1, 4, 5, 8, 9, 11, 12, 22, 23
   L: 3, 4, 5, (6), 7, 8, (9), (15), (16), 17, 18, 23
   M: 2, 3, 4, 5, 8, 9, 10, 11, 17
   N: 1, 3, 5, 6, 8, 10, (15), 16, 23

2. A581.2, Hero returns and aids his people in battle: 3
   D113.1, Transformation of man to wolf: 15, cf. 12
   E261, Wandering ghost makes attack: 5, 8, 18
   E422, Living corpse: 8
   E441, Ghost laid by burial: 8
   E433, Ghost placated by sacrifice: 5, (7), 9, 22
   E446.5, Ghost laid by pushing it into water: 5, cf. 4, 6
   E466, Ghost laid by being killed: 5
   E721,723, Soul journeys from the body, wraith of person
     separate from body: 16
   F624,624.1,624.2,624.2.02, Mighty lifter lifts ox, lifts
     large stone, moves enormous rock: 4, 5, 10, 11, 12
   F627, Strong man pulls down building: 1
   G262.0.1, Lamia: 6, 7
   G302, Malevolent demon: 5, 6, 7, 8, 9, 18
   G303.20, Evil demons kill people: 5, 6, 7, 8
   M305, Ambiguous oracle: 2, 4, 20, 21
   M310.1, Prophecy of future greatness and fame: 10, 20
   N847, Prophet as helper: 20
   Q115, Grant of any boon asked: 21
   Q552.10, Plague as punishment: 2, 4, 7, 9, 22
   Q556, Curse as punishment: 3
   R185, Hero fights death to save somebody: 5, 6, 7, 10
   S262, Periodic sacrifices to a monster: 5, 6

University of California
Berkeley

Themistocles' Place in Athenian Politics

The search for the political Themistocles has not been rewarding. The nature of the testimony makes it too easy to accept one or another of a set of clichés, which have the advantage of being immediately understood. Thus, Themistocles is seen as a *novus homo*,[1] or a "democrat"[2] or as "the great radical."[3] The trouble with all these labels is that they give the picture of politics in the Marathon generation a vividness, a sharpness of focus that no one has a right to expect, considering the state of our evidence.[4] It is my aim in this paper to examine the literature of the fifth and fourth centuries to determine how impressions of Themistocles' political position might have evolved, and then to review what is known of his public career to see if there is any justification for giving him a meaningful political label.

[1] E. M. Walker, *CAH* IV 167–172; H. Berve, "Fürstliche Herren zur Zeit der Perserkriege," *Die Antike* 12 (1936) 16; V. Ehrenberg, "Die Generation von Marathon, *Ost und West* (Prague 1935) 114; M. F. McGregor, "The Pro-Persian Party at Athens," *Athenian Studies*, HSCP Suppl. I (1940) 85; A. W. Gomme, *Historical Commentary on Thucydides* I 261.

[2] C. A. Robinson, "The Struggle for Power at Athens," *AJP* 60 (1939) 232–237; Robinson, "Athenian Politics, 510–486," *AJP* 66 (1945) 243–254, passim; W. G. Forrest, "Themistokles and Argos," *CQ* 10 (1960) 235 and passim; A. R. Burn, *Persia and the Greeks* (London 1962) 279–296.

[3] Robinson, *AJP* 66, 251.

[4] The works cited in the first two notes are representative. Gomme, "Athenian Politics," *AJP* 65 (1944) 321ff, in arguing with Robinson and McGregor was drawn into a tacit acceptance of their terms. C. Hignett, *History of the Athenian Constitution* (Oxford 1952) 183, refused to see Themistocles as a democrat, followed by G. T. Griffith, "Isegoria in the Assembly at Athens, "*Ehrenberg Studies* (Oxford 1966) 137, n. 55.

THE EARLIER WRITERS

The earliest information about Themistocles comes from two poets of his own generation. His friend Simonides must have dealt at length, in various lost works, with his feats during the Persian Wars;[5] we owe to him the knowledge that Themistocles was a member of the ancient and noble clan of the Lycomidae.[6] The poet Timocreon of Ialysus, on the other hand, was forced to endure exile because of Themistocles, and he did his best to ensure that future generations would remember the general's reputation for avarice and corruption (in Plut. *Them.* 21).

There is nothing political here so far as we can see, but later writers such as Critias and Theopompus may have drawn political inferences from Timocreon's bitter verses. Simonides' identification of Themistocles as a Lycomid, on the other hand, seems to have been ignored by Hellenistic times in favor of vague but more dramatic reports of low origins on his mother's side.[7]

Nor is Herodotus useful on the details of political activity in Athens. As far as the historian was concerned, the form of government was established when Cleisthenes invited the Demos to participate. If he knew of partisan debate of any kind after this date he gave no indication, describing domestic politics only as a series of clashes between individual personalities, with nothing implied as to party, faction or program.[8]

The two greatest minds of the next generation may be excused at once from this inquiry. Thucydides is in general contemptuous of political labels, seeing in them only disguises with which man masks his eternal quest for power.[9] To Plato, the argument would have been irrelevant, as he thought that with the exception of Aristeides, *all*

---

[5] Lost works on the battles of Artemisium and Salamis are known by title from Suidas, *s.v.* Simonides. On his friendship with Themistocles see Cicero *De Finibus* 2, 32; Plutarch *Them.* 1.4, 5.6.

[6] In Plut. *Them.* 1.4; the Lycomidae are discussed at greater length infra.

[7] The earliest extant reports of her foreign origin are from IV–III B.C., Phanias and Neanthes (Plut. *Them.* 1.2), who identify her as Euterpe of Halicarnassus. At some later date the story was improved by making her a Thracian slave girl: Plut. *Them.* 1.1 = Amphicrates, in Athenaeus 13.576C; *Anth. Pal.* 7.306.

[8] Hdt. 5.66, 78; 6.131; on Herodotus' conception of Athenian democracy, see V. Ehrenberg, "Origins of Democracy," *Historia* 1 (1950) 527–528.

[9] Thuc. 3.82.8. To Thucydides, the supreme realist, there are only two political parties anywhere: those in power and those out of power. The *fact* of coming to power interests him more than the means of doing so.

politicians—Miltiades and Cimon as well as Themistocles—were false statesmen, teaching the commons materialism instead of virtue.[10]

It was probably during the latter half of the Peloponnesian War that Themistocles began to be thought of in some circles as one of the founders of radical democracy. First of all, he was the creator of the navy. That strange figure, Stesimbrotus of Thasos, whose motives must remain unknown, wrote a treatise of some kind, in which he recreated a debate between Miltiades and Themistocles over the building of the fleet.[11] Some modern scholars have interpreted this debate as a confrontation between hoplite conservatism and naval democracy.[12] The Old Oligarch, after all, had so clearly pointed out the naval basis of sovereign democracy (Ps. Xen. AP I, 2) and critics of democracy, who were beginning to gather real strength in the oligarchic clubs at this time, may have assigned responsibility for what they considered mob rule to Themistocles, who by fortifying the Piraeus and creating the navy had shifted the balance of power to the lower classes.[13]

Second, some oligarchs seem to have professed admiration, on a theoretical level at least, for the Spartan constitution and the Spartan way of life.[14] In remembering Themistocles as the originator of an anti-Spartan foreign policy they may have come to the logical conclusion that he was therefore the natural enemy of an oligarchic polity as well.

But as far as direct evidence is concerned, the only representative of the oligarchs who mentions Themistocles critically is Critias, and there are no obvious political implications in his claim that the general had increased his fortune from three to a hundred talents

[10] Plato Gorgias 455e, 519a; cf. M. Pavan, La Grecità politica da Tucidide ad Aristotele (Rome 1958) 173.

[11] Plut. Them. 4.5 (F. Jacoby, Fragmente der griechischen Historiker [hereafter cited as FGrHist] 107, F 2).

[12] U. von Wilamowitz-Moellendorf, Aristoteles und Athen II (Berlin 1893) 84, n. 20; B. Perrin, Plutarch's Themistocles and Aristeides (New York 1901) 186–187; cf. G. Gottlieb, Das Verhältnis der ausserherodoteischen Überlieferung zu Herodot (Frankfurt 1963) 99–100.

[13] Plutarch quotes a slogan: ἡ κατὰ θάλατταν ἀρχὴ γένεσίς ἐστι δημοκρατίας (Them. 19.6), which he may have found in oligarchic literature of the period. This, at least, is what the context implies. Although Plutarch (Them. 4.4) cites Plato to the effect that Themistocles created naval democracy (Leges 706c and probably thinking of 707c as well), the philosopher did not actually mention the general's name; cf. G. Morrow, Plato's Cretan City (Princeton 1960) 97–100, and A. Momigliano, "Sea-Power in Greek Thought," CR 58 (1944) 1–7.

[14] See the references in E. R. Dodds, Plato: Gorgias (Oxford 1959) 357 (ad 515e8).

during the course of his career (Aelian *VH* 10.17). There is even an indication that some of the political clubs may have remembered Themistocles favorably, for in describing the Athenian desecration of his grave, Andocides hoped to inflame the oligarchs against the Demos.[15]

There is a curious tale from the Atthis of Cleidemus, which has been thought to show a partisan attitude to Themistocles. Aristotle said (*AP* 23.1) that the Areopagus, on the eve of the battle of Salamis, had given eight drachmae to each man boarding the triremes. But Cleidemus, whose work will have appeared twenty or so years earlier (ca. 350),[16] said that Themistocles was responsible for this largesse, having used the disappearance of the gorgoneion from Athena's statue as a pretext, ransacking the luggage of those waiting to embark, and thus finding enough money to pay the fleet. One would be hard put to explain just what this story is supposed to mean, as in the present state it is nonsense.[17] Both versions were reported by Plutarch (*Them.* 10.6–7) and modern scholarship has tended to see the difference between them as a difference in fourth-century party attitudes: Aristotle's anti-democratic source, whoever it was,[18] defending the conservative Areopagus, Cleidemus supporting the democrat Themistocles.[19] There are no other fragments of Cleidemus to indicate his political preferences; therefore, commentators have made the most of this one. But the above interpretation inevitably reads into Plutarch's account all sorts of nuances that were not there to begin with; if one considers the story carefully, all it really proves is that Cleidemus believed Themistocles capable of a shabby trick.

Despite the suspicion that oligarchic literature down to mid-fourth century must have condemned Themistocles as the founder of radical, naval democracy, this brief survey exhausts extant references

---

[15] Cited by Plutarch *Them.* 32.4; cf. D. MacDowell, *Andokides on the Mysteries* (London 1962) 191.

[16] For the publication date, see Jacoby, *Atthis* (Oxford 1949) 74; *FGrHist* IIIb Suppl. 58–59.

[17] Jacoby, *Atthis* 81–82; the absurdity of the story is also well exposed by J Labarbe, *La loi navale de Thémistocle* (Paris 1957) 137–138.

[18] The source will have been someone who followed the reasoning of Isocrates' *De Pace* and *Areopagiticus*—perhaps his student Androtion; so Jacoby, *Atthis* 74; J. Day and M. Chambers, *Aristotle's History of Athenian Democracy* (Berkeley, Los Angeles 1962) 7–11.

[19] Jacoby, *Atthis* 75–76, followed with some doubts by Day and Chambers (supra, n. 18) 10.

which can be interpreted as partisan bias of any kind. Impressions die hard, but it must be admitted that down to the time of Aristotle not one single extant writer speaks of Themistocles as a democrat opposing a more aristocratic polity.[20]

In fact, articulate spokesmen of the fifth and fourth centuries seem to be unanimous in viewing the general as a non-political statesman and hero of Athens' greatest hour. To Lysias, he stands between Solon and Pericles as one of Athens' great lawgivers; the orator implies as well that he was of good family.[21] The later orators echo this praise: Themistocles was the modest hero of an older, better Athens,[22] whose wise counsel led to the victory at Salamis,[23] and to the building of the walls.[24] Demosthenes admitted that an older and virtuous Athens never hesitated to punish even its greatest heroes—Themistocles, for example—for thinking themselves better than others (23.205). He also claimed that the rebuilding of the walls by Conon was a greater accomplishment than the original construction by Themistocles, because the latter had worked by stealth (20.73–74). But in general, the memory of the great man was such that all factions within the fourth-century democracy evoked his name to support their arguments.[25]

Not even men who are otherwise critical of radical democracy depart from this estimate. To Isocrates, Themistocles remained the great hero of the Persian Wars and there is no hint that the philosopher saw him responsible for naval imperialism, or for the weakening of the Areopagus.[26] And the Socrates portrayed in Xenophon's *Memorabilia* said in so many words that anyone planning a career as a statesman

[20] There are several references to Themistocles in Theopompus' digression on the Athenian demagogues (*FGrHist* 115 FF 85–87, all in Plut. *Them.*), but there is no reason to believe that the historian distinguished between politicians of whatever political coloration; see the comment on F 90 by W. R. Connor, "Theopompos' Treatment of Cimon," *Greek Roman Byzantine Studies* 4 (1963) 107ff.

[21] Lysias 30.27–28. He emphasized Nicomachus' servile origins and compared them to the family background of the older nomothetae.

[22] Demosthenes 23.196–98; [Dem.] 13.21–22, 29; Aeschines 1.25.

[23] Dem. 18.204; 19.303.

[24] Dem. 20.73–74; Dinarchus *Dem.* 1.37; for other praise, see Aeschines 2.9; 3.181, 259; Hyperides *Epitaph.* 6.37.

[25] Pointed out by Pavan (supra, n. 10) 170–172.

[26] Isocrates *Panegyricus* 154, *De Pace* 75–76, *Antidosis* 233, *Panathenaicus* 51–52. For Isocrates, Athenian naval imperialism had not yet been corrupted under Themistocles and Pericles; cf. Pavan (supra, n. 10) 101, 106.

should first study Themistocles and try to emulate him.[27] The same theme was developed at greater length by Aeschines the Socratic.[28]

ARISTOTLE

But the most detailed portrait of Themistocles that has survived is that drawn by Plutarch, and his impression of the general is that of a radical democrat who looked to the mob for support of his innovations.[29] Plutarch's portraits are seductive and deceptively compelling. More than one modern scholar can recall a distinct impression that some piece of information is based on good and frequent authority, only to find after rigorous searching that his memory has tricked him and that the story exists only in Plutarch. But in these cases the information in question is of little more value than the biographer's source. Here, specifically, one need look no further than the majestic fabric of political theory created by Aristotle and expanded upon by disciples like Theophrastus. The Aristotelian political corpus was well known to Plutarch and the infallibility of its basic premises was taken for granted by him, as it was by the majority of ancient writers.[30]

The Aristotelian *Athenaion Politeia* in particular became for antiquity the standard reference work on Athenian political history; but for modern scholars it remains an enigma. In chapters 22 to 25, especially, it is often very difficult to ascertain just what Aristotle is trying to say, or to decide whether some of the confusion is due to his sources or to a lack of clarity in his own thinking. Generations ago it was almost heresy to suggest that Aristotle could be anything less than clear, and some of these passages, when the treatise was first discovered on papyrus, were used as arguments to show that the great philosopher could not possibly have written such a web of errors. Criticism since that time has shown that previous generations underestimated the extent to which Aristotle was dominated by his theories of political behavior, and the extent to which he forced an interpretation of the facts to fit his theories.[31]

---

[27] Xenophon *Mem.* 4.2.2. cf. 2.6.13, *Symp.* 8.39.

[28] In Aristides *Or.* 46, II 292ff Dindorf, with *Oxyrhynchus Papyri* XIII, No. 1608; commentary by H. Dittmar, *Aischines von Sphettos* (Berlin 1912) 155–158; E. G. Berry, *TAPA* 81 (1950) 1–8.

[29] E.g., *Them.* 3.3; *Arist.* 2.1.

[30] For Plutarch's reliance on Aristotle, see my remarks in *Historia* 13 (1964) 386–387. Cf. R. Flacelière, *Plutarque: Vies* II 6–7; E. Meinhardt, *Perikles bei Plutarch* (Frankfurt 1957) 29, n. 70; K. Ziegler, *Plutarchos von Chaironeia* (*RE* separate impression, 1949) 284.

[31] K. Beloch, *Griechische Geschichte* (Strassburg 1893–1904) II.2, 134–135;

It is now clear that he believed the whole human political experience could be reduced to symmetry and order, like any other field of human knowledge; that polities could be ranged in some sort of spectrum; and that certain opposing forces were at work within every polity, causing it to incline now toward rule by the few and now toward rule by the many. In Athens specifically, he saw two parties emerging after the Cleisthenic reform, one of the *gnorimoi* and one of the Demos, and he seems to have assigned every famous Athenian leader to one or the other party. Modern scholarship has done valuable work in showing where he found his historical data;[32] but it is not so clear that his political interpretations are anything but his own, except for the canon of political forms derived from the constitutional theory of the Academy.[33]

His concept of the years between the Cleisthenic constitution and the restriction of the Areopagus (ca. 508–462) seems to be as follows. The constitution of Cleisthenes introduced radical democracy. Ostracism—a democratic institution—was established at the start, and was followed by election to the archonship by lot (487/6) and Themistocles' creation of naval power, both of which Aristotle considered harmful to a sound polity.[34] During much of this period, Miltiades was the leader of the *gnorimoi* and Xanthippus was leader of the Demos; later in the period Aristeides and Themistocles also became leaders of the Demos (*AP* 28.2).[35]

After Salamis, there was a *metabole*, a change of constitution because of the prestige which the Areopagus had won through their provisioning of the fleet, and this body was prominent for seventeen years. While the Areopagus now presided over the *gnorimoi*, Aristeides and Themistocles continued to be leaders of the Demos. Aristeides proposed that the revenue of the empire be used to support a movement of people into the city where they would be put on the public

---

Day and Chambers (supra, n. 18) 17–24; K. von Fritz and E. Kapp, *Aristotle's Constitution of Athens* (New York 1950) 32ff; Pavan (supra, n. 10) 161–168.

[32] Most recent survey, citing older literature, in Day and Chambers (supra, n. 18) 5–11; cf. Jacoby, *Atthis* 234–235, long note 36.

[33] Plato *Politicus* 291d *sq.* and see Diogenes Laertius 3.82.

[34] Ostracism: *AP* 22.1, *Pol.* 3.1284a17–18; sortition: *AP* 22.5, *Pol.* 4.1294b8, 6.1317b20; naval democracy: *Pol.* 5.1304a22, 7.1327b7.

[35] Προστάτης τοῦ δήμου, which Aristotle took to mean party leader, meant at this time only patron of the whole people against the tyrants; H. Schaefer, "Prostates," *RE* Supplb. 9 (1962) 1293–1296; cf. Ehrenberg (supra, n. 8) 529 and note.

payroll in one capacity or another (*AP* 24); Themistocles finally aided Ephialtes in the attack on the Areopagus (*AP* 25). This brought an end to the Areopagus constitution and left the way open for a radical democracy again, in which the assembly and courts became sovereign.

Themistocles thus emerges in the *Athenaion Politeia* as a democrat by definition. First, although Aristotle admits he was ἐπιεικής —that is, a member of the aristocracy[36]—some tradition of his hostility to Miltiades made it necessary that he be assigned to the opposite side of the political aisle. Second, he was one of the leaders of the Demos at a time when the Demos was adopting institutions typical of radical democracy: sortition, ostracism, and a large navy, and he was specifically responsible for introducing the naval bill. Third, after the Persian Wars, he continued as democratic leader, and with Aristeides opposed the party of the Areopagus.[37] Finally, he cooperated with Ephialtes in putting an end to the Areopagus constitution.

It is easy to reject this interpretation on the basis of method alone; the idea that human behavior—especially political behavior— can be explained by some sort of logic is now rejected by all but the most incurable optimists. And yet there is no question that the polity of the Athenians came into the fifth century with an aristocratic orientation— the preserve of princely persons who felt themselves beyond the Law, as Berve has put it (see supra, n. 1)—but on the eve of the Peloponnesian War had become dominated by a Demos jealous of its authority and prerogatives. Aristotle saw Themistocles as a force tending toward this change in polity. Can we in fact argue that he was not?

THEMISTOCLES

At the time of the Cleisthenic deme organization, when Themistocles was perhaps an adolescent,[38] his family's legal residence was the deme of Phrearrioi, of the tribe Leontis, in the Laureion mining

---

[36] *AP* 28.1: the Demos first chose leaders from those who were not ἐπιεικής after the death of Pericles. For the meaning of this term and the natural opposition between ἐπιεικής and πλῆθος, see *Pol.* 5 1308b27.

[37] In Aristotle's system of opposites, this is what seems to be meant: Aristeides and Themistocles are both democratic leaders opposing the Areopagus (*AP* 23.3, 28.2).

[38] I accept here and later R. Lenardon's reasons for accepting 493/2 as the year of Themistocles' archonship, and for putting his birthdate somewhere around 525 (*Historia* 5 [1956] 401ff), *pace* Flacelière, "Points obscurs de la vie de Thémistocle," *REA* 55 (1953) 15–19.

district. Nepos (1.2) says his father Neocles was *generosus*, and in fact he was a Lycomid. The main branch of the Lycomidae continued to reside in the deme Phyla,[39] where they are said to have celebrated rites older than those of the Kerykes at Eleusis.[40] The nobility of the clan is therefore not in question. Themistocles' mother is perhaps to be identified as Euterpe of Halicarnassus (see supra, n. 7), making her son *nothos* by both later and earlier reckoning, but a full citizen by Peisistratid fiat and Cleisthenic law.

The uncertainty of the exact location of Phrearrioi makes it impossible to know the nature of Themistocles' family interest, which could have been either mining[41] or agricultural, depending on whether the deme lay entirely in the hills around the modern Plaka, or if it included some of the valley to the northwest as well.[42] If Critias was correct in claiming that the statesman started his public career with a patrimony of three talents he would not have been among those reckoned truly wealthy (like Callias), but three talents still meant a rich man to Isaeus;[43] we should assume this sum to have been worth much more in Themistocles' own day. At any rate, neither residence in an isolated deme nor moderate income would have affected his status as an aristocrat as long as he came from a noble family and had not made his money in trade of a baser sort.[44]

It was perhaps a desire to escape the remoteness of southeastern Attica that led Themistocles to maintain a house in the heart of the city, and to marry the daughter of Lysander of Alopeke. The deme fairly bristles with important persons[45] and if the marriage took place before 490 or so it might have meant an improvement in Themistocles' social and economic position.

[39] Plut. *Them.* 15.3; *IG* i² 302.29, ii² 2670.

[40] Hippolytus, *Refutatio omnium haeresium* 5.20.4–6. See the note on this passage in A. Bauer and F. Frost, *Themistocles: Testimonia* (Chicago 1968) 128.

[41] *SEG* XVI 123.36 locates a mine at Phrearrioi.

[42] E. Kirsten, in *Westermanns Atlas zur Weltgeschichte* (Braunschweig 1963) 13; Kirsten-Philippson, *Die griechischen Landschaften* (Frankfort 1950–1959) I. 3, 850, n. 2; 988.

[43] Isaeus 3.18, 3.25.

[44] On this prejudice, see Aristophanes *Equites* 128ff; V. Ehrenberg, *The People of Aristophanes* (Oxford 1943) 120ff.

[45] Melesias, father of the politician Thucydides: Plut. *Per.* 11.1; Callias and Hipponicus: B. Meritt, *Hesperia* 5 (1936) 400 (no. 10.110), and *IG* ii² 2407.31, 43, as read by D. M. Lewis, *BSA* 50 (1955) 13–14; Megacles and Hippocrates: *AP* 22.5 and numerous ostraca; Aristeides: Plut. *Arist.* 1.1. Further comment and an interpretation of ἀλωπεκίζειν (Ar. *Vesp.* 1241) in Lewis, "Cleisthenes and Attica," *Historia* 12 (1963) 23.

We are informed, by the reliable testimony of Dionysius of Halicarnassus,[46] that Themistocles was the archon of the year 493/2. Many have wondered how an Athenian statesman could attain "the highest office in the state" in 493/2, only to drop out of sight for a decade.[47] It seems to me that our assumptions about the nature of the office of archon ought to be reconsidered.

First, almost all the archons from 507–487 are unknown persons. Second, those who are known seem to have been young: Themistocles, Aristeides, Hipparchus—and going back to the period of the tyrants—Miltiades and the younger Peisistratus.[48] This despite the fact that the Athenians generally put a premium on age and experience. Third, if the archonship had been largely an honorary position under the Peisistratids, nothing could better have convinced the Athenians that it was better left that way than the archonship of Isagoras, during which he expelled Cleisthenes and numerous other families and tried to destroy the council of 400 (Hdt. 5.72; *AP* 20).

Finally, one cannot escape the impression that the really important people in Athens made themselves felt without any official position (or at most, during times of crisis, as *strategoi*). Political stature was not a matter of office-holding but of confidence and consensus. Athenians throughout their history seem to have an intuitive distrust of office-holders, surrounding them with scrutinies and audits while reserving their trust for the mature, responsible (and answerable) private citizen: Cleisthenes, Themistocles in 483 and again in 479, Ephialtes and Pericles two decades later, to say nothing of Aristeides in 476. I believe that the archonship did not lose its importance only after it became subject to the lot in 487/6 (*AP* 22.5); rather that its real significance, which had once made it worth fighting over (*AP* 13.2), had been ruined by Peisistratid *adlectio*. I would therefore regard the archonship as a proving-ground for young men of promise, and see Themis-

---

[46] *Ant. Rom.* 6.34. Of the thirty-three archon years given by Dionysius, not one has been shown to be incorrect and twenty-two are reinforced by other testimonia. The date 493/2 is particularly firm as Dionysius also gives the date of the next year *AUC* and the name of the Olympic victor. For other arguments supporting 493/2 see Lenardon, loc. cit. (supra, n. 38).

[47] E.g., Gomme (supra, n. 1) I 261, followed by Flacelière (supra, n. 38) 18.

[48] All noted by H. T. Wade-Gery, *Essays in Greek History* (Oxford 1958) 146, n. 1; 171, n. 1, who suggests that young men of thirty became archons more or less *ad annum*. So also H. Schaefer, "Besonderheit u. Begriff d. attischen Demokratie im V. Jahrhundert," *Probleme der Alten Geschichte* (Göttingen 1963) 142.

tocles in 493/2 more as a quaestor than as a consul. It would be apposite here to repeat the judgment made thirty years ago by Helmut Berve:

> Aufstrebende Naturen ohne Rückhalt an Besitz und Geschlecht wie Themistokles benutzten das Archontat als erste Stufe auf der Leiter zur Macht, während den fürstlichen Herren an einem Amt, das ihnen keine neuen Machtmittel in die Hand gab, nichts gelegen war. Weder Kleisthenes noch Megakles noch Miltiades sind Archonten gewesen, und doch waren sie es, die den Staat leiteten, nicht die jeweiligen Träger des Oberamtes mit seinen geringen Kompetenzen.[49]

At the time Berve wrote he was not aware that an inscription had just been found which would prove that Cleisthenes and Miltiades had in fact been archons.[50] But the relative youth of both men when they held office (Cleisthenes 525/4, Miltiades 524/3) would tend to reinforce his impression of the archonship, correcting it only in the detail that it was not only the obscure who used the office as the first rung on the ladder to power.

Consequent to this reappraisal of the archonship are the following corollaries:

That Herodotus' description of Themistocles' status in 483 (7.143: ἐς πρώτους νεωστὶ παριών) is in fact a correct one, because archons and junior Areopagites were not considered to be among the *protoi*.

That the fortification of the Piraeus begun during Themistocles' archonship[51] was not necessarily a policy or a project proposed by the archon himself but a precaution considered advisable by the leaders of the *Boule* after the failure of the Ionian revolt, and entrusted to the supervision of the archon. It is entirely understandable that Themistocles would later have taken credit for the project himself.

Incidental to any discussion of the archon year 493/2 are the trials of the tragedian Phrynichus for disturbing the Athenians with

---

49 Op. cit. (supra, n. 1) 13. My only objection is to Berve's conception of Themistocles as a man without wealth or family. Gomme (supra, n. 4) n. 13, admits with doubts the possibility that the archonship had lost importance already and that Themistocles' tenure of the office does not prove a political victory.

50 B. Meritt, *Hesperia* 8 (1939) 59–65.

51 Thuc. 1.93.3; Pausanias 1.1.2; Eusebius *Chron.* Vers.Arm. Ol. 71.1 (496/5, the right Olympiad but the wrong year).

The Capture of Miletus (Hdt. 6.21) and Miltiades for tyranny in the Chersonese (6.104). There have been frequent attempts to connect Themistocles with one or another of these events.[52] But the general's sponsorship of Phrynichus in 476 is the only evidence on which to base a possible earlier collaboration. Again, it is only an assumption that Miltiades was attacked by the Alcmeonidae this year and was thus forced into an alliance with Themistocles, who helped him get off. It is true that the victor of Marathon was successfully prosecuted by Xanthippus, an Alcmeonid in-law, in 489/8 (Hdt. 6.136), but theories of an earlier prosecution by the same element are patently *post eventum* and rest on various other assumptions: that Athenian *gene* and their marriage connections act throughout with solidarity; that if Themistocles was anti-Alcmeonid in the 480's he will have been earlier as well; that he will therefore have taken Miltiades' side against the common enemy, and so forth. An assumption based upon so many hypotheses has a final and logical ring to it, because it explains so many things. The trouble is that the various items which are supposed to have been explained are themselves only speculations, each and every one of them more vulnerable to criticism than the final assumption, whose only virtue is that it holds the whole structure together. Again and again we are reminded how little we know of the politics of this period; it is safe to say only that whatever Themistocles' attitude to Miltiades, the return of the baron of Chersonese meant a momentary eclipse for all men of ambition, particularly after the triumph at Marathon.

The most arresting feature of internal politics in Athens in the 480's is the series of ostracisms. The evidence is twofold. According to the *Athenaion Politeia*, Hipparchus son of Charmus was ostracized in 488/7 (22.3–4), Megacles in 487/6 (22.5) and "friends of the tyrants" for the next two years (22.6). But in 484/3 they ostracized Xanthippus, the first exile who had nothing to do with the tyranny.[53] Finally, in 483/2, Aristeides was ostracized (22.7).

All these names have been found on ostraca,[54] and from the frequency of those bearing the name of Themistocles, including 190

---

[52] Walker, *CAH* IV 171f (both trials); Wade-Gery (supra, n. 48) 177f (both); Ehrenberg (supra, n. 1) 117 (Phrynichus); Forrest (supra, n. 2) 235f (Phrynichus); McGregor (supra, n. 1) 94 (Miltiades); Burn (supra, n. 2) 226 (Miltiades).

[53] This statement has always been a puzzle, as it would seem we must believe that the Alcmeonid Megacles was one of the "friends of the tyrants."

[54] E. Vanderpool, "Ostraka from the Athenian Agora," *Hesperia* Suppl. 8 (1949) 408–409.

prepared in advance and seemingly never used,[55] one could conclude that he was politically quite active in the 480's. But issues, factions, and personalities must remain as unknown as ever, as one example will suffice to show. In section NN of the great drain, between the slope of the Areopagus and Kolonos Agoraios, ostraca with the following names were found in conjunction: Themistocles (69), Callixenus (45),[56] Hippocrates Alcmeonidou (44), Aristeides (2), Cydrocles (2), Habron, Eratyllus, Andronichus (1 each). Of this list, only Themistocles and Aristeides are any more than mere names to us; the last four men are utterly unknown.[57]

      With so little evidence, it is useless to speculate about the reasons why these men became candidates for ostracophoriae (but see additional note, at end). If an analogy is permitted, a chess game may proceed until an exchange becomes logical. But it does no good to know that knight takes knight on the twelfth move. We must see the whole board to understand the logic, and it is exactly the whole board which is missing in this case.

      For the contest between Themistocles and Aristeides we are on slightly firmer ground, as far as *early* evidence is concerned. Ostraca bearing their names have been found together elsewhere,[58] Herodotus said they were bitter enemies (8.79), and it would seem probable that they clashed over Themistocles' proposal to spend the state revenue from the Laureion mines on the construction of a new fleet of triremes. The literature on this episode is overwhelming,[59] therefore I will concentrate on the specific question: what was the major consideration of policy, as it was presented to the Athenians? It seems to me that it cannot have been merely the narrow issue of triremes versus public distribution,[60] or, as later political theorists saw it, the impossibly

[55] O. Broneer, *Hesperia* 7 (1938) 228–243.

[56] Identified as an Alcmeonid by Stamires and Vanderpool, *Hesperia* 19 (1950) 376ff.

[57] Vanderpool (supra, n. 54) 395.

[58] H. Thompson, *AJA* 37 (1933) 296.

[59] It will suffice to mention here only J. Labarbe, *La loi navale de Thémistocle*, (supra, n. 17) an impressive study of the evidence and earlier literature, if sometimes the interpretations are questionable; cf. T. J. Cadoux, *JHS* 79 (1959) 184f.

[60] The ignorant and indigent may have thought so, and the opposition may have appealed to them on this basis, but such arguments will have been merely a smoke-screen. It is interesting to note that according to the classical concept of Themistocles as a demagogue, this would have been the class from which he drew his support. For the view that cash distributions had been carried out frequently in the past, see W. P. Wallace, *NC* ser. 7, no. 2 (1962) 28–35.

farsighted creation of naval democracy, naval empire, and Periclean imperialism. To the forceful and calculating political leaders of Athens it must have been the practical and immediate consideration of whether or not to expand the war with Aegina, for which the ships were to be merely a means to an end.[61]

This is in fact the reason put foward by Themistocles,[62] the war had been going badly,[63] it was obvious it could never be won without sea power, and there was the additional fear that Aegina (which had given earth and water to Darius in 491) would become a base for the Persian armada, about which the Athenians may have begun to hear rumours. But there existed at Athens a faction opposed to war with Aegina, including perhaps a segment of the sporting gentry,[64] and Aristeides may have been its leader; he was entrusted with a mission of some sort to Aegina on the eve of Salamis, a function generally assigned to proxenoi and others with friendly foreign connections.[65] Themistocles most strenuously urged passage of the Navy bill, perhaps with special warnings of the threat of Aeginetan medism (Hdt. 8.92 suggests this), and it may have seemed to him and his supporters after passage, that it was impossible to permit the leader of the opposition to remain in Athens because of future divisive obstructionism.[66]

It is not until the year of Salamis that Themistocles emerges as a living personality. His accomplishments during this year were so impressive that both ancient and modern writers have fre-

[61] As we are reminded most recently by Ida Calabi Limentani, *Plutarchi vita Aristidis* (Florence 1964) lxiv.

[62] Hdt. 7.144; Thuc. 1.14.3. One assumes the later testimonia are based on one or another of these two writers; cf. Plut. *Them.* 4.1; Polyaenus 1.30.6; Aristides *Or.* 46, II 250f Dindorf.

[63] Hdt. 6.87–93, which I think must be dated to the period after Marathon, *pace* Andrewes, *BSA* 37 (1936/7) 1–7.

[64] χρὴ δ'ἀπ' 'Αθανᾶν τέκτον 'ἀθληταῖσιν ἔμμεν, . . . Pindar *Nem.* 5.49; cf. Melesias, trainer of Aeginetan athletes, in *Ol.* 8; *Nem.* 4 and 6; Wade-Gery's remarks in *Essays* (supra, n. 48) 243–246.

[65] The statement of [Demosthenes] 26 ii, 6, that Aristeides lived in Aegina during his exile, is denied by many modern scholars, although I can see nothing against the claim. But Aristeides will have returned to Athens before this mission (*AP* 22.8) from wherever he spent his exile. See W. W. How and T. Wells, *Commentary on Herodotus* (Oxford 1928) *ad* 8.79; other references in Calabi Limentani (supra, n. 61) *ad Arist.* 8.2.

[66] Plutarch tells us Aristeides opposed Themistocles on issues he otherwise would have supported, a not unusual phenomenon in the history of politics. *Arist.* 3, of course, is late and anecdotal, but the situation described therein is quite likely.

quently made deductions about both earlier and later activities from what they know of this period.

The war meant a closing of ranks at Athens and the exiles were brought home. If the Themistocles Decree is accepted as genuine, the general himself was responsible for this reconciliation; later tradition at any rate believed so.[67] Themistocles' *boule* and *dynamis* during this crucial year made his reputation for all time. First, he successfully challenged the vested interests of the Delphic interpreters by persuading the Athenians to accept his reading of the Wooden Wall response. Second, he masterminded the Artemisium and Salamis campaigns despite his subordinate position in the councils of war, Finally, he acted on behalf of unity and sound strategy throughout in the face of the defeatism, stupidity and shortsightedness of those in command. The most convincing proof of his genius is that we are compelled to these judgments by the narrative of a historian who disliked him and made every attempt to belittle his accomplishments.[68]

The only indication that politics were pursuing a normal course during this period is the unexplained absence of Themistocles from the winter of 480/79 to the year after the war. A later tradition held that he had been relieved of his command because he had been so signally honored by Sparta after Salamis, but this may be only a rationalizing attempt by later writers to explain his disappearance from the account of Herodotus.[69]

After the war Themistocles reappears in our sources. Acting probably as a private citizen, he persuaded the Athenians to send him to Sparta on his famous mission of deception and delay while the city walls were being rebuilt (Thuc. 1.90–92). It is a measure of the man that having obtained unprecedented status as a "friend" of Sparta (Hdt. 8.124; Thuc. 1.91.1)—an honor and advantage in both international and domestic politics that would have been treasured for life by most men—he chose to sacrifice it in one moment for the advantage of his city. That Athens was adamant and unified on the issue of fortifications seems demonstrated by the fact that they also risked the lives of

---

[67] Plut. *Them.* 11.1; Aristides *Or.* 46, II 248 Dindorf.

[68] This is the usual interpretation of Herodotus' treatment of the general, from Plutarch *De Hdt.Mal.* 37, to the present, e.g., How and Wells (supra, n. 65) I 42–43. Herodotus is defended by H. Strasburger, "Herodot und das perikleische Athen," *Historia* 4 (1955) 21–22.

[69] Diodorus 11.27.3, on which see C. Hignett, *Xerxes' Invasion of Greece* (Oxford 1963) 275–277.

Aristeides and Habronichus, another diplomat with a special relationship with Sparta (Hdt. 8.21).

Perhaps on his return from Sparta Themistocles persuaded the Athenians to fortify Piraeus as well. His intentions, made clear by Thucydides (1.93.7), were strictly strategic and extramural, as it were, and once more we must deny any purposeful and partisan strengthening of the thetes or commercial interests as a political force (the one is a concern of fourth-century theorists; the other, of the 1920's and 1930's, which I regard as self-explanatory). As far as we know there was no significant opposition to making Piraeus and the fleet a new center of gravity in Athenian foreign policy, with Xanthippus already on the high seas as admiral, Cimon preparing to start his career and Aristeides high in the councils of the new imperialism.[70]

Only Plutarch reports the attempt of Themistocles to redress the balance of power by restoring Thebes, Argos, and Thessaly as voting members of the Amphictyonic Council (*Them.* 20.3–4). Nevertheless, modern scholars have shown good reason to credit the story.[71]

From 478 to his ostracism we are almost without reliable evidence for the statesman's activities. There are the following possible exceptions.

Themistocles had built a shrine to Artemis Aristoboule near the agora. The report by Plutarch (*Them.* 22.2) is confirmed by the recent discovery of the building;[72] that Athenians were consequently angered by Themistocles' pride rests again on Plutarch's authority alone, but this would seem reasonable.

In 477/6 Themistocles produced a play by Phrynichus,[73] which scholars since Nauck have assumed to be the *Phoenissae*, commemorating the crushing of the Persian fleet at Salamis. Athenian reaction at this time may have contributed to the later tradition that Themistocles made himself tiresome by continually reminding his fellow citizens of his achievements. During this same year new statues

---

[70] On Aristeides, see *AP* 23.4-24.2. If there was discontent it may have been of the type described by Plutarch *Arist.* 13. The leaders, as noted by Calabi Limentani, *ad loc.*, were country squires, malignant and ineffectual.

[71] Full commentary on this episode by H. Bengtson, "Themistokles u. d. delphische Amphiktyonie," *Eranos* 49 (1951) 85–92; Flacelière (supra, n. 38) 19–28; cf. B. D. Meritt, H. T. Wade-Gery, M. F. McGregor, edd., *The Athenian Tribute Lists* III (Cambridge, Mass. 1939–1953) 105, 302, n. 6.

[72] Threpsiades and Vanderpool, *Deltion* 19 (1964) 26–36.

[73] Plut. *Them.* 5.4, probably quoting from the *didaskalia*.

of the tyrannicides were dedicated and this has recently been seen as an anti-Alcmeonid gesture by Themistocles, who hoped to minimize Cleisthenes' part in overthrowing the tyrants.[74] Attractive as this thesis is, it is still conjecture and must not be made the basis for further speculation.

Perhaps it was during this year that Themistocles appeared at Olympia and received the tumultuous acclaim of the crowd. But the story rests entirely on the authority of later writers and one can almost see the details being added century after century by enthusiastic raconteurs.[75]

One final event is firmly established but cannot be certainly dated: Themistocles' arbitration of a dispute between Corinth and Corcyra.[76]

To bring this survey to an end, sometime late in the 470's, Themistocles was ostracized, and when the Spartans brought an accusation of medism against him he was prosecuted *in absentia* by an otherwise unknown member of the Alcmeonid family.[77]

As far as I can see, none of this behavior, taken at face value, provides any revelations about Themistocles as *novus homo*, democrat, egalitarian, or any other term in the lexica of political scientists, ancient or modern. This brings up a question which is so often avoided: what, really, does the word "democrat" mean in the political context of the Marathon generation? The present age is neither so preoccupied with theory nor so semantically handicapped as Aristotle and should be able to arrive at more meaningful qualifications.

I think most modern scholars would now agree that Athens in the first third of the fifth century continued to be manipulated by an aristocratic elite. Although the nobles were now constrained to operate within the confines of the Cleisthenic constitution, that instrument, like most successful and enduring institutions of its kind, was

---

[74] Anthony Podlecki, "The Political Significance of the Athenian 'Tyrannicide' Cult," *Historia* 15 (1966) 138–140.

[75] Earliest evidence for his presence at Olympia, Theophrastus in Plut. *Them.* 25.1. Other details: *Them.* 17.4; Paus. 8.50.3; Aelian, *VH* 13.43; [Themistocles] *Epistle* 8, p. 748 Hercher.

[76] Hinted at by Thuc. 1.136.1 and amplified by Theophrastus in *POxy* VII, no. 1012, C ii 22–23, which is probably the source of Plut. *Them.* 24.1. Cf. Burn (supra, n. 2) 293ff, on Themistocles' western interests.

[77] Craterus, *FGrHist* 342 F 11; Plut. *Them.* 23.1.

permissive and was designed to be a reflection of tempora and mores rather than of doctrine. We would assume that most far-reaching questions of domestic and foreign policy were settled informally by discussion in the houses of the great, that the final decision was written up *pro forma* by the *Boule* and given perfunctory acclamation by the Ecclesia. Only when there was irreconcilable disagreement among the clans (or such *aporia* that it was felt best to spread responsibility for a decision) would the Demos be invited to take sides. Even in these cases the Demos would be lending its support to one aristocrat or another. When the herald asked: τις ἀγορεύειν βούλεται; citizens over fifty years of age were invited to speak first, and it is almost certain that only men of unquestionable stature would be recognized: Areopagites, present and previous *strategoi*, phratry chiefs, and so forth.[78] The threat of using popular support was always there but we should assume that all factions within the aristocracy were prepared to go to the people (τὸν δῆμον προσεταιρίζεσθαι, as Cleisthenes had done), either to arouse enthusiasm for a disputed policy—as Themistocles seems to have done for the Navy bill in 483 and for his interpretation of the oracle in 481/0—or to attack a rival in the courts (e.g., Miltiades) or in an ostracophoria (e.g., Themistocles, several times).

A "democrat" during this period, then, would be a man who lacked the needed influence to assert his views in the councils of the great families and who therefore made it a practice to initiate action before the People, seeking popularity with those elements who were most likely to come to the Ecclesia.

But as I have shown, all our *evidence* that Themistocles did in fact act this way is impressionistic, based as it is on Aristotle's backward projection of the behavior of fourth-century demagogues and Plutarch's embellishment of the Aristotelian thesis with revealing anecdotes. Everything we know about Themistocles indicates that his talents lay in converting the mighty to his purpose. His ability to suffer fools gladly, to compromise, to come to terms with political enemies are all signs of a man who works with the system rather than against it. His enemies are but dimly perceived; but we generally assume him to be a foe of the Alcmeonidae, who are in turn supposed to be popularity-seekers and to have invented the idea of taking the Demos as a client. His friends are totally unknown, and it is interesting to note that the one

[78] The herald's question in Dem. 18.170; Aeschines 3.4; cf. G. T. Griffith on *isegoria* (supra, n. 4) 115–138, and A. G. Woodhead, *Historia* 16 (1967) 129–140.

political compact often proposed is with the princely Miltiades—at which point the proposers are forced to concede that it was an "unlikely alliance." Such are the paradoxes created by political science and its accomplice, historicism. The fact is, that if we had only the testimony of Herodotus and Thucydides, and no preconceptions about class warfare and party politics, we should never have thought of Themistocles as a radical in the first place. The first Athenian who actually behaved the way a "democrat" is supposed to behave is that grass-roots fascist Cleon, who was the first to speak the language of the agora and to turn a fraudulent egalitarianism and resentment of wealth, style, and privilege into a potent political weapon.

I would suggest instead, although the suggestion brings up a subject outside the scope of this paper, that the eventual impetus toward a broader based democracy in the fifth century was psychological: during the century, the commons lost its awe for the *gnorimoi*, who were after all the founders of the democracy, in the same way that Americans in the early nineteenth century lost their awe for *their* founding fathers. The chief medium of change was the empire, which by creating a new class of wealthy persons diluted aristocratic control of the economy, and by creating a bureaucracy, diluted aristocratic control of public business.

For the political tendencies of the Marathon generation, however, it remains almost impossible to make positive statements, and it will suffice here to stress the negative point: that Aristotle's picture of left-wing and right-wing politics in fifth-century Athens is based on false premises, and that his portrayal of Themistocles as a leader of the left is merely this general fallacy carried out to a particular fallacious conclusion.

But anyone who attempts to use the testimony of writers subsequent to Aristotle—and I am thinking here particularly of Plutarch—should note the extent to which his logic imposed on subsequent generations. Partly because of the stature of the great polymath, and partly because the Athenian Demos itself did not survive him, subsequent inquiry into the Athenian polities was persuaded to accept his view, not as one generation's contribution to a continuing organic debate, but as a final summation, a sort of fossilized logos no longer subject to revision. Future thinkers might question Aristotle's judgment— whether sovereign democracy was all that unsound—but never the rigid symmetry of the structure he gave to politics, never the roles he assigned to the various players within the political spectrum, never the logic that made Themistocles a democrat.

University of California
Santa Barbara

ADDENDUM

Since this paper was submitted, our evidence for the ostracophoriae has been increased by thousands of new ostraca, unearthed by the Deutsches Archäologisches Institut in its Kerameikos excavations. I am indebted to the Institute and to Professor Franz Willemsen for allowing me to inspect these ostraca during the summer of 1967 and for permission to make a few brief statements about them.

It can now be shown that Themistocles was in fact a candidate in the contest that saw the ostracism of Megacles (487/6), and so was his friend and mentor, Mnesiphilus of Phrearrioi. Demonstration rests on ostraca inscribed with the different names, but broken from the same vase.

I am relieved to be able to say that the first impression of all the new evidence in no way changes my opinion about Themistocles' political position; in fact it confirms my conviction that the contests were highly personal, rather than partisan-political.

ARTHUR E. GORDON

Notes on the *Res Gestae* of Augustus*

It is seldom that we have the advantage of possessing both an ancient Latin inscription and two ancient literary references to it, as we have in the case of the *Index rerum gestarum* (or simply the *Res Gestae*) of Augustus.[1] In Suetonius[2] we have a mention and brief explanation of it (as well as some apparently direct borrowings)[3] written hardly more than a century after the event by one who had undoubtedly seen the original in Rome. In Dio we have a similar statement about a century later,[4] which may or may not depend on Suetonius.

* A revised version of a paper presented at the annual meeting of the Philological Association of the Pacific Coast, Victoria, B.C., November 24, 1967.

[1] For a similar case, involving a speech of Claudius, cf. Tac. *Ann.* 11.23.1–25.1 with *CIL* 13.1668 (= Dessau 212), on which see Arnaldo Momigliano, *Claudius: The Emperor and His Achievement*, transl. by W. D. Hogarth (Oxford 1934; with new pref., bibliog., and minor corrections, Cambridge 1961) 10–19, and Ronald Syme, *Tacitus* (Oxford 1958) 1.317–319, 2.703 with n. 3. The question of the original title of the *Res Gestae* is a vexed one: cf. Jean Gagé in ed. 2 (1950) of his *Res Gestae Divi Augusti* (Publ. de la Fac. des Lettres de l'Univ. de Strasbourg, Textes d'Étude, 5) 9.

[2] *Testamentum L. Planco C. Silio cons.* [A.D. 13] *III. Non. Apriles, ante annum et quattuor menses quam decederet* [i.e., Augustus], *factum ab eo ac duobus codicibus partim ipsius partim libertorum Polybi et Hilarionis manu scriptum depositumque apud se virgines Vestales cum tribus signatis aeque voluminibus protulerunt. Quae omnia in senatu aperta atque recitata sunt. . . . Tribus voluminibus, uno mandata de funere suo complexus est, altero indicem rerum a se gestarum, quem vellet incidi in aeneis tabulis, quae ante Mausoleum statuerentur, tertio breviarium totius imperii, quantum militum sub signis ubique esset, quantum pecuniae in aerario et fiscis et vectigaliorum residuis.* (Suet. *Aug.* 101.1, 4 ed. Ihm).

[3] For a list of the chief correspondences between the *Res Gestae* and Suetonius' *Augustus*, see Gagé (supra, n. 1) 210.

[4] Dio-Xiph. 56.33.1: ἐγέγραπτο δὲ ἐν μὲν τῷ πρώτῳ ὅσα τῆς ταφῆς εἴχετο, ἐν δὲ τῷ δευτέρῳ τὰ ἔργα ἃ ἔπραξε πάντα, ἃ καὶ ἐς χαλκὰς στήλας πρὸς τῷ ἡρώῳ αὐτοῦ σταθείσας ἀναγραφῆναι ἐκέλευσε, τὸ τρίτον, etc.

Seldom also do we have an autobiographical document composed by the chief of a great state such as Rome while he is still at the head of it. Disappointing though we may find the *Res Gestae* as an account of the author's public career, we must yet—so far as we are interested in the history of his age—regret the loss of his earlier and undoubtedly much longer account "of his life down to the Cantabrian War" (presumably that of 26–25 B.C.), mentioned also by Suetonius.[5] Why did this not survive whereas the later account did?

The fact is that all the Roman political apologias to which we have reference, except the two of Julius Caesar and this second one of Augustus (if it is a political apologia), are lost save for later quotations.[6] It may be reasonably conjectured that the preservation of Caesar's two was due to their having what was perhaps lacking to all the lost ones (those of Sulla and Varro, for example, and even Cicero's autobiographical pieces, both prose and verse),[7] namely style, a quality attested by Cicero himself for Caesar's *Gallic War*,[8] as well as by Hirtius,[9] and clear even in his *Civil War*, unrevised as it is.

[5] Suet. *Aug.* 85, *init.*: *Multa varii generis prosa oratione composuit, ex quibus . . . aliqua de vita sua, quam tredecim libris Cantabrico tenus bello nec ultra exposuit.*

[6] Exceptional in being preserved is the Εἰς ἑαυτόν of the emperor Marcus Aurelius, but this of course is far from being a political apologia. On what sort of document the *Res Gestae* is—a much-discussed question—see infra, n. 51.

[7] For Sulla see H. Peter (ed.), *Historicorum Romanorum fragmenta* (Leipzig 1883) 127–134; for Varro, *op. cit.*, 236; for Cicero, *op. cit.*, 206–210, and Willy Morel (ed.), *Fragmenta poetarum Latinorum epicorum et lyricorum praeter Ennium et Lucilium* (ed. 2, Leipzig 1927) 68–73; cf. Schanz-Hosius, *Geschichte der römischen Literatur . . .*, 1[4] (Munich 1927) 530–534, 535–537; Karl Büchner, *Paulys Realencyclopädie der classischen Altertumswissenschaft*, Neue Bearbeitung (Stuttgart 1894—) (hereafter cited as *P-W*) 2 R., Bd. 7:1 (1939), *s.v.* M. Tullius Cicero, no. 29, cols. 1245–1256, 1267–1269.

[8] Cic. *Brut.* 75.262, *Tum Brutus: . . . Compluris* (sc. *orationes eius*, i.e., Caesar's) *autem legi atque etiam commentarios quos idem scripsit rerum suarum. Valde quidem, inquam* (i.e., Cicero), *probandos; nudi enim sunt, recti et venusti, omni ornatu orationis tamquam veste detracta. Sed dum voluit habere parata unde sumerent qui vellent scribere historiam, ineptis gratum fortasse fecit qui illa volent calamistris inurere: sanos quidem homines a scribendo deterruit; nihil est enim in historia pura et inlustri brevitate dulcius.* See also Suetonius' report (*Divus Iulius* 55) of further testimony on Cicero's part.

[9] Hirtius, pref. to Caes. *B. G.* bk. 8, sect. 4–7: *Constat enim inter omnes nihil tam operose ab aliis esse perfectum quod non horum elegantia commentariorum superetur. Qui sunt editi ne scientia tantarum rerum scriptoribus deesset, adeoque probantur omnium iudicio ut praerepta, non praebita, facultas scriptoribus videatur. Cuius tamen rei maior nostra quam reliquorum est admiratio; ceteri enim quam bene atque emendate, nos etiam quam facile atque celeriter eos perfecerit scimus. Erat autem in Caesare cum facultas atque elegantia summa scribendi, tum verissima scientia suorum consiliorum explicandorum.* For ancient as well as modern comparisons between Caesar's and Augustus' styles, see infra, n. 10 and n. 61.

On the other hand, I suggest heretically, the circumstances to which we owe the preservation of Augustus' *Res Gestae*, as against the loss of his earlier account of himself, are not its literary character or style (of which it seems to me to have none, despite Jean Gagé's praise of it as "ce beau latin d'Auguste")[10] or its author's great name, but first the fact that the *Res Gestae* was inscribed, and second the fact that the original inscription in bronze was—no doubt within a short time—duplicated in stone, being cut on at least three public buildings or monuments. Ironically, Augustus had ordered the *Res Gestae* to be cut in bronze after his death and set up in front of his Mausoleum in Rome,[11] as though thinking the *Res Gestae* as precious as a legal document worth

[10] On p. II of ed. 2 of his *Res Gestae Divi Augusti* (cited in full supra, n. 2), which I find the most useful edition now available of the *Res Gestae*, with long introduction, text, apparatus criticus, commentary, etc., though Mommsen's ed. 2 (see infra, n. 12) is still indispensable. Gagé's high opinion is in general accord with the views expressed by editors and commentators since Mommsen and Kaibel wrote in 1883 (Mommsen[2] 189, 194, 197; cf. Mommsen, *Historische Zeitschrift*, 57 [N. F. 21, 1887] 396), though I find no one else calling the work "beau." Suetonius, after listing Augustus' prose and verse pieces (*Aug.* 85) but not mentioning the *Res Gestae*, writes (ch. 86 *init.*): *Genus eloquendi secutus est elegans et temperatum vitatis sententiarum ineptiis atque concinnitate et reconditorum verborum, ut ipse dicit, fetoribus; praecipuamque curam duxit sensum animi quam apertissime exprimere* . . . But Tacitus (*Ann.* 13.3) puts Caesar and Augustus together, as speakers: *Nam dictator Caesar summis oratoribus aemulus; et Augusto prompta ac profluens quae deceret principem eloquentia fuit* ("the ready and fluent diction appropriate to a monarch," John Jackson), as also Fronto in 163 (*Ad Verum Imp.* 2.1 [Naber, p. 119; Haines, Loeb ed., vol. 2, pp. 136–139]): . . . *Caesari quidem facultatem dicendi video imperatoriam fuisse, Augustum vero saeculi residua elegantia et Latinae linguae etiam tum integro lepore potius quam dicendi ubertate praeditum puto* ("the master of but the dying elegance of his times and such charm as the Latin tongue still retained unimpaired, rather than of opulent diction," Haines). For the most detailed comparison of Caesar's and Augustus' styles, see Ed. v. Wölfflin, *Sitzungsb. d. phil.-phil. u. hist. Cl. der k. b. Akad. d. Wiss. zu München*, 1896 (1897) 161 *fin.*–184 (he thinks that Augustus emulated Caesar). For other views of the style of the *Res Gestae*, cf. Wilamowitz, *Hermes*, 21 (1886) 625; Ed. Norden, *Die antike Kunstprosa*, 1 (Leipzig 1898) 268; V. Gardthausen, *Augustus u. seine Zeit*, 1:3 (Leipzig 1904) 1283f, 1288; W. L. Westermann, *Amer. Hist. Rev.* 17 (1911) 5; F. W. Shipley (ed. and transl.), Velleius Paterculus . . ., *Res Gestae* Divi Augusti (Loeb Class. Libr. 1924) 336; T. Rice Holmes, *The Architect of the Roman Empire* (Oxford 1928) 181f; Georg Misch, *Geschichte der Autobiographie*[2] 1 (Leipzig, Berlin 1931) index, p. 471, *s.v.* Augustus, esp. p. 164 ("Hier ist Stil ohne Phantasie und Leidenschaft," etc.); Schanz-Hosius, *Gesch. der röm. Lit.*[4] 2 (Munich 1935) 14f; H. J. Rose, *A Handbook of Latin Literature* (New York 1936 and reprinted) 304 (in the 1960 paperback); Wilhelm Weber, *Princeps, Studien zur Gesch. des Augustus*, 1 (Stuttgart-Berlin 1936) 105; Concetta Barini (ed.), *Res Gestae divi Augusti* (Rome 1937) p. v; Ronald Syme, *The Roman Revolution* (Oxford 1939 and reprinted) 522–524; Henry Bardon, *Les empereurs et les lettres latines d'Auguste à Hadrien* (Paris 1940) 54, 62; S. Riccobono (ed.), *Acta Divi Augusti* (Rome 1945) 7f; Enrica Malcovati (ed.), Imp. Caes. Augusti *Operum fragmenta*[3] (Turin etc. 1947 [*Corpus Script. Lat. Paravianum*]) p. LIII; Karl Hönn, *Augustus u. seine Zeit*[4] (Vienna 1953) 292; O. A. W. Dilke, in *Greece and Rome*, ser. 2, IV (1957) 79f. (See infra, n. 61.)

[11] See supra, n. 2.

preserving forever. But the very fact that bronze was the material inscribed is probably what led to its loss, bronze having been too valuable a metal not to be melted down for other purposes in due course, with the result that only a small number of inscribed Roman bronzes have survived, in contrast with the very many thousands of inscribed stones.

Another unusual quality of this "titulus inter Latinos primarius" (as Mommsen calls the *Res Gestae*)[12] is the fact, mentioned above, that it exists in three more or less complete copies, all of them in Turkey, in what was the Roman province of Galatia; but one of these— the one located at Ankara, the capital of Turkey, as it was also of Galatia—is so relatively complete that the *Res Gestae* is sometimes referred to as the *Monumentum Ancyranum*. This copy exists in both the original Latin—or, presumably at least, a fairly accurate copy of it (there are a few slips,[13] due probably to some copyist or the cutter)[14]— and a Greek version; the Latin was rediscovered, and its rediscovery made known to the West, in 1555, but the reading of the complete Greek text had to wait till the nineteenth century and the destruction of house walls that had concealed it.[15] The other two copies are only fragmentary, the remnants thus far found at Apollonia (in Pisidia) being only in Greek,[16] those at so-called Pisidian Antioch only in Latin.[17]

There may, of course, have been other copies, not yet dis-

[12] *Res Gestae Divi Augusti ex monumentis Ancyrano et Apolloniensi*, iterum ed. Th. Mommsen. Accedunt tabulae undecim (separately bound) (Berlin 1883), p. xxxviii. His much-quoted phrase, "the Queen of Latin inscriptions," occurs on p. 385 of his article in the *Historische Zeitschrift* listed supra, n. 10.

[13] Apart from such things as *aede* (for *aedem*), *quinquens* (for *-iens*), *provicia[s]*, *provincis*, *perpetum* and *exercitum* (for *-uum*), *praerant* and *sexsiens*, which may be errors of spelling or cutting, or may echo current pronunciation or be attested in literature (see H. Dessau, ed., *Inscriptiones Latinae selectae*, 3:2 [Berlin 1916] pp. 811, 822 *init.*, 835, 805, 837f, and F. Sommer, *Handbuch der lateinischen Laut- und Formenlehre* . . .2⁻³ [Heidelberg 1914] pp. 301, 274 *fin.*, 331, 392f [sect. 231], 281), there is one mistake in case form: *ducenti* for *-tos*, following the correct *octingentos*, ch. 23.

[14] For Gagé's reconstruction of the *Res Gestae* from Augustus himself to the Ankara and other copies, see his ed. (supra, n. 1) 42–54; cf. G. A. Harrer, "*Res Gestae Divi Augusti*," *Studies in Philology*, 23 (Chapel Hill 1926) 387–403, esp. 398 (summary); E. Kornemann, *P-W* 16:1 (1933) 215–223, *s.v.* Monumentum Ancyranum, sects. 2f; for the most complicated one, see Weber (supra, n. 10) 106ff.

[15] See, most fully, Mommsen (supra, n. 12), pp. xvi, xxxiif.

[16] See, besides Mommsen (ed. 2), W. H. Buckler, W. M. Calder, W. K. C. Guthrie, *Mon. Asiae Min. ant.* 4 (Manchester 1933) 49–56, no. 143; Kornemann (supra, n. 14) 212 (lines 48ff), 213 (lines 63ff)–214 (line 3); Weber (supra, n. 10) 111, 114–116, 111*f, n. 466; Gagé (supra, n. 1) 6, 47, 53f, 56, 63f.

[17] See W. M. Ramsay and Anton von Premerstein (edd.), *Monumentum Antiochenum* . . . (Leipzig 1927 [*Klio*, Beiheft XIX (N. F., Heft VI)]); Gagé (supra, n. 1) 7, 64.

covered. E. G. Hardy, for example, wrote that it seemed "probable that Tiberius caused copies of the document to be engraved on the walls of all temples of Rome and Augustus existing at the time of his accession, and that in the Greek-speaking parts of the empire he had a Greek translation appended,"[18] and Wilhelm Weber, "Überall, wo Caesareen, Augusteen, Denkmäler gleich dem in Apollonia, Feste, Spiele zum Gedächtnis des Augustus vorhanden waren, ist mindestens die Möglichkeit der Existenz eines Exemplars gegeben."[19]

But the fact that the only copies found to date are in Galatia raises the question whether this is due merely to chance or "to the very remoteness of that country, where ancient monuments have a greater chance of escaping destruction than in cities lying more directly in the stream of historic changes and more exposed to vicissitudes of fortune" (as Hardy wrote)[20] or to some special connection between Augustus and Galatia (as W. M. Ramsay, V. Ehrenberg, and Gagé have argued)[21] based on Augustus' having been the one who made a Roman province of Galatia and also, as he himself notes in the *Res Gestae*, settled colonies of soldiers in Pisidia, among other places.[22] I agree rather with Dessau[23] that the explanation may lie rather in the identity of the Roman governor of the province of Galatia at the beginning of the reign of Tiberius, who may have been induced by personal motives— gratitude to Augustus? desire to make favor with Tiberius?—to urge or order the duplication and Greek translation of the *Res Gestae* at various places in Galatia; but even if his identity should ever become known through the discovery or interpretation of some pertinent information,[24] we should still wish to know that he was in fact responsible for

18 E. G. Hardy (ed.), *The Monumentum Ancyranum* (Oxford 1923) 10.

19 Weber (supra, n. 10) 111, cf. 109 *fin.*–111.

20 Hardy, *ibid.* (supra, n. 18).

21 Ramsay, *JRS* 6 (1916) 105 (for his dating of Colonia Caesarea Antiochea, which is conjectural, cf. *JRS* 14 [1924] 172, 16 [1926] 111—he lowered the date from ca. 25 to ca. 21–19 B.C.); V. Ehrenberg, *Klio* 19 (1925) 200; Gagé (supra, n. 1) 23.

22 *Res Gestae*, 28.1 (edd. Volkmann [see infra, n. 25] and Gagé, ed. 2, and so hereafter unless otherwise indicated): *Colonias in Africa, Sicilia, [M]acedonia, utraque Hispania, Achai[a], Asia, S[y]ria, Gallia Narbonensi, Pi[si]dia militum deduxi.* Cf. Mommsen (supra, n. 12) 119–121; Gagé (supra, n. 1) 133f. For Augustus' making Galatia a province, see David Magie, *Roman Rule in Asia Minor . . .* (Princeton 1950) 1.453ff.

23 Hermann Dessau, *Geschichte der römischen Kaiserzeit*, 1 (Berlin 1924) 484. Harrer (supra, n. 14), 388f, calls this explanation "very reasonable, though it may not be conclusive."

24 No governors of Galatia under Tiberius or at the end of Augustus' reign seem to be known with certainty, though W. M. Ramsay maintained, on the strength of the

the work in question; the likely place for divulging such a fact would be either the so-called *Praescriptio* (or Title) or the Appendix (or *Summa*) of the *Res Gestae* as inscribed, both of which seem to be local additions, of a summary character, to the original text;[25] but in fact none of the three copies has any mention of local responsibility—certainly not the one at Ankara, nor either of the others so far as their fragments reveal. Nevertheless this explanation of Galatia's being the provenience of all three copies seems to me the most probable of those thus far advanced.

However many copies of the *Res Gestae* (with or without Greek translation) may have been inscribed in Galatia (or elsewhere in the Greek world), they all no doubt were cut on public monuments somehow connected with the cult of Rome and Augustus (alone or with members of his family); the one at Ankara, for example, was cut on the walls of the Temple of Rome and Augustus, which, like the Parthenon, later became a Christian church and in the fifteenth century was attached to a Turkish mosque;[26] hence perhaps the fact that this Ankara copy (with its translation) is so much better preserved, so much more complete, than the other two copies, which seem not to have been cut on temple walls.[27]

Mommsen's second edition of the *Res Gestae*, of 1883, valuable and indispensable as it is,[28] is based on only the Ankara and

fragmentary *CIG* 3.3990 [= *IGR* 3.249], lines 1f, and the equally fragmentary *JRS* 2 (1912) 101, no. 42 (emended *JRS* 6 [1916] 134) and other considerations, that a L. Calpurnius Piso (?) Frugi was the governor A.D. 12–15 (or, alternatively, ca. 13–15): cf. Ramsay, *JRS* 6 (1916) 134, *JHS* 38 (1918) 172–175, no. XIV, and in *Anatolian Studies Presented to William Hepburn Buckler*, edd. W. M. Calder and Josef Keil (Manchester 1939) 210; Wm. F. Shaffer, *The Administration of the Roman Province of Galatia from 25 B.C. to A.D. 72* (Princeton diss. 1945, seen in microfilm) 162, 177 (where he conjectures L. Calpurnius (Piso?) Frugi as governor for perhaps ca. A.D. 14–17 and as perhaps the one whose name is lost in *CIG* 3.4039 *init.*), 289, n. 5 (with ref. to *PIR*2 2.61, no. 288 *fin.*, where Groag rejects the attribution of *IGR* 3.249 to a Piso, in favor of Ti. Iulius Frugi [*PIR*2 4:3, 217, no. 329]); Magie (supra, n. 22) 2.1596 (list of governors). Dessau had previously (*PIR* 3, ed. 1, 499, no. 31) been uncertain whether -υγει (the basis of "Frugi") was part of a name.

[25] For a summary of various views see Hans Volkmann, *Res gestae divi Augusti, Bericht*, Teil II (Leipzig 1943 [Bursian's *Jahresbericht* . . ., 1942, vol. 279]) 50–52.

[26] See Mommsen, ed. 2, p. XIII.

[27] For the *Mon. Apoll.* see Buckler, Calder, and Guthrie (supra, n. 16) 53; for the *Mon. Ant.*, Ramsay-Premerstein (supra, n. 17) 4, 13–16.

[28] For the strongest tribute to Mommsen's great achievement in thrice editing the *Res Gestae* (ed. 1 1865 and 1873 [*CIL* vol. 3], ed. 2 1883), as well as to Domaszewski's "helle Augen und eindringenden Spürsinn," see Weber (supra, n. 10) p. 108*.

Apollonia copies (neither of which he saw directly),[29] the Antioch copy
not being found until 1914 and 1924;[30] and there seems to be as yet no
single edition that may properly be called the standard, embodying a
text based on the editor's (or editors') autopsy of both Latin copies and
both Greek versions, supplemented by squeezes (or other equally good
reproductions), photographs, and on-the-spot notes and measurements.
So far as I am aware, no one who has edited the *Res Gestae* as a whole, or
even the *Monumentum Ancyranum* or *Antiochenum* separately,[31] has seen
and examined all the extant remains of the three monuments.

The text of neither the Latin nor the Greek is certain at all
points, since even when the Greek is extant (at Ankara or Apollonia)
where the Latin is missing (or vice versa, at Ankara or Antioch), we
cannot be sure exactly what Latin (or Greek) was originally cut, for
several reasons: a mistake of some sort is always possible; the Greek is
not, and cannot be, a word-for-word translation of the Latin (e.g., for
the Latin *in libertatem vindicavi*, ch. 1.1, the Greek seems to have had only
the one word ἠλευθέρωσα, only two letters out of ten being extant at
latest report);[32] there are inconsistencies of spelling in both the Latin
and the Greek (e.g., *cl]aussum*, with two S's, vs. *clausum*, with one, in the
same sentence, ch. 13); sometimes in the Latin a number is written as a
word, sometimes as a numeral (e.g., *tribuniciae potestatis duodevicensimum,
consul xii*, ch. 15.2—the Greek seems never to write a number as a
numeral); the order of words is variable, therefore often indeterminable
in a restoration; abbreviation in the Latin (there seems to be none in
the Greek), while infrequent except in the praenomina (where it is
regular when the praenomen is followed by nomen or cognomen), is
inconsistent elsewhere, not only between the Ankara and Antioch
copies (e.g., *Rom.* in *Mon. Anc.*, *Romani* in *Mon. Ant.*, in the *Praescr.*), but

29 For ed. 1 and *CIL* 3 Mommsen relied chiefly on drawings prepared in
1861, at Ankara, by Georges Perrot and Edmond Guillaume (Mommsen, ed. 2, pp. xvii,
xxviif), for ed. 2 on a plaster-of-Paris copy, in 194 pieces, made in 1882 by Carl Humann
(Mommsen, *op. cit.*, xvii, xxviii–xxxii).

30 See Ramsay-Premerstein (supra, n. 17) 1–5.

31 Apparently the *Monumentum Apolloniense* has never been separately edited.
Of the editors of the *Mon. Antiochenum*, one at least—D. M. Robinson, *AJP* 47 (1926) 1–54,
with seven plates—had some firsthand knowledge of the *Mon. Ancyranum* (he speaks, p. 4, of
spending "some time at Angora studying and taking squeezes of parts of the *Mon. Anc.*"), but
it is clear that for their text of the *Mon. Anc.*, which was basic to their texts of the *Mon. Ant.*,
they all used previously published editions of the former, chiefly Mommsen's second.

32 For the Greek of the *Mon. Anc.* vs. that of the *Mon. Apol.* see Gagé (supra,
n. 1) 53f.

even within the same copy (e.g., *consulibus* three times, *cos.* twice, in the same sentence in *Mon. Anc.*, ch. 16.2); the spacing between words, sentences, and paragraphs is variable. At one time it was my tentative belief that no editor, not even Mommsen, in suggesting restorations had given adequate thought to spatial considerations, but I am now less confident of my doubt. Nevertheless the restorations remain the most debatable element in establishing the text. For example, in chapter 1, sections 1–2, Mommsen in ed. 2 restores 11 letters, two other editors 14, five others (including Mommsen in ed. 1) 16, and one editor 17,[33] for the same space, which Mommsen himself measured as large enough for 16 letters (5 of which are beyond question except for possible errors) but which contains the end of one sentence (sect. 1) and the beginning of the next (sect. 2), where there may well have been extra space left. In fact, the Antioch copy, though incomplete here, seems to lack only 4 letters[34] and to show that the 16-letter space in the Ankara copy contained only 13 letters. One must conclude, and emphasize, that all the restorations (as in all other incomplete inscriptions) are more or less conjectural, but one must add that there is only one small place—a single word—where, for lack of other evidence, it is possible to know as yet what the reading of neither the Latin nor the Greek was: in chapter 32, at the end of section 1, in the name of a German king perhaps otherwise unattested, the Latin is entirely missing, and the Greek has only the last three letters, -ρος.[35]

Despite all that has been said above about the difficulties of presenting a perfect text of either the Latin or the Greek, the general character of the document is clear enough. It is simple in structure, flat, without style (in my own opinion), not in the least reflective or philosophical in tone, as Augustus looks back over some fifty-seven years of public life,[36] and so highly self-centered that few sentences lack

---

[33] See Gagé, *op. cit.*, p. 72, *ad loc.*

[34] See Ramsay-Premerstein (supra, n. 17) Tab. I, col. 1, lines 3f, and pp. 41 *fin.*–42.

[35] Cf. Gagé (supra, n. 1) 55 *init.* (read "32" for "33"). The most attention to spatial considerations in restoring missing material since Mommsen[2] seems to be given by H. Markowski, *Eos*, 31 (1928) 219–235, 32 (1929) 347–370.

[36] Fifty-seven years if we subtract 19 from 76: 19 because he was in his 19th year (Sept. 23, 63–Sept. 22, 62 B.C., by the pre-Julian calendar) when he returned to Italy, accepted his inheritance, and got together an army *privato consilio et privata impensa* (*Res Gestae, init.*), 76 because he was in his 76th year (Sept. 23, A.D. 13—) when he wrote the last sentence of the *Res Gestae*—so at least the text reads: *Cum scri*]*psi haec, annum agebam septua-gensu*[*mum sextum*] (the restorations are confirmed by the Greek, which is complete here). I

a reference to himself,[37] and he seldom bothers to use the "editorial" or "diplomatic" plural, and only by means of *noster*,[38] never with verbs or pronouns. There is at least one ambiguity—the meaning of the first sentence of chapter 34[39]—and at least one mistaken statement, where Augustus, apparently in order to avoid mentioning Antony, says (ch. 2 *fin.*) that he himself twice defeated the forces of Brutus and Cassius at Philippi.[40] There are also a few examples of awkward phrasing, where, it seems, the Latin could be improved in economy or clarity of expression; for example, chapters 3.4,[41] 20.3,[42] 25.3,[43] 27.3,[44] 30.2,[45] 33 *init.*,[46] and 34.2.[47]

am aware of the controversy about the date of composition of the *Res Gestae* (see esp. Mommsen[2], pp. 1f, 59, 193f; Kornemann [supra, n. 14] 217–223, sect. 3; Volkmann (supra, n. 25] 63–74, sect. II 3; Gagé [supra, n. 1] 16–23, 211) and am prepared to accept the view that the framework of the *Res Gestae* and the bulk of the composition date from many years before the end of Augustus' life (perhaps as early as 27–23 B.C., perhaps not until a few years before the beginning of the Christian era) and that thereafter Augustus made only small additions and corrections to it. But I must add two points: (1) I see no reason why Augustus himself could not have composed and added the latest chronological data in the document (ch. 4.4, his 37th year of tribunician power [A.D. 14, June 26— (so Degrassi, *Inscr. Italiae*, 13:1 [Rome 1947] 157, col. 1, year 23; L. Petersen, *PIR*[2] 4:3 [Berlin 1966] 162, 2nd par., *s.v.* Iulius no. 215]); 7.2, *princeps senatus* for 40 years [28 B.C.— (cf. Mommsen[2], p. 32 *init.*)]; 8.4, his third census, A.D. 14 [cf. Suet. *Aug.* 97, ca. 100 days before his death, i.e. ca. May 11]; 35.2, his 76th year [A.D. 13, Sept. 23—]) in the summer of A.D. 14, before his last journey to Campania, on which he died on Aug. 19; and (2) the Latin used by Suetonius at the beginning of chapter 101 shows that the date he gives, April 3, A.D. 13, applies only to Augustus' *testamentum*, not to the *tria signata aeque volumina* (including the *Index rerum a se gestarum*, sect. 4) which the Vestal Virgins produced, along with his testament, after his death.

[37] I count 11 or 12 according to Mommsen's punctuation in ed. 2; 10 or 11 according to Gagé's, 5 of these being relative sentences that might be attached by an editor to the preceding sentences as relative clauses. After this, one may better appreciate Caesar's third-person references to himself.

[38] Perhaps the most striking examples of *meus* where *noster* would have been proper are *classis mea* in ch. 26.4 *init.*, and *ex[ercitus me]u[s]* (the Greek is complete) in 30.2. But note that *ego* seems never to be used here, and *ipse* referring to himself only three times (twice restored from the Greek).

[39] See Volkmann (supra, n. 25) 92f, and esp. H. U. Instinsky, "Consensus Universorum," *Hermes* 75 (1940) 265–278; more recently, F. E. Adcock, "The Interpretation of *Res Gestae Divi Augusti*, 34.1," *CQ*, n.s. 1 (1951) 130–135.

[40] Noted by Mommsen[2], p. 5, *ad loc.*; cf. Gagé (supra, n. 1) p. 75, *ad loc.*

[41] Ch. 3.4: for *Naves cepi sescen[tas praeter] eas, si quae minore[s quam trir]emes fuerunt*, why not simply omit the *si* and delete the editors' comma? (But cf. Wölfflin [supra, n. 10 1886 [1887] 268f.)

[42] Ch. 20.3: to *coepta profligataque opera a patre meo*, I should prefer *opera a patre meo coepta profligataque.*

For footnotes 43 to 47 see page 134.

Some other qualities of the Latin of the *Res Gestae* deserve mention: the succession of sentences beginning with first-person emphasis in chapters 31 to 33 (*Ad me* ..., *Nostram amicitiam* ..., *Ad me* ..., *Ad me* ...; then, after one "normally" structured sentence, *A me* ...); the simple style, with only one or two periodic sentences and, by my count, twenty-two subjunctives (including a few restored). But two of these subjunctives are particularly interesting. In chapter 5.2 Volkmann is correct, I believe, in following Markowski, against Mommsen and all the other editors so far as I have observed, in restoring the perfect subjunctive *liberarim*, instead of Mommsen's imperfect *liberarem*, in a consecutive or result clause in secondary sequence, on the strength of the perfect tense in the only other such clause in the *Res Gestae*, in chapter 17.1. The two sentences for comparison are: (ch. 5.2) *Non sum] depreca[tus] in s[umma f]rum[enti p]enuria curatio[n]em an[non]ae, [qu]am ita ad[min]ist[ravi ut intra] die[s] paucos metu et periclo* (sic) *p[r]aesenti*

---

43 Ch. 25.3: for *Qui sub [signis meis tum] militaverint fuerunt senatores plures quam DCC, in ii[s qui vel antea vel pos]tea consules facti sunt ad eum diem quo scripta su[nt haec, LXXXIII, sacerdo]tes ci[rc]iter CLXX* (if these are good restorations—their substance is partly assured by the Greek, which, however, is no clearer) I would suggest the addition of two antecedents, *eorum* (or *ex eis*) before the first *qui*, *ei* before the second. (The addition of a comma after *militaverint*, with Mommsen[2] and others, and of another after *iis*, with Volkmann, but not Mommsen or Gagé, for example, would not affect the present argument.) I assume the meaning to be, *not* "Those who at that time fought under my standards were more than 700 senators; among those who either previously or later became consuls ... 83, priests about 170," but rather "Of those who ... fought ... there were more than 700 senators, among them those who either ... became consuls ... 83 ...," or (better) "among them 83 who either ... became consuls ... (and) about 170 priests." (Similarly also Wm. Fairley in his ed. and transl. of the *Mon. Ancyranum* [Philadelphia 1898] 60: "There were more than 700 senators who ..., and among these ... 83 have ... been made consuls," etc., and Shipley [supra, n. 10] 387: "Those who served ... included more than 700 senators, and among them 83 who ... consuls," etc.)

44 Ch. 27.3: for *Provincias omnis quae ... vergunt ad Orien[te]m, Cyrenasque, iam ex parte magna regibus ea possidentibus*, I would suggest ... *iam ex parte magna a regibus possessa*.

45 Ch. 30.2: in *Citr[a] quod* (the Danube) *[D]a[cor]u[m tr]an[s]gressus exercitus*, I would transpose *Dacorum* and *transgressus*. (H. Markowski, *Eos*, 32 [1929] 357, proposes *citr[a] quod a[mpl]u[s ⟨Dacorum⟩ tr]an[s]gressus*, etc., *Dacorum* having been, he suggests, omitted by the stonecutter by error.)

46 Ch. 33 *init.*: to *A me gentes Parthorum et Medoru[m per legatos] principes earum gentium reges pet[i]tos acceperunt*, I would prefer *a me gentes P. et M. reges per legatos principes suos petitos acceperunt*.

47 Ch. 34.2 *fin.*: for *clu]peus [aureu]s in [c]uria Iulia positus* (sc. *est*), *quem mihi senatum pop[ulumq]ue Rom[anu]m dare virtutis clementiaeque e]t* (or without *et*) *iustitiae et pieta[tis cau]sa* (or *caus]sa*) *testatu[m] est pe[r e]ius clupei [inscription]em*, I would suggest *clupeus ... positus, qui per inscriptionem testatus est se senatum populumque R. mihi dare virtutis ... causa*, or else *clupeus ... positus, cuius inscriptio testata est senatum populumque R. mihi eum dare virtutis ... causa*.

civitatem univ[ersam liberarem (Mommsen *et al.*), *liberarim* (Markowski, Volkmann) *impensa et] cura mea*; (ch. 17.1) *Quater [pe]cunia mea iuvi aerarium, ita ut sestertium milliens et quing[en]tie(n)s ad eos qui praerant* (sic) *aerario detulerim.* Not only is the *detulerim* a good parallel, but the perfect or completed aspect of the two verbs suggests the perfect subjunctive rather than the imperfect.[48] The only other perfect subjunctive in the *Res Gestae* seems to me a peculiarly nice and delicate example of the relative clause of characteristic (there are only two such clauses—the second one restored by Mommsen—in the whole document, and they come in successive sentences), additionally noteworthy in that it comes first in its sentence, preceding the main verb. In chapter 25.3, Augustus, after saying that all Italy voluntarily took an oath of allegiance to him and demanded him as leader in the war in which he was victorious at Actium and that all the western provinces took the same oath of allegiance, then says, beginning a new sentence, *Qui sub [signis meis tum] militaverint*[49] *fuerunt senatores plures quam DCC . . .*, as though to say, "Of those who [I supply *eorum* or *ex eis* as the antecedent of *qui*][50] were of such quality as to serve under me at that time, there were more than 700 senators," etc.

What Augustus tells us may be the truth, except for the mistake noted above, but it is certainly not the whole truth—in accordance, one supposes, with the type of political apologia that it seems to me to belong to.[51] There is considerable suppression of facts that even a man in his seventy-sixth year can hardly have forgotten.[52] His enemies and opponents, such as Brutus and Mark Antony, are nowhere named, nor is there mention of the proscription of those whom the middle-aged

---

[48] For imperfect vs. perfect in such clauses cf. S. A. Handford, *The Latin Subjunctive . . .* (London 1947) 143f, sect. 157 (*b*), (1)f; E. C. Woodcock, *A New Latin Syntax* (London and Cambridge, Mass. 1959) 122f, sect. 164.

[49] This form, in -*int*, is sufficiently clear in Mommsen's plate of column 5 of the Latin, *exempli Latini pagina V*, line 6. Though the I is not perfectly clear, there is not enough room for the V of the perfect indicative in place of it.

[50] See supra, n. 40. Robert S. Rogers, Kenneth Scott, Margaret M. Ward (edd.), *Caesaris Augusti Res Gestae et Fragmenta* (Boston, etc. 1935) 66, simply call *militaverint* "a subjunctive of characteristic."

[51] For summaries of views concerning the character of the *Res Gestae*, see Volkmann (supra, n. 25) 74–80, and Gagé (supra, n. 1) 23–34, 211; add J. E. Sandys, *Latin Epigraphy*, ed. 2, rev. by S. G. Campbell (Cambridge 1927) 259 ("a posthumous political manifesto in the retrospective form of a dignified narrative of the emperor's public career"), Syme (supra, n. 10) 522–524, and Ettore Paratore, *Storia della letteratura latina* (Florence 1951) 439 ("un riassunto apologetico della propria vita").

[52] On the date of composition see supra, n. 36.

Antony and the young Octavian had considered too dangerous to be allowed to survive in the year 43, among them the great republican Cicero; no mention of the various instances of enforced exile to which Augustus felt obliged to resort, including that of his own daughter and later her daughter, as well as the exile of Ovid,[53] who, year after year, in poem after poem, appealed to the emperor—and later to Germanicus —not indeed to bring him back from exile, but to allow him to live somewhere nearer to Rome than the god-forsaken shores of the Black Sea,[54] where he says he has to talk to himself to hear Latin.[55]

On the positive side, however, there are a good many interesting pieces of information, such as—to name only two—the census figures of Roman citizens (census populi, civium Romanorum capita, by whom I suppose Augustus to mean only male citizens of military age) for the years 28 and 8 B.C. and A.D. 14 (ch. 8) and the naming of embassies from as far away as India, some 3,000 to 4,000 miles away as the crow flies and by caravan considerably farther.[56] But what the Res Gestae fails most to do justice to are what modern historians tend to consider the author's real points of greatness, such as his intelligence and skill in feeling his way forward against opponents and obstacles, in establishing what amounted to a monarchy while using all the old Republican forms possible and avoiding any new or obsolete terms of bad omen or bad odor (no specific title for himself except princeps[57] or princeps senatus,[58] but a cleverly invented new name of the traditional three elements, imperator Caesar Augustus),[59] and in making good use of men like Agrippa and Maecenas, Vergil and Horace; his reorganization of the army into a professional one; his reorganization of the provincial administration and his treatment of Egypt; his reorganization and de-

[53] For Ovid, see most recently Robert Samuel Rogers, "The Emperor's Displeasure and Ovid," TAPA 97 (1966) 373–378.

[54] Ovid Tristia 2.183–186, 4.4.51–54; Ex Ponto 1.2.127f and 150, 1.8.73f, 3.9.3, 4.8.83–88 (this to Germanicus); cf. Ex Ponto 2.2.65f, 96, 110; 2.8.36 and 72; 3.1.1–4, 29f, 85, 151; 3.3.63f; 3.7.29f; 3.9.37f; 4.13.47–50; 4.14.7–14.

[55] Tristia 5.7.61–64; cf. 4.1.89–91, 5.2.67, 5.10.37f, 5.12.57.

[56] Ch. 31.1, where the Latin is nearly all lost, but the Greek is complete and says "frequently," though only two such embassies from India, one to Augustus at Tarraco in Spain, the other to him on Samos, are otherwise attested, by Orosius 6.21.19, and Dio 54.9.7f (cf. Suet. Aug. 21.3).

[57] Res Gestae, ch. 13 fin., 30.1, 32.3.

[58] Op. cit., ch. 7.2.

[59] See Ronald Syme, "Imperator Caesar: A Study in Nomenclature," Historia, 7 (1958) 172–188.

velopment of the civil service, with some use for the first time (except for tax-collecting) of the equestrian class; [60] in short, his establishment of the empire on foundations so solid and stable as to last for centuries— though probably not in the shape he had envisaged—after having looked kaput.

I finally list the points made above that have some claim to originality: the suggestion that the *Res Gestae* would have gone the way of all the other political apologias of ancient Rome (if this is what it is) except Caesar's *Bellum Gallicum* and *Civile* (which have style) and would have failed to survive, had not Augustus requested that it be inscribed, but that it was the inscription's being reproduced in stone that preserved it; endorsement of Dessau's conjecture that the most reasonable explanation of why the two Latin copies and the two Greek versions have turned up in central Turkey is that the Roman governor of Galatia at the beginning of Tiberius' reign was personally responsible for having the original Roman inscription copied in stone (with, some- times, a Greek version) in his province; a suggestion that the bronze original became lost because it was bronze; comparison of the Temple of Rome and Augustus at Ankara with the Parthenon in respect to their survival as buildings and to the *Monumentum Ancyranum's* being much the best preserved of the *Res Gestae* copies; the lack of a standard edition and its severe requirements; the difficulties of restoration; my heretical view of the lack of style of the *Res Gestae*, with a list of references to two ancient and many modern views for comparison; [61] emphasis on the

---

[60] See G. H. Stevenson, *CAH* 10 (1934, 2nd impr. 1952) 185–189.

[61] The modern views (see supra, n. 10, for the references) speak most often of its clarity (Mommsen, Wilamowitz, Wölfflin, Gardthausen, Barini), its brevity and con- ciseness (Wilamowitz, Mommsen, Gardthausen, Shipley, Misch, Hönn), its plainness, simplicity, lack of exaggeration and of any attempt at literary embellishment (Kaibel, Westermann, Shipley, Misch, Schanz-Hosius, Dilke), its cool dignity, formality, and majesty (Norden, Gardthausen, Sandys [see supra, n. 51], Rice Holmes, Schanz-Hosius, Dilke). Some see Augustus as emulating Caesar (Wölfflin, Riccobono, Hönn), and Wölfflin sees him successful in this, rating him next to Caesar among the Julian-Claudian emperors. Mommsen thought that the *Res Gestae* confirmed the judgment of Suetonius and Fronto, quoted supra, n. 10. Other views of its style are: correct, proper, suitable to the circumstances (Mommsen, Kaibel, Wölfflin), sure, calm, objective (Gardthausen, Shipley, Misch), smooth (Gardt- hausen, Schanz-Hosius), proud (Westermann, Bardon), self-conscious (Bardon). Gardt- hausen speaks of its "lapidary brevity," Bardon of the style as "so much influenced by epi- graphic tradition," Dilke of the style's often recalling that of inscriptions, Malcovati of the *Res Gestae*, whatever type of literature it belongs to, as "something great and new in the history of literature," which "mira quadam reverentia animos nostros imbuere fatendum

self-centered character of the *Res Gestae* and mention of several awkward places in the Latin, as well as of one particularly nice example of the perfect subjunctive; endorsing R. S. Rogers' view of Ovid as a victim of the emperor's "displeasure," with a picture of the poet's having to talk to himself to hear Latin; finally, a listing of some of Augustus' major accomplishments not described in the *Res Gestae*.

University of California
Berkeley

ADDENDUM

On note 7. On Cicero's poetry, add now G. B. Townend's chapter, "The Poems," in *Cicero*, ed. by T. A. Dorey (London 1965) 109–134.

On note 10. To the list of ancient *testimonia* on Augustus' style, add Aulus Gellius, 10.24.2: *Divus etiam Augustus, linguae Latinae non nescius munditiarumque patris sui in sermonibus sectator*, etc.

On note 24. For Ramsay's and Shaffer's L. Calpurnius Piso Frugi as governor of Galatia at the beginning of Tiberius' reign, see now Barbara Levick, in *Anatolian Studies* 17 (1967) 102 (a reference I owe to my colleague, P. D. A. Garnsey): "an insubstantial figure . . . rightly neglected in standard lists of Galatian governors." I should have cited R. K. Sherk's *The Legates of Galatia from Augustus to Diocletian* (Baltimore 1951 [*The Johns Hopkins Univ. Studies in Historical and Political Science* 69:2], which I had known but forgotten), where (pp. 26–28) as governor "early in the reign of Tiberius (ca. 14–17 A.D.?)" is listed a certain Metilius ("or Meteilius": "no further identification is possible," with reff. to *P-W*, Syme, and Ramsay), who is named, obviously as governor of Galatia ('Επὶ Μετειλίου), in an almost completely legible Greek inscription cut on the left anta of the same temple in Ankara that bears the *Res Gestae* of Augustus (D. Krencker and M. Schede, *Der Tempel in Ankara* [Berlin-Leipzig 1936] 52ff, pl. 43, 44a [= *Orientis Graeci inscriptiones selectae*, ed. W. Dittenberger (Leipzig 1903–1905) 2.533]).

est." Rice Holmes' verdict also deserves quoting in full: "that laconic monument the majesty of which impresses all who have the sense of style." Gagé's "ce beau latin d'Auguste" has been quoted above. Gardthausen notes some roughnesses that should have been removed in editing, but he seems not to specify them. To most of these points I would agree—certainly to the brevity, plainness, matter-of-factness, clarity (with the exceptions noted above)—while still finding the work without "style" and not particularly "beau."

CRAWFORD H. GREENEWALT, JR.

9

Lydian Vases from Western Asia Minor

Our understanding of Lydian painted pottery of the seventh and sixth centuries B.C. is based primarily on material recovered in excavations at Sardis, the Lydian capital. Some Lydian pottery also has been found outside Lydia in western Asia Minor: in Caria, Ionia, Aeolis, Mysia, Phrygia, Cappodocia and Pisidia. The two vases with which this article is concerned were recovered in clandestine excavations somewhere in western Asia Minor; they expand our understanding of the techniques and styles used by Lydian, or "Lydianizing," vase painters of the seventh and sixth centuries.

A two-handled cup, or *kantharos*, which is reported to have been found at Düver in the Burdur region, is now in the collection of Hüseyin Kocabaş in Istanbul.[1]

Istanbul, Kocabaş Collection, 2372.
H. .235, D. mouth .141, D. foot .545, H. neck .1415.
Mended; parts of the neck and body are missing.

[1] Bay Hüseyin Kocabaş permitted me to draw, photograph, and publish the kantharos and the vases which are said to have been found with it. I am very grateful to Bay Kocabaş for his generosity and hospitality on several occasions in 1963 and 1964. Unfortunately, however, although I was allowed ample time to examine the vases, my notes on all seven are incomplete.

It is a pleasure to acknowledge here the kindness and encouragement of Dr. Nezih Fıratlı, Curator of Greek and Roman Antiquities at the Istanbul Archaeological Museum, who introduced me to Bay Kocabaş in the autumn of 1963.

This paper has benefited from suggestions and comments made by Mrs. George Dimmler, Mrs. Peter King, Mrs. Herbert Knill, and Mr. Terry Small.

Professor D. A. Amyx has been kind enough to read the manuscript and to suggest improvements, for which I am very grateful.

The neck is high and outflaring. The shoulder slight and rounded. The lower body tapers downward and is slightly convex. The foot is low and outflaring. Walls very thin. Handles of the double-roll type.

Glaze, dark brown to light orange where thin, and matt, has been applied evenly on the handles, in horizontal strokes on the foot, and in vertical "marbled" stripes on the neck interior. Over the body, the glaze has been brushed in seven rows of overlapping curls (started at the base, brushed from right to left). The neck is painted cream-white.

A figured scene is painted on the neck between the handles; both sides are the same. Two deer, couchant, face each other. A shrub with almond-shaped leaves grows between them. The main stalk springs from three shallow roots, and puts forth drooping, leafy branches, which fill the spaces in front of the animals under their chins. Above, the stalk divides into undulating, leafy tendrils, which cover the animals and fill the background space.

Each animals has a slender, pointed ear; almond eye with vertically-dashed iris; two neck bands, one articulating head from neck, the other neck from body; spotted neck, and body; hoofed hind foot; two "tails," one dart-shaped at the end of the spine, the other long and thin, curled around the haunch.

Outlines are dark brown.[2] Animals' heads, neck bands, feet, and thin "tails" are reserved. Leaves and hide spots are orange-brown. Necks and bodies are tan.

Cups with high, vertical handles and deep bowls are conventionally called kantharoi, and the name kantharos may reasonably be given to the cup in the Kocabaş Collection. In form and structure, there is a general similarity between the Kocabaş kantharos, some

_____

[2] These outlines may have been painted in manganese glaze; cf. infra, p. 153, and note 28.

Boeotian Archaic kantharoi from Rhitsona,[3] and two Rhodian Geometric kantharoi from Exochi in Rhodes and from southwest Asia Minor.[4] Double-roll handles do not appear on Greek kantharoi, but they do on other shapes made in Eastern Greece in the seventh and sixth centuries, and in Phrygia in the eighth century. The delicate construction of the Kocabaş kantharos may be compared with late seventh and early sixth-century Chiot chalices, "Ionian" and Vroulian cups. I do not know of parallels to the shape in any Anatolian Iron-Age pottery.

Technical and stylistic elements in the painted decoration of the katharos may be found in Lydian and Eastern Greek vase painting.

The body of the kantharos is decorated with a pattern motive of overlapping curls. This motive was executed in the Lydian decorative technique commonly called "marbling." In Lydian marbling, dilute glaze was applied with a multiple or single brush to the surface of a pot, and was unevenly deposited by a brush in thick and thin amounts. The amount of deposit was governed by the pressure borne on the brush and/or by the pressure made by individual brush hairs. The patterns which the vase painter created with his brush were made of different thicknesses of dilute glaze. Color and light make these patterns visible: the thickly-deposited glaze is opaque, and turned red or brown-black in the firing; thinly-deposited dilute glaze is translucent, and combines with the lighter-colored background surface, which is seen through the glaze, to produce different color tones; these tones may range from deep orange and brown to pale yellow, depending on the thickness of glaze deposit and the color of the pot surface.[5]

---

[3] P. N. Ure, *Sixth and Fifth Century Pottery from Rhitsona* (London 1927) 19–20, 34–35, pls. 7 (102.3, 130.1), 10 (36.18).

[4] K. F. Johanson, *Exochi ein fruehrodisches Graeberfeld* (Copenhagen 1957) 14, 16, Abb. 10. The Exochi kantharos was found in a grave together with two Protocorinthian skyphoi.

[5] Mr. J. V. Noble has kindly written me (September 1966) on this subject as follows: "The brownish coloring on this ware [i.e., marbled ware] is chemically the same as the Greek black glaze. It is brown because it has not been fired under a reducing atmosphere long enough to turn it black, and part of it is dilute which always fires to a golden brown . . ." On some marbled pottery, concentrated deposits of glaze are black.

Marbled effects sometimes appear in Attic Red-figure, where dilute glaze was used for shading. Dionysos' leopard-skin cloak on the Pointed Amphora by the Kleophrades Painter in Munich is a good example; P. Arias, B. B. Shefton, M. Hirmer, *A History of Greek Vase Painting* (London 1962) pl. XXX.

The technique of children's finger-painting is similar to marbling. In finger-painting, however, the slickness of the paper permits the paint to be played into pat-

Marbled zigzag bands and stripes, like those on the inside of the neck of the kantharos, are familiar elements in Lydian pottery decoration. The marbled overlapping-curl pattern motive is attested on only a few sherds, which have been found at Sardis, Daskyleion, Midas City, and Gordion in seventh to fifth-century deposits.[6]

The figural scene on the neck of the kantharos is curious. Certain elements, such as the axial, symmetrically-balanced composition and the choice and arrangement of motives (animals flanking a vegetable form) appear in the shoulder decoration of "Rhodian"[7] Wild Goat-style oinochoai. The vegetable form, which is represented as a natural growth, however, does not appear in "Rhodian" vase painting, and has no close parallel in any other Greek orientalizing style or school of vase painting. Leafy branches are represented on a few shreds of painted pottery from Asia Minor, Midas City in Phrygia and Patnos in Urartu.[8]

terns and deposits of uneven concentration. In marbling, I believe that some element in the glaze itself may have permitted this play.

On many pieces of ancient marbled ware which I have examined, the glaze had been applied to a surface which clearly had been neither slipped nor burnished. When I attempted to reproduce marbled effects with clay and an AMCO engobe solution, however, I found that an unburnished clay surface absorbed the engobe before it could be brushed into a pattern; unless the glaze was applied in generous amounts, in which case it lost the translucence necessary for the pattern to be visible. Perhaps honey, or the like, was mixed with the dilute glaze so that the glaze would be more resistant to absorption; cf. Noble's experiments with Red-figure relief lines: J. V. Noble, *The Techniques of Painted Attic Pottery* (New York 1965) 58.

I am most grateful to Miss Mary T. Souther, Instructor in Art at Tower Hill School (Wilmington, Delaware), for the encouragement and help which she gave me to experiment in reproducing marbled effects, and to the Trustees of Tower Hill School for the use of Art Department facilities and materials.

[6] Only the pieces from Midas City have been published: C. H. E. Haspels, *Phrygie*, III: *La Cité de Midas: Céramique et Trouvailles Diverses* (Paris 1951) 29–30, pl. 8b. 4–5.

The most interesting examples of marbled curl patterning appear on two delicate skyphos fragments found at Sardis (inventoried P61.159 / 3427 and P61.557 / 4084; probably from the same skyphos). Marbled overlapping curl pattern covers the inside and outside of each fragment. The slip is a highly micaceous solution which shows through the glaze where it is thin and gives a golden metallic effect. Micaceous-slipped wares (without marbling) are common at Sardis: G. M. A. Hanfmann, "The Fourth Campaign at Sardis (1961)," *BASOR* 166 (1962) 8. Many fragments of another skyphos decorated with marbled curl patterning, but over cream-white slip, were found at Sardis during the 1967 excavations.

[7] I understand "Rhodian" to include several styles and schools of Eastern Greek vase painting, as it has been defined by R. M. Cook, "Fikellura Pottery," *BSA* 34, (1933–1934) 2, n. 1.

[8] These leafy twigs and branches are outlined in dark and filled in light brown over a cream-coloured slip: C. H. E. Haspels, *Phrygie*, III: *La Cité de Midas: Céramique*

Representations of animals in a recumbent, couchant posture with their forelegs folded do not appear in seventh- and sixth-century Greek vase painting; they do appear in contemporary Greek and Etruscan theriomorphic alabastra, in Greek and Etruscan ivories, and in Eastern Greek or Lydian jewelry.[9] The couchant posture also is common in "nomadic" art.[10] Since a few ivory and bone objects carved in a "nomadic" style and datable to the seventh and sixth centuries have been found in Asia Minor, at Ephesos and Sardis,[11] it is possible that "nomadic" art could have had some influence on the arts of Asia Minor in the seventh and sixth centuries. Might the iconography of the couchant deer on the Kocabaş kantharos reflect the influence of "nomadic" art?

Certain peculiarities in the animals' anatomy and the mannered style of drawing suggest that the artist who decorated the kantharos copied parts of the figural motives from another source. The short, diagonal line which connects the back of the foreleg hoof with the underbelly suggests that he did not understand, or was not interested in,

---

et Trouvailles Diverses (Paris 1951) 27–29, pls. 7d, 8a; M. J. Mellink in *Art Treasures of Turkey* (Washington 1966) 83, no. 88 (the leaves do not appear in the illustration).

9 For Corinthian, Eastern Greek, and Etruscan theriomorphic aryballoi (deer, sheep, lions, oxen), R. A. Higgins, *British Museum Catalogue of the Terra-cottas in the Department of Greek and Roman Antiquities* (London 1959) II, 53–54.

Ivory couchant animals (rams, lions, oxen; with heads turned aside) have been found in sanctuaries at Ephesos, Sparta, and Perachora: J. M. Stubbings, in *Perachora* (Oxford 1962) II, 407–410. An unpublished example from Erythrai is now in the Fuar Museum in Izmir.

Ivory couchant lions, with heads facing forward, were found in the Bernadini and the Barberini Tombs: C. D. Curtis, "The Bernadini Tomb," *MAAR* 3 (1919) 62–65, pls. 38, 39, 41; *idem*, "The Barberini Tomb," *MAAR* 5 (1925) 34–35, pl. 17.

Gold earring pendants in the form of couchant lions with their heads facing forward and a couchant ram with its head turned aside have been found at Sardis: C. D. Curtis, *Sardis*, XIII: *Jewellery and Gold Work*, 1 (Rome 1925) 34, pl. 8; the ram earring was found in 1967 excavations.

For a couchant camel and rider in bronze from Camiros, L. Curtius, "Sardanapal," *JdI* 43 (1928) 286–287.

10 P. Amandry, "Un Motif 'Scythe' en Iran et en Grèce," *JNES* 24 (1965) 149–160.

11 For the ivories carved in "nomadic" style from Ephesos: D. G. Hogarth, *Excavations at Ephesus: The Archaic Artemisia* (London 1908) 163, 164, pls. 21, 23, 36; E. Akurgal, *Die Kunst Anatoliens* (Berlin 1961) 216 and references; P. Amandry, *op. cit.* (supra, n. 10).

For the "nomadic" (Cimmerian?) bone plaque from Sardis: G. M. A. Hanfmann, "The Eighth Campaign at Sardis (1965)," *BASOR* 182 (1966) 13–14, fig. 9. On Cimmerians in western Asia Minor, G. L. Huxley, *The Early Ionians* (London 1966) 53–54 and references.

the articulation of the foreleg. Furthermore, each animal apparently possesses two tails: a short, leaf-shaped brown tail at the end of the spine, and a long, narrow, white tail, which curls around the haunch. The pronounced curl at the tip suggests that the artist thought of the latter as a tail, even though deer do not normally have long sinuous tails. He must either have confused the deer with some representation of a feline; or copied an animal whose haunch was outlined in reserve, and misunderstood the significance of the reserve outline. In a similar way, he could have copied the neck bands from reserved jaw and shoulder outlines. Reserved jaw, shoulder, and haunch outlines were conventional in "Rhodian" Wild Goat and Fikellura styles of vase painting.[12]

The leafy tendrils of the shrub fill most of the space above and behind the deer. If the artist composed the shrub in this way because of *horror vacui*, his method of eliminating vacant space is more sophisticated than that employed by Greek Orientalizing vase painters: instead of introducing abstract motives into his composition, he filled the background with a landscape element (or created a landscape element out of a filling motive).

Where was the kantharos made? The shape has no exact parallel among Greek kantharoi, but it appears to be more Greek than Anatolian. The decorative technique and, I think, the pattern decoration on the body are Lydian. The figure decoration on the neck seems to have been inspired to a considerable extent by Eastern Greek art, but painted by an artist who was either unfamiliar with or unconscious of the course of his inspiration. The kantharos could have been made in Lydia, although probably not so far west as Sardis, where the local pottery was strongly influenced by Eastern Greek style; or it might have been made further East, in southwest Phrygia, northwest Caria, or Pisidia.

The dealer who sold the kantharos to Bay Kocabaş told him that it had been found in a grave, which overlay a stratum of Chalkolithic burials, at Düver in the Burdur region of southeastern Anatolia. This region was a part of Pisidia in ancient times. The same

[12] For reserved jaw and shoulder outlines on deer: K. F. Kinch, *Vroulia* (Berlin 1914) 233–234, fig. 118; W. Schiering, *Werkstaetten Orientalisierender Keramik auf Rhodos* (Berlin 1957) Taf. 12.6, 7; R. M. Cook, "Fikellura Pottery," *BSA* 34 (1933–1934) 17, fig. 1, pl. 2.b.

Reserved haunch outlines occur on seated animals: W. Schiering, *op. cit.*, Taf. 17.2; 16.1, 6.

dealer later sold Bay Kocabaş six other vases, which he said had been found together with the kantharos in the same grave. These vases are: a Lakonian skyphos, three lydia, lekythos-arbybalos, and a cup painted with pendent concentric semicircles.

Lakonian skyphos. Kocabaş Collection, 2568. Plates 1:4, 2:1, and 2:2.
H. pr. .081, D. foot .0643.

Broken; the body is mended up to the shoulder. One handle (the left in pl. 4) has been restored. Five fragments of the rim are preserved.

The clay is buff-tan, coarse and gritty. The glaze is black and slightly metallic. Cream-white and purple paint are used.

The inside is black.

On the outside, the upper part of the rim is cream-white, decorated in black with a "dot-and-square" motive and a narrow band. The lower part of the rim and shoulder are black. Two narrow white bands on either side of a broad purple band encircle the body just under the handles. The lower body is decorated with black rays on a cream-white ground. Above the foot are four bands: two narrow white bands, a broad purple, and a narrow white band.

Concentric rings decorate the underside of the bowl: on the foot edge, a narrow black band; towards the center, two narrow black bands, one broad purple, and one narrow black band.

Cup. Kocabaş Collection, not inventoried.
Only a few rim fragments are preserved.

The shape is evidently a skyphos type.

The inside has been painted with dark glaze, and decorated under the rim with one white band.

The outside has been painted cream-white and decorated in dilute (sepia-colored) glaze with a scale pattern. Each scale is made up of three concentric pendent half-circles.

Lydion. Kocabaş Collection, 2373.
H. .086, D. belly .0715.

Fine scoring lines appear on the shoulder.

Glaze, fired black to red, covers the inside of the neck and the entire outside of the lydion.

Lydion. Kocabaş Collection, 3541.
Plate 2:3.

H. .108, D. belly .095.

Similar to 2569.

Lydion. Kocabaş Collection, 2569.
Plate 2:3.

H. .12, D. belly .118.

Dark glaze is streakily applied over the body.

Lekythos-Aryballos. Kocabaş Collection, 2374.
Plate 2:3.

H. (without handle) .09, D. belly .076.

Preserved intact. There is encrustation on the mouth and parts of the body.

The sides of the handle are ridged.

The clay is fired reddish. The body is slipped in yellow-tan; decorated with glaze which is brown and metallic.

Glaze is solidly painted over the handle, lip, and foot; it is slopped around the base of the neck; and painted in narrow-broad-narrow bands around the shoulder.

If these six pots and the kantharos were deposited together with one interment, as the alleged circumstances of their provenance suggest, they all ought to have been made within a ten- to twenty-year period; the skyphos and the kantharos, because of their exotic character, might be as much as twenty years older than the others. If the kantharos' alleged context pieces could be dated, they might help to establish the date when the kantharos was made.

Of the six pots, the Lakonian skyphos can be the most precisely dated. It belongs to a type which is associated with the stylistic and chronological phases of Lakonian painted pottery known as Lakonian I and II. The profile and decoration of the rim suggest that the skyphos should be identified with Lakonian I rather than with II;[13] if these rim features constitute valid dating criteria,[14] the skyphos ought to have been made in the second quarter of the seventh century, or shortly thereafter, ca. 650–620, according to Boardman's chronology. If the skyphos is Lakonian II, however, it might date ca. 620-560.[15]

The type of lydion with globular body and low, conical foot, to which the three in the Kocabaş collection belong, seems to have

[13] E. A. Lane, "Lakonian Vase-Painting," *BSA* 34 (1933–1934) 16, 117. Lane believed that a straight rim profile and squares and spaces of the same size in the "dot-and-square" pattern on the rim appear in Lakonian I-type skyphoi; that a curved, outflaring rim profile and more widely-spaced squares in the "dot-and-square" pattern appear in Lakonian II-type skyphoi.

[14] B. B. Shefton, who has seen the photographs and drawing of the Kocabaş skyphos, has remarked that the spacing of the squares is closer than normal in sixth-century pieces, but that this may not be a safe criterion for dating (letter of January, 1966).

Shefton has called my attention (in the letter mentioned above) to other examples of Lakonian pottery decorated with purple bands like the one on the underside of the Kocabaş skyphos: aryballoi from Perachora, for which he has suggested a date generally within the first half of the sixth century (B. B. Shefton in *Perachora* [Oxford 1962] II, 383–384) and a plate from Tocra in Libya, which the excavators are inclined to date around the second quarter of the sixth century (J. Boardman, J. Hayes, "Excavations at Tocra 1963–1965: The Archaic Deposits 1," *JHS Suppl.* 4 (1966) pl. 69, no. 1021).

[15] J. Boardman, "Artemis Orthia and Chronology," *BSA* 58, (1963) 1–7. A Lakonian II-type skyphos has been found with Middle and Late Corinthian pots in a grave at Taranto: P. Pelagatti, "La Ceramica Laconica del Museo di Taranto," *ASAtene* 17–18 (1955–1956) 19–20, fig. 12. Another has been found at Tocra: J. Boardman, J. Hayes, "Excavations at Tocra 1963–1965: The Archaic Deposits 1," *BSA Suppl.* 4 (1966) 89, 91, pl. 67 (no. 987).

been used throughout the sixth century. There is no positive evidence which suggests that this type was made earlier than ca. 600, but the chronology of Lydian pottery before ca. 575 is uncertain.[16] The lekythos-aryballos and the cup painted with pendent semicircles probably were made in the sixth century, but might also be somewhat earlier or later.[17]

If the skyphos is Lakonian I or II, it cannot have reached Asia Minor much before ca. 640; and it ought not to have remained in circulation, even in as remote a region as Pisidia, much after ca. 550. If it is Lakonian I, and if ten years be allowed for its travel to and use in

[16] I have discussed lydion types and chronology in my dissertation, "Lydian Pottery of the Sixth Century B.C.: The Lydion and Marbled Ware" (University of Pennsylvania 1966). Lydia have been found together with Corinthian, Attic, Lakonian, and Eastern Greek vases in grave deposits at Gordion, Sardis, an Aeolian site, Ialysos, Taranto, and Caere. These deposits suggest that the type of lydion with globular body and conical or keg-shaped foot was in use through the sixth century.

One of the earliest examples of this type may be one from a grave at Taranto. The Corinthian and Lakonian vases found in the same grave have suggested a date sometime in the first quarter of the sixth century for the grave deposit: P. Pelagatti, "La Ceramica Laconica del Museo di Taranto," *ASAtene* 33–34 (1955–1956) 23–25, fig. 17 on 22.

Lydia of this type evidently were still in use ca. 525 (nine were found in the Gordion Tumulus "A" burial deposit, which has been dated ca. 525 on the stylistic evidence of context material by E. Kohler) and perhaps even in the early fifth century: A sarcophagus burial at Sardis, excavated by H. C. Butler between 1910 and 1914, contained seven lydia of this type and an Attic lekythos decorated in black glaze with a palmette motive. A photograph of one of the lydia (decorated with marbling) and detailed notes made by G. H. Chase on all the pots and the circumstances of their discovery are now in the Fogg Art Museum in Cambridge, Massachusetts. On the basis of Chase's written description of the black-glazed lekythos, G. M. A. Hanfmann has compared it to lekythoi which may be dated to the first half of the fifth century: C. H. E. Haspels, *Attic Black-figured Lekythoi* (Paris 1936) pl. 36.5; C. W. Blegen, H. Palmer, R. S. Young, "The North Cemetery," *Corinth* (1964) XIII 165, pl. 52 (no. 339.5).

I subscribe to the tradition that lydia originated in Lydia and were exported and imitated abroad: A. Rumpf, "Lydische Salbgefaesse," *AM* 45 (1920) 163–170; C. Roebuck, *Ionian Trade and Colonization* (New York 1959) 3, 56; that lydia were made to contain an unguent or powder, which may have been *bakkaris* (mentioned as early as the middle of the sixth century, by Hipponax as preserved in Athenaeus, *Deipnosophistai* 12.553; 15.690–691). The plant *bakkaris* has been identified most frequently with *Gnaphalium sanguineum*: J. Berendes, *Des Pedanios Dioskurides aus Anazarbos Arzneimittellehre* (Stuttgart 1902).

[17] An unpublished lekythos-aryballos in Heidelberg is nearly identical in shape and decoration to the example in the Kocabaş collection. One in Leipzig is less similar: W. Mueller, *CVA* (Berlin 1959) Deutschland 14, Leipzig 1, 54–55, Taf. 50, no. 3 (dated to the early sixth century).

The decoration (pendent concentric half-circles in glaze over white slip) of the cup fragments in the Kocabaş collection is matched on a skyphos from Gordion (inventoried 6332 P2401) and on krateriskos and lekythos fragments from Sardis (the krateriskos inventoried P64.263 / 6338).

Pisidia before interment, it might have been deposited in a grave at Düver ca. 640–610; if Lakonian II, ca. 610–550.

The only evidence for the integrity of the group as a single deposit, of course, is the word of the dealer who sold the pots to Bay Kocabaş. Nevertheless, the pots would make a homogeneous group: the decoration and/or shape of five out of seven is Lydian; the lekythos-aryballos might well be Eastern Greek, or an Anatolian imitation of an Eastern Greek type; and a Lakonian skyphos in company with Eastern Greek and Lydian pots is likely enough, for Lakonian pottery has been found at several sites in Eastern Greece and western Asia Minor (Samos, Smyrna, an Aeolian site, Daskyleion, Sardis, Gordion). Furthermore, Düver is not an unlikely place of discovery for pots such as these. The mixture of Greek and non-Greek elements in the painted decoration of the kantharos is paralleled in the painted relief decoration of Archaic architectural tiles which were found in great numbers together with some pottery and stone sculpture at Düver in 1962.[18] The kantharos and the other pots could have been found in the cemetery of the settlement in which the tiles and other objects were recovered.

The only dependable criteria which can be used to date the kantharos, however, have to be provided by the kantharos itself.

Kantharos shapes generally similar to that of the Kocabaş kantharos may be found in Rhodian Geometric and Boeotian seventh- and sixth-century pottery. I think that the delicate construction, and to some extent the shapes, of Chiot chalices and "Ionian" and Vroulian cups, which have been dated ca. 625–550, offer more significant parallels.[19]

[18] The architectural tiles from Düver are now in museums in Istanbul, Birmingham, and Stockholm, and in a private collection in Switzerland. For the examples in the museums: E. Akurgal, *Orient und Okzident* (Baden-Baden 1966) 220, Abb. 68; N. Thomas, "Recent Acquisitions by Birmingham City Museum," *Archaeological Reports* (1964–1965) 64–70; Å. Åkerström, *Die Architektonischen Terra-kotten Kleinasiens* (Lund 1965) 218ff.

Some pottery from Düver, lydia and fragments of large painted vessels, are now in the Archaeological Museum in Istanbul.

The site of Düver has been described briefly by M. J. Mellink, "Archaeology in Asia Minor," *AJA* 68 (1964) 159. For the location, see the map in G. E. Bean, "Notes and Inscriptions from Pisidia. Part I," *Anatolian Studies* 9 (1959) 69, fig. 1.

[19] Chiot chalices: R. M. Cook, *Greek Painted Pottery* (London 1960) 127–129; J. Boardman, "Excavations in Chios 1952–1955: Greek Emporio," *BSA Suppl.* 6 (1967) 119–122. "Ionian" cups: F. Villard, G. Vallet, "Megara Hyblaea," *MélRome* 65 (1955) 23–27. Vroulian cups: R. M. Cook, *op. cit.* 140–141; K. F. Kinch, *Vroulia* (Berlin, 1914) 170ff.

The marbling technique was used apparently as early as the first quarter of the sixth century and as late as the first quarter or first half of the fifth century; there is nothing which suggests that it was used before ca. 600, but, as was remarked above, the chronology of Lydian pottery before ca. 575 is uncertain.[20] The general composition of the figural scene may be paralleled in "Rhodian" Orientalizing vase painting of the second half of the seventh and first half of the sixth centuries.

If the branches and leaves of the tree were composed for the purpose of filling vacant background space, they constitute a more naturalistic filling motive than those normally used in Greek vase painting of the later seventh and early sixth centuries. This naturalism, however, might not necessarily indicate that the date of the kantharos is later than the period when the use of filling ornament was conventional in Greek painting. Organic plant forms seldom were used as space fillers in Greek vase painting; a rare example is the flowering plant on the neck of the Middle Protoattic Nessos Amphora in New York, which Miss Richter has dated early in the second quarter of the seventh century.[21] Leafy-branch motives appear on a few examples of Anatolian vase painting; it is not clear whether they were intended to be fillers, or symbols, or landscape elements.[22] Indeed, the composition of the tree on the Kocabaş kantharos may have been intended not so much to fill space as to emphasize the luxuriance of foliage (as in the "Ionian" cup in the Louvre),[23] or perhaps to suggest the concealment of the animals under a bower.

Stylistic features suggest to me that the kantharos was made sometime in the last decade of the seventh century or the first half of the sixth century.

[20] See supra, p. 148 and note 16.

[21] Metropolitan Museum of Art 11.210.1: G. M. A. Richter, "A New Early Attic Vase," *JHS* 32 (1912) 376–377, fig. 3; *idem The Metropolitan Museum of Art Handbook of the Greek Collection* (Cambridge, Mass. 1953) 40, pl. 27; P. Jacobsthal, *Ornamente griechischer Vasen* (Berlin 1927) 27, pl. 48.

For landscape elements in early Greek vase painting, M. Heinemann, *Landschaftliche Elemente in der griechischen Kunst bis Polygnot* (Bonn 1910); to the examples cited by Heinemann should be added a skyphos fragment from Megara Hyblaea: G. Vallet, F. Villard, *Megara Hyblaea* II: *La Céramique Archaique* (Paris 1964) 40, pl. 39, fig. 14, pl. 22.

[22] Supra, n. 8.

[23] Louvre F68: P. E. Arias, B. B. Shefton, *A History of Greek Vase Painting* (London 1962) 295–296, pl. 51 (Mrs. Bonnie Kingsley reminded me of this piece).

In the autumn of 1965, an unusual oinochoe was purchased from Sotheby's by the University Museum of the University of
Pennsylvania.[24]

Philadelphia, University Museum, 66.1.1.
    Plates 2:4, 3:1, and 3:2.

    H. .241, D. belly .168.

    Small chip off spout, mended; otherwise intact. Clay fairly
    fine with some pocks and grits; non-micaceous; hard;
    light pink-buff.

    Trefoil mouth, double-roll handle, tall neck; round body
    with continuous curve from shoulder to belly; thick ring
    foot.

    The oinochoe is decorated with three kinds of paint or
    glaze: a white slip; a glaze of the "Greek glaze" type,
    which has fired brick-red to dark sepia, and is non-
    metallic; and a glaze which has fired a purple-chocolate
    color, matt, and which must have a high manganese
    content.[25]

    The neck, shoulder, and upper body are covered with
    white slip. The trefoil lip, handle, lower body, and foot
    are painted with the sepia glaze; as are nine narrow bands
    which ring the body in three groups of three. Thirteen
    pendent, overlapping hooks are marbled on the shoulder
    in a dilute solution of this glaze (the hooks curve to the
    left, and overlap from right to left).

[24] I wish to thank Dr. Froelich Rainey, Director of the University Museum,
and Professor Rodney S. Young, Curator of the Mediterranean Section of the Museum,
for their permission to publish this oinochoe. Professor David G. Mitten of Harvard
University informed Dr. Young and myself that the piece was to be sold at auction, and
so is partially responsible for its acquisition by the University Museum. The photographs
were taken by Mr. George M. Quay.

[25] Professor G. Roger Edwards pointed out to me that manganese glaze
had been used to paint the outlines of the animals. The properties of manganese glaze have
been discussed by M. Farnesworth and I. Simmons in their article "Coloring Agents for
Greek Glazes," *AJA* 67 (1963) 396.

A figured scene is painted on the neck. Two gazelles, couchant, are on the front axis. Between them is a filling ornament, which is composed of a cross with solid triangles in the angles.

The animals are outlined in manganese glaze. The necks and rumps of the animals are painted solidly with sepia glaze; the same was used to make two rows of dots which crisscross each flank, and the filling ornament.

Sotheby and Co.: *Catalogue of Highly Important Egyptian, Western Asiatic, Greek and Roman Antiquities* (Sale of November 29, 1965) lot 124, p. 50.

The oinochoe in Philadelphia and the Kocabaş kantharos have several features in common: Greek shape, Lydian marbling; a figural motive on the front axis of the neck; heraldic arrangement of figures; and couchant deer, painted in outline.

The shape of the oinochoe in Philadelphia, with the trefoil lip, double-rolled handle, and low ring foot, generally resembles that of oinochoai decorated in the "Rhodian" Wild Goat style, ca. 630–575. The proportions are close to "Rhodian" examples which have been dated to the decades before and after ca. 600 B.C.[26]

---

[26] I am thinking of oinochoai decorated in the style which Miss Kardara has called "Classical Camiran"; an example is Louvre E 319 (Ch. Kardara, *Rodiake Angeiographeia* (Athens 1963) 100, no. 7, pl. B, 'delta'). R. M. Cook has dated the "Classical Camiran" style ca. 625–600 (*idem, Gnomon* 37 (1963) 504, 506).

A group of "Rhodian" oinochoai, which seem to be later in date than "Classical Camiran" oinochoai, is distinguished by a more slender shape, with taller body and high neck and lip. Schiering included this group with his "Vlastos" style (W. Schiering, *Werkstaetten Orientalisierender Keramik auf Rhodos* [Berlin 1957] 24, 25, Taf. 6.4. R. M. Cook has dated the "Vlatos" style "c. 600 through the first quarter of the 6th century," but has noted "a lacuna in the evidence of grave groups and stratification" for the second quarter (*idem, Gnomon* 30, (1958) 71–72).

The only published example of a "Vlastos"-style oinochoai which was found with datable context material comes from a grave at Ialysos: G. Jacopi, "Scavi nelle Necropoli di Jalisso" *Clara Rhodos* (1929) III, 72–80 (grave no. 377). The integrity of the group published in Clara Rhodos has been questioned, however (R. M. Cook, "Ionia and Greece in the Eighth and Seventh Centuries B.C.," *JHS* 66 [1946] 73, n. 55; an alabastron, inventoried no. 11598, is recorded in *Clara Rhodos* as having come from grave no. 380, and in *CVA* Rodi 1 as having come from grave no. 377).

2. Istanbul, Kocabaş Collection, 2372. Lydian Kantharos.

4. Istanbul, Kocabaş Collection, 2568. Lakonian Skyphos.

1. Istanbul, Kocabaş Collection, 2372. Lydian Kantharos.

3. Istanbul, Kocabaş Collection, 2372. Lydian Kantharos.

Plate 2   Greenewalt

2. Istanbul, Kocabaş Collection, 2568. Lako-nian Skyphos.

4. Philadelphia, University Museum 66.1.1. Lydian Oinochoe.

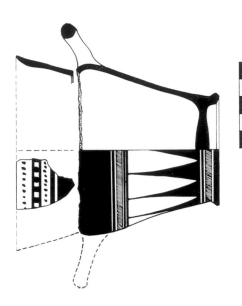

1. Istanbul, Kocabaş Collection, 2568. Lakonian Skyphos.

3. Istanbul, Kocabaş Collection (left to right), 2373, 3541, 2569, 2374. Lydia and Lekythos-Aryballos.

2. Philadelphia, University Museum 66.1.1. Lydian Oinochoe.

1. Philadelphia, University Museum 66.1.1. Lydian Oinochoe.

The shoulder of the oinochoe is decorated with marbled overlapping pendent hooks. Pendent hooks and marbling are standard decorative elements of Lydian painted pottery,[27] but I know of no other vase or sherd on which these two elements are combined. The hooks were evidently brushed from right to left, while the pot rested on the potter's wheel.

The axial position, symmetrical arrangement and stance of the deer on the neck recalls the Kocabaş kantharos. On the oinochoe, however, the deer are carelessly drawn; their folded forelegs are convincingly, if sketchily, articulated; and their bodies are colored in an abstract manner.

The axial position and heraldic arrangement of the figures, the use of outline and abstract coloring for the animals, and the "filling" motive are characteristic features of the "Rhodian" Wild Goat style of vase painting, ca. 630–575.

In the "Rhodian" schools of the Wild Goat style, manganese glaze was seldom, if ever, used: all outlines were painted in iron-oxide glaze. Orange/red or purple/crimson paint was used for details, but not for the outline of filling motives. On the oinochoe, however, manganese glaze was used for the animals' outlines, and iron-oxide glaze for their body coloring and for the filling motive. Manganese and iron-oxide glazes used in precisely this way appear in Wild Goat pottery which has been found, and apparently was made, at Sardis.[28]

Several oinochoai belonging to this group have been found with datable context material in Asia Minor; some of these are discussed and illustrated in my dissertation (supra, n. 16) 193–198, pls. 11, 12.

Whether the shape of all "Rhodian" oinochai became more slender after ca. 600, or whether oinochoai with more slender shapes were produced in a particular region or workshop is not clear (R. M. Cook has suggested that the "Vlastos" style was practiced outside of Rhodes; idem, Gnomon 30 [1958] 72). The shape of the University Museum oinochoe may represent, of course, a late survival of the "Classical Camiran" oinochoe shape-type.

[27] In the usual Lydian pendent-hook motive, each hook is composed of five to ten separate lines. A compass instrument with several drawing nibs was used to draw the hooks. Each nib was probably a tightly-bound brush, which released just enough glaze to mark the line: the lines are always uniform in width and spacing, and have never dribbled.

These hooks appear most often on the shoulders of amphorae, oinochoai, and hydriai; the only published illustration of them which I have been able to locate shows them on the underbelly of an amphora: G. M. A. Hanfmann, "Excavations at Sardis, 1958," BASOR 154, (1959) 28, 33, fig. 15.

[28] On Wild Goat-style pottery found and apparently made at Sardis, filling ornament often was drawn in the additional color: red, when the animals were drawn in

6—c.s.c.a.

The marbled hooks and certain elements in the figural decoration, therefore, suggest that the oinochoe was made in western Asia Minor, in an area influenced by the Lydians in the seventh and sixth centuries. Since Eastern Greek style is more pronounced in the shape and decoration of the oinochoe than in the kantharos which is said to come from Düver, one might suppose that the oinochoe was made somewhere closer to the Eastern Greek world than Düver in Pisidia. It was evidently not made at Sardis, for the clay is not the coarse, micaceous, reddish sort which is distinctive of Sardian pottery. The excellent state of the oinochoe's preservation indicates that it was recovered from a grave: graves containing Lydian and Eastern Greek pottery of the Archaic period have recently been opened near the villages of Menye (Maeonia), Kemaliye (Pentechoria), Kula, and Mersinli, all located east of Sardis. The University Museum oinochoe may very well have been found and made in this part of Lydia. Close "Rhodian" shape parallels suggest that it should date ca. 610–580.

University of California
Berkeley

iron-oxide glaze; iron-oxide, when the animals were drawn in manganese glaze. Two Sardian Wild Goat sherds on which manganese glaze was used for outlines and iron-oxide glaze for additional color are illustrated in Professor Hanfmann's preliminary report on the eighth Sardis campaign: G. M. A. Hanfmann, "The Eighth Campaign at Sardis (1965)," *BASOR* 182 (1966) 15, fig. 11; 22, fig. 18 (inventoried P65.6 / 6593 and P65.109 / 6737).

I hope to discuss the character of the Sardian Wild Goat style in a later article.

10

Pompey and the Pisones

Is it legitimate to speak of "family politics" in late Republican Rome? If by that is meant that members of an aristocratic *gens* cooperated as a monolith, the answer must be firmly in the negative. Those who seek to construct political alignments along familial lines confront (though not many have acknowledged it) an increasingly embarrassing dilemma. Where evidence is scanty, historians have, with some impunity, discerned (or imposed) patterns of political collaboration. For such an endeavor, refutation is as difficult as demonstration. But when information becomes plentiful in the Ciceronian age, these reconstructions become more slippery and more vulnerable. The facts stubbornly resist simplistic cataloguing into compartments labeled by *gentes*.

The family of the Calpurnii Pisones provides a striking *exemplum*. That proud and powerful clan could by the Ciceronian era look back to four generations of distinguished *consulares*. Yet as evidence unfolds in more imposing quantity for the 60's and 50's B.C., ostensible paradox and inconsistency baffle the inquirer. One Piso emerges as a relentless enemy of Julius Caesar; another was Caesar's father-in-law. The latter was lambasted mercilessly in Cicero's most vicious invective; but still another Piso was son-in-law of Cicero himself. Two further Pisones are remembered for their relations with Pompeius Magnus: one suffered assassination, so it was said, at the hands of Pompey's agents or friends; the other, by contrast, was a loyal legate of Pompey and received consular rank through the general's favor. Here is bewildering paradox indeed. It is hardly surprising that in the vast literature on

Republican politics, the Pisones of this period, despite their prominence, have received no systematic treatment. Critics of the prosopographical approach have gleefully pointed to this and other instances in order to undermine theories of a familial structure in Roman politics.[1] But negative carping from the sidelines is not a particularly fruitful enterprise. And the criticism can be excessive. What distinguishes the Ciceronian period from earlier eras is not simply that evidence becomes more abundant and thereby more embarrassing. The fact is that politics had become more complicated.

Sulla potuit, ego non potero? Things were not the same after Sulla; nor could they ever be again. He had marched his army on Rome, shattering tradition and sacred precedent. He had proscribed enemies and erased the old lines that once divided senatorial families. Restoration of the institutional structure was no permanent solution. A potential second Sulla was discernible already shortly after the death of the dictator. Given the experience of the 80's, no one could be blind to the implications contained in the meteoric rise of Pompeius Magnus. Roman *nobiles* would have to make their plans accordingly. Some might hitch their fortunes to Pompey's ascending star; others could attempt to raise up a successful counterweight; still others hoped to perpetuate an older system, a closed oligarchic corporation to resist the claims of Pompey and the Pompeians. It should not elicit surprise if this involved the severing of previous ties or even the splitting of families. Attitudes toward Pompey in senatorial circles must have been an overriding issue in the two decades and more that followed the death of Sulla. An investigation of the Calpurnii Pisones in this context may prove illuminating. It reveals greater consistency than has hitherto been noticed (or acknowledged).

One may profitably begin with C. Calpurnius Piso, the consul of 67. His activities in that year are reasonably well documented, though almost nothing is known of him before and very little after. Lamentably, the *fasti* do not preserve his filiation. Hence, stemmata of the Pisones customarily leave him on one side, a lonely isolated figure. That is excessive caution. He was in the inner ring of the nobility in the 60's, a friend of Lucullus, Hortensius, and Bibulus.[2] Such a man will

---

[1] See especially now the remarks of C. Meier, *Res Publica Amissa* (Wiesbaden 1966) 7–23; 162–200.

[2] Clodius attacked him in 61, linking him with Lucullus and Hortensius; Cic. *Ad Att.* 1.14.5. Association with Bibulus is attested by Cic. *Ad Att.* 1.17.11.

not have lacked distinguished ancestors. A plausible hypothesis offers itself: Piso may have been the younger son of L. Piso Frugi, praetor in 112, who perished during his praetorship. That would make him grandson of the consul of 133, the eminent historian, moralist, and author of the *lex Calpurnia repetundarum* which instituted Rome's first criminal court. An older brother then would be the praetor of 74, whose office indicates precedence of birth by four or five years. C. Piso thus finds a place (admittedly conjectural) in the Pisonian stemma.[3]

The company of Lucullus, Hortensius, and Bibulus suggests a conservative disposition for C. Piso. And the surviving evidence is abundant on that score. As an orator Piso preferred a low-key, conversational tone, relying more on imposing appearance than on rhetoric. But when confronted by popular agitators, he was stalwart and unbending in resistance, sometimes to the point of violence. The *popularis* tribunes of 67, A. Gabinius and C. Cornelius, found Piso a resolute foe. And when Lollius Palicanus, branded by oligarchic tradition as a *seditiosissimus homo*, sought a consular post for 66, Piso, in the teeth of popular outcry, refused to countenance his candidacy. It was a stormy consulship. Piso was in the midst of at least two open riots in the course of the year. While blocking an *ambitus* measure of Cornelius, his *fasces* were broken and he was fortunate to escape with his life. And again while opposing Gabinius' legislation, he faced a hostile crowd which threatened to tear him to pieces. His enemies were barely dissuaded from deposing him from office.[4]

More important for our purposes, however, is the evidence which these activities provide for Piso's attitude toward Pompey. It has a clear pattern. In 67, after two years of comparative idleness, Pompey once again occupied the center of the stage as debate raged over an

[3] On the consul of 133, see F. Münzer and C. Cichorius, "Calpurnius," no. 96, *RE* 3 (1899) 1392–1395; the praetor of 112, Münzer, "Calpurnius," no. 97, *RE* 3 (1899) 1395; the praetor of 74, Münzer, "Calpurnius" no. 97, *RE* 3 (1899) 1395; the praetor of 74, Münzer, "Calpurnius," no. 98, *RE* 3 (1899) 1395–1396.

[4] On Piso's oratory, see Cic. *Brutus* 239. The opposition to Cornelius and the consequent riots are recorded by Asconius 58; 75 (Clark), and Dio 36.38–39. Cornelius' effort was thwarted and Piso succeeded in passing a substitute *lex de ambitu*; T. R. S. Broughton, *The Magistrates of the Roman Republic* (New York 1952) (hereafter cited as *MRR*) II, 142–143. On this see W. McDonald, *CQ* 23 (1929) 196–208. Some, it seems, sneered at Piso's hypocrisy, alleging that Piso had himself gained election only by buying off *accusatores* who had levelled an *ambitus* charge against him in 68; Sallust *Hist.* 4.81 (Maur.); Dio 36.38.3. For Piso's vigorous but fruitless opposition to Gabinius, see Dio 36.24.3; 36.37.2; Plut. *Pomp.* 25.4; 27.1–2. His blocking of Palicanus' candidature is given by Val. Max. 3.8.3. For other references to Piso, not relevant here, see Münzer, "Calpurnius," no. 63, *RE* (1899) 1376–1377.

extraordinary command against Mediterranean piracy. It can be no coincidence that all of the men with whom Piso clashed so violently in that year show close connection with Pompey. C. Cornelius had been his quaestor in the Spanish wars of the late 70's. Lollius Palicanus had agitated for tribunician reform in 71 in cooperation with Pompey, who brought it to fruition in the succeeding year. Documentation is hardly necessary for A. Gabinius. He was a steady Pompeian throughout his career. Piso's contest with Gabinius in 67, in fact, was over the latter's measure to award *imperium infinitum* in the Mediterranean to Pompey. The consul did not give up resistance even when the bill was passed over his objections. He sought to block Pompey's levies and interfered with the equipment and recruitment of his fleets. And, as if that were not enough, Piso challenged the great man to his face: "if Pompey was going to emulate Romulus, he would also suffer Romulus' fate."[5]

There is more to be said on C. Piso in this connection. Among those who spoke for Gabinius' bill, in defiance of Piso and other *principes*, was C. Julius Caesar.[6] Caesar's political stance in the 60's shows consistent advocacy of Pompeian causes in the interests of his own future career.[7] And there is further consistency: a bitter *inimicitia* between Caesar and Piso. In 63 Caesar launched an unsuccessful prosecution against Piso for extortion allegedly committed in the latter's provincial governorship in Gaul. In retaliation, Piso did his best to implicate Caesar in the Catilinarian conspiracy.[8] That effort was abortive, but Piso brought more substantial evidence against genuine conspirators, spoke up in the senatorial debate apparently for summary

---

[5] For the latter statement, see Plut. *Pomp.* 25.4: ʽΡωμύλον ζηλῶν οὐ φεύξεται ταὐτὸν ἐκείνῳ τέλος. Plutarch ascribes the remark simply to τῶν μὲν ὑπάτων ἅτερος, but adds that he was subsequently almost torn to pieces by the mob; evidently, that consul was Piso. On the efforts to undermine Pompey's recruitment, see Plut. *Pomp.* 27.1; Dio 36.37.2. For Cornelius' quaestorship, see Asconius 57 (Clark); for Palicanus' connection with Pompey, Ps-Asconius 189; 220 (Stangl).

[6] Plut. *Pomp.* 25.4.

[7] Cf. the acute remarks of L. R. Taylor, *TAPA* 73 (1942) 1–24.

[8] On the trial of Piso, see Sallust *Cat.* 49.2. Cicero was counsel for the defense; Cic. *Pro Flacco* 98. Cf. E. Ciaceri, *Cicerone e i suoi tempi* (Milano etc. 1939–1941) I, 216–217. The formal charge was *res repetundae*. The allegation *Transpadani supplicium iniustum* will have been added by Caesar in the course of the *accusatio*. Piso's assertion of Caesar's complicity with Catiline: Sallust *Cat.* 49.2; Plut. *Caes.* 7.3. Cicero's defense speech for Piso was the fruit of an earlier and apparently close connection; Cic. *Ad Att.* 1.1.2. The orator's daughter was married to C. Piso, quaestor in 58. If the above reconstruction is correct (p. 157), this Piso was nephew of the consul of 67, and the Ciceronian association lends further credence to that reconstruction.

punishment, and later praised Cicero for his deed. He hoped for speed in snuffing out the conspiracy. It may be surmised that among his motives was a desire to forestall Pompey, lest he add the conquest of Catiline to his laurels.[9] Piso receives no further mention in the extant evidence after the year 61. Death shortly afterwards is a reasonable hypothesis. But it admits of no doubt that Pompey had had a relentless foe in C. Calpurnius Piso.

Another Piso has fared badly in the ancient tradition: Cn. Calpurnius Piso, alleged accomplice of Catiline in the so-called "1st Catilinarian Conspiracy." Sallust denounces him as a ruined young aristocrat goaded by poverty into recklessness and insurrection. The picture persists in later sources.[10] He was, however, a *nobilis*. His filiation is known, C.f., though neither father nor grandfather made an appearance in recorded history. The consul of 139, also Cn. Calpurnius Piso, may well be *proavus*.[11] The actual involvement of Piso in abortive schemes of 66–65 to murder consuls or senators rests on inconclusive testimony. The "1st Conspiracy" has provoked endless controversy which shows little sign of abating.[12] It will serve no purpose to add fuel to that particular fire here. That there was any "plot" at all remains murky and obscure; its possible aims even more so. Later embellishments make the events almost impossible to reconstruct. With regard to Piso, it will be prudent to report only that rumors of an association with Catiline had reached Cicero's ears by 64 when he delivered the *In Toga Candida*.[13]

Catilinarian intrigues can be left aside. But there is more substantial and revealing information on Cn. Piso. He received appointment to Spain in 65 with the title *quaestor pro praetore* and the matter was managed by M. Crassus. Implacable hostility between Pompey and Crassus is, of course, notorious. Attitudes toward Pompey linked

[9] Piso's bringing up of information: Plut. *Cic.* 19.1; participation in the debate: Cic. *Ad Att.* 12.21.1; praise for Cicero: Cic. *Phil.* 2.12. On Pompey's hopes to quell the uprising himself, see Meier, *Athenaeum* 40 (1962) 103–125.

[10] Sallust *Cat.* 18.4: *adulescens nobilis, summae audaciae, egens, factiosus, quem ad perturbandam rem publicam inopia atque mali mores stimulabant*; Asconius 66 (Clark): *adulescens potens et turbulentus*; cf. Dio 36.44.5.

[11] The filiation is in *ILS* 875.

[12] Cf., e.g., G. DeBenedetti, *Historia* 3 (1929) 333–344; F. L. Jones, *CJ* 34 (1939) 410–422; H. Frisch, *Class et Med* 9 (1947) 10–36; P. A. Brunt, *CR* 7 (1957) 193–195; C. E. Stevens, *Latomus* 22 (1963) 397–435; R. Seager, *Historia* 13 (1964) 338–347; R. Syme, *Sallust* (Berkeley, Los Angeles 1964) 86–102.

[13] Cic. *In Tog. Cand., apud* Asconius 92 (Clark).

Crassus and Piso. Young Piso, so Sallust reports, was awarded his Spanish post precisely because he was known as a bitter foe of Pompey.[14] Nor was it Crassus alone who urged that appointment. Some senators were happy to be rid of Piso for a time; his was not a character which they found congenial. But *boni complures* saw in him a safe and useful man in Spain: the province could be a bulwark against Pompeius Magnus.[15] Whatever the purpose of the mission, however, Piso perished mysteriously in the course of it. The Spaniards themselves, it seems, were responsible for his murder. Cruelty and insolence may have been the provocation. Piso was a harsh taskmaster. But many suspected that clients and retainers of Pompey performed the deed. That Pompey himself, far off in the east, ordered Piso's slaying is hardly credible. But Pompeian *clientelae* in Spain were widespread, and there is much evidence for Calpurnii and Crassi there as well. It will not be rash to imagine that Crassus and Piso had hoped to expand their Spanish following at the expense of Pompey and that this rivalry played a part in Piso's demise.[16]

Piso's actions in Spain and his fate are familiar. But there is another item which has not been exploited. Valerius Maximus tells the story. A certain Cn. Piso, a young man, brought prosecution against Manilius Crispus, who, though evidently guilty (the charge is unspecified), was shielded by the imposing presence of his backer, Pompeius Magnus. Nothing daunted, the zealous young prosecutor showered invective upon Pompey himself. When the general, imperturbable as ever, inquired why Piso did not prosecute him as well as Manilius, Piso shot back a swift reply: "Guarantee the republic that you will not

---

[14] Sallust *Cat.* 19.1: *Postea Piso in citeriorem Hispaniam quaestor pro praetore missus est adnitente Crasso, quod eum infestum inimicum Cn. Pompeio cognoverat.* On the connection between Piso and Crassus, cf. also Asconius 83 (Clark).

[15] Sallust *Cat.* 19.2: *boni complures praesidium in eo putabant et iam tum potentia Pompei formidulosa erat.* Anti-Caesarian authors later sought to implicate Piso and Caesar in nefarious plots; the fantasies are transmitted by Suet. *Iul.* 9.3. Other evidence on the Spanish command is noted in Broughton, *MRR* II, 159. J. P. V. D. Balsdon, *JRS* 52 (1962) 134–135, strains credulity in arguing that a quaestor was dispatched to Spain only because no other governors were available; cf. also Syme, *Sallust* 89.

[16] On the murder of Piso, see Sallust *Cat.* 19.4–5: *Sunt qui ita dicant, imperia eius iniusta, superba, crudelia barbaros nequivisse pati; alii autem equites illos Cn. Pompei veteres fidosque clientis voluntate eius Pisonem aggressos;* Asconius 92 (Clark): *Ibi quidem dum iniurias provincialibus facit, occisus erat, ut quidam credebant, a Cn. Pompeii clientibus Pompeio non invito;* Dio 36.44.5 ascribes the death penalty simply to Piso's harshness toward the Spaniards. On the Spanish *clientelae*, see E. Badian, *Foreign Clientelae* (Oxford 1958) 312; 316; 318; cf. Stevens, *Latomus* 22 (1963) 417.

bring civil war in the wake of a prosecution, and I will have you up on a capital charge before I get Manilius." [17]

That is information which no historian should have missed. Who is Cn. Piso the prosecutor? Identification has been made with Cn. Calpurnius Piso, Cn. f. Cn. n., the future consul of 23 and son of the quaestor of 65.[18] On that view, the trial took place after conclusion of the Mithridatic War and Pompey's triumphant return: hence ca. 60 B.C. Perhaps so. Yet Valerius Maximus gives no date and there are other problems. The younger Piso later found himself on the Pompeian side in the civil war, not the most likely spot for the man who had heaped insults on Magnus and had feared above all his initiation of a *bellum civile*. Moreover, a consul of 23 B.C. would hardly be old enough to undertake a prosecution in 60, much less to hurl a challenge at Pompey. His father was only of quaestorian age in 65. And who is Manilius Crispus? He nowhere else appears on record. But temptation is strong to see in him C. Manilius, the tribune of 66, whose *lex* in that year transferred the Mithridatic command onto the shoulders of Pompey. To believe that this Manilius suffered a prosecution in 60 demands faith. He was condemned on a *maiestas* charge in 65. No evidence suggests that he was fortunate enough to be recalled later and unfortunate enough to be prosecuted again. The multiplication of ad hoc hypotheses is rarely sound methodology.[19] A solution lies ready at hand. The trial fits in 69 or 68 before Pompey sailed off against the pirates. In that event, the young prosecutor, of course, was Cn. Piso himself, the future quaestor of 65. There need be no doubt that some men feared civil war from Pompey at so early a time. Even earlier, in the winter of 75–74, he had sent a menacing dispatch to the senate from Spain: "If you don't send aid, my army will march right into Italy and bring the whole Spanish war with it."[20] The implications of that message were unmistakable. It may be asserted with some confidence that Manilius Crispus' accuser was the quaestor of 65. The picture falls neatly into place. Cn. Piso is described as an *infestus inimicus* of Pompey in 65. His

---

[17] Val. Max. 6.2.4: '*da*' inquit, '*praedes rei publicae te, si postulatus fueris, civile bellum non excitaturum, etiam te tuo prius quam de Manilii capite in consilium iudices mittam*'.

[18] Münzer, "Calpurnius," no. 95, *RE* 3 (1899) 1391–1392.

[19] On the younger Piso's service with Pompey, see *Bell. Afr.* 3.1; 18.1; Tac. *Ann.* 2.43. Sources on the trial of Manilius are collected by Broughton, *MRR* II, 153.

[20] Sallust *Epist. Pomp.* 10: *qui nisi subvenitis, invito et praedicente me exercitus hinc et cum eo omne bellum Hispaniae in Italiam transgradientur.* Cf. 8: *quod ego vos moneo quaesoque ut animadvortatis neu cogitatis necessitatibus privatim mihi consulere.*

fearless public denunciation of the general a few years before forms the perfect backdrop.

So far the evidence is consistent. But there is not much relevant information on the next individual who merits inquiry, C. Calpurnius Piso Frugi, L.f., the son-in-law of Cicero. C. Piso could trace his descent back in a straight line to the consul of 133. The reconstruction suggested earlier would make him nephew of C. Piso, the consul of 67 and *inimicus* of Pompey. On his character testimony is plentiful, but almost exclusively from Cicero. That will not get us far. Piso was quaestor in 58 and during that year and the following he worked tirelessly to secure Cicero's recall from exile. His boundless energy played no small role in making the campaign for recall successful. Unfortunately, Piso, who had given up a provincial assignment to remain in Rome and advocate Cicero's cause, did not live even to witness his father-in-law's return. Under the circumstances, Cicero's references to him will only naturally have been filled with the most extravagant praise: filial piety and unselfish devotion of the highest order, a natural talent for oratory and persuasion, grace of manner, surpassing all others of his generation in self-control, prestige and virtue.[21]

Ciceronian laudation can be taken for what it is worth. But what of Piso's attitude toward Pompey? Two pieces of information warrant mention. The first is inconclusive but interesting. Not long before the year 70 a L. Piso brought charges of *res repetundae* on behalf of the Greeks against P. Gabinius.[22] Such is the sum of our evidence on that matter. The prosecutor, however, may well be L. Piso, the praetor of 74 and father of C. Piso.[23] A feud with the Gabinii is suggested. C. Piso, consul 67, as we have seen, engaged in a violent clash with another Gabinius, the agent of Pompey the Great.

The second item is more substantial. In 59 the informer Vettius revealed (or fabricated) a plot aimed at the murder of Pompey.

---

[21] Praise is most effusive in Cic. *Brutus* 272; also *In Vat.* 26; *P. red. in sen.* 38; *P. red. ad Quir.* 7; *Ad Fam.* 14.1.4. Other references in Münzer, "Calpurnius," no. 93, *RE* 3 (1899) 1391.

[22] Cic. *Div. in Caec.* 64.

[23] Badian, *Studies in Greek and Roman History* (New York 1964) 82, 100, argues that this L. Piso is the future consul of 58, seeking renown at the bar as a young man. The argument has plausibility and the question must remain open. But Cicero twice more in the *Verrines* refers to L. Piso and the references there are definitely to the praetor of 74; *Verr.* 2.1.119; 2.4.56. That inclines the balance toward this same man as the subject of *Div. in Caec.* 64.

Among the individuals named as privy to the intrigue was C. Piso, Cicero's son-in-law. This "Vettius affair," of course, has been subjected to interminable debate.[24] It is beyond our purpose to investigate the substance of the charges or the mysterious motives that may have lain behind Vettius' testimony. What is significant is the inclusion of Piso in the company of men like Lucullus, Bibulus, Curio, and Domitius. That Piso was regarded as a plausible conspirator is the irreducible minimum of this affair, and that is sufficient. Cicero's son-in-law, like the other Pisones so far examined, may be reckoned among those aristocrats for whom the *potentia* of Pompey was obnoxious.[25]

Investigation must turn now to the best known of the Pisones. L. Calpurnius Piso Caesoninus, the consul of 58, is infamous as the object of Cicero's railing denunciation. The portrait conveyed is unforgettable. Piso was grim, taciturn, and imposing, with wrinkled forehead, hairy cheeks and formidable eyebrows. He was the image of sternness and solemnity, but in fact wallowed in lasciviousness, gluttony, and orgiastic parties. His fondness for Epicurianism was not philosophic interest, but intoxication with the slogan of "pleasure."[26] Such is the Ciceronian picture. But Cicero's exaggerated insults need be taken no more seriously than his lavish praise. L. Piso reckoned three consulars among his ancestors in a direct line, the consuls of 180, 148, and 112. Actions later in his life, during the civil war and then in the struggles after Caesar's death, showed him moderate and independent, and earned him eventually the plaudits of Cicero himself.[27] But we are concerned here with an earlier phase of his career and actions of a more dubious character. Does L. Piso fit the pattern discerned above for his

---

[24] The bibliography continues to grow. A few of the more recent contributions may be noted: W. C. McDermott, *TAPA* 80 (1949) 351–367; L. R. Taylor, *Historia* 1 (1950) 45–51; W. Allen, *TAPA* 81 (1950) 153–163; R. Rossi, *Annali Triestini* 21 (1951) 247–260; C. Meier, *Historia* 10 (1961) 68–98; R. Seager, *Latomus* 24 (1965) 519–531. The naming of Piso appears in Cic. *Ad Att.* 2.24.3; *In Vat.* 26

[25] Plutarch, to be sure, remarks that in 58 Cicero sent Piso to Pompey in order to beg assistance for the orator in his plight; *Cic.* 31.2. But no issue is reported for the interview and Plutarch himself omits it when speaking elsewhere of these events; *Pomp.* 46.5. In all probability it is a confusion with the equally fruitless pleas which Piso addressed to the consuls on Cicero's behalf; Cic. *In Pis.* 12–13; *Pro Sest.* 54; 68; *P. red. in sen.* 17. Cf. E. Meyer, *Caesars Monarchie und das Principat des Pompeius* (Stuttgart and Berlin 1922) 97–99.

[26] See, e.g., Cic. *In Pis.* 1; 13; 22; 66–69; *P. red. in sen.* 13–16; *Pro Sest.* 19; 21–23. Other references in Münzer, "Calpurnius," no. 90, *RE* 3 (1899) 1387–1390; see also R. G. M. Nisbet, *Cicero, In L. Calpurniam Pisonem Oratio* (Oxford 1961) v–xvii; 192–197, and P. Grimal, *Cicéron, Discours Contre Pison* (Paris 1966) 44–65.

[27] Münzer, "Calpurnius," no. 90, *RE* 3 (1899) 1389–1390.

adfines? The familiar evidence would seem to argue the contrary, as do the standard modern accounts. Piso became father-in-law of Julius Caesar in 59, part of the network of alliances formed by the "1st triumvirate." He secured the consulship of 58 together with Pompey's devoted ally A. Gabinius. The two consuls then cooperated with Clodius in securing the exile of Cicero for which both received lucrative provincial commands. Such, of course, is the root of Cicero's fierce hostility which ultimately issued in the *In Pisonem* delivered in 55 after Piso's recall from Macedon. Did Piso then stand apart from other members of his clan and attach himself to Pompey and the triumvirate? A careful examination of the evidence might lead to a different conclusion.

The year 59 was evidently a sharp turning point in the career of L. Piso. It was the year of Caesar's dramatic and domineering consulship. Connection with Caesar brought promise for the future and the immediate benefit of a chief magistracy. Caesar's marriage to Calpurnia came some time during 59; whether before or after Piso's election for the following year is uncertain.[28] There can be no doubt, however, that the dual arrangement signals a bargain. As late as April 59, when Cicero speculated on the consular candidates, Piso did not even receive a mention.[29] By October he was consul-elect. Marriage or betrothal of his daughter was surely instrumental.

How far did this affect Piso's political stance? The attitude of Cicero is revealing. He was certainly no inveterate foe of the Pisones, as we have seen already in his relations with the consul of 67 and with his son-in-law the quaestor of 58. More to the point, however, he was no inveterate foe of L. Piso himself. Quite the contrary. Cicero was under heavy fire for his execution of the Catilinarians. But he had no reason to fear Piso on this score. The latter had heaped praise upon the deeds of Cicero's consulship.[30] Nor did the marriage tie to Caesar necessarily bode evil. Indeed Cicero, linked to Piso through his own son-in-law, supported him actively for the consulship of 58. At the elections Cicero served Piso's interests during the crucial voting of the *centuria praerogativa*.[31] With Piso as chief magistrate, the orator had high

---

[28] Sources are divided: Suet. *Iul.* 21 and Dio 38.9.1 seem to put the election first; Plut. *Caes.* 14.4 and Appian *BC* 2.14 put the marriage first. None makes any pretense at exactitude and it does not matter much. The connection is clear in all.

[29] Cic. *Ad Att.* 2.5.2.

[30] Cic. *In Pis.* 72.

[31] Cic. *P. red. in sen.* 17: *Tu misericors me, adfinem tuum, quem comitiis praerogativae primum custodem praefeceras;* also *In Pis.* 11.

hopes that his cause would be defended and advanced. Men congratulated Cicero because a friend and kinsman would now be his advocate
in the consulship.[32] There was obviously no reason to suspect that Piso
would collaborate with Cicero's *inimicus* Clodius, especially since
Clodius had already threatened to rescind the legislation of Piso's
father-in-law Caesar.[33] Certainly no evidence would suggest a prior
connection with Clodius.[34] But Clodius' pyrotechnics in 58 promised
advantage to Piso. The tribune, at the height of his popular prestige,
could secure a profitable provincial assignment for Piso. Hence the
latter conveniently looked the other way when Clodius carried out his
campaign of vilification against Cicero and eventually brought about
the orator's exile.[35] Cicero could not at first believe it. He went himself
to Piso; and along with him came C. Piso, the consul's kinsman and
Cicero's faithful son-in-law. But their pleas were in vain. The bargain
had been made and L. Piso was looking forward to his tenure in
Macedon.[36]

Cicero could justify righteous indignation. The violent
epithets of the *In Pisonem* may be excessive, but Piso was certainly no
paragon of virtue. A marriage compact with Caesar guaranteed his
consulship, and cooperation with Clodius was the price of a provincial
post. But had Piso moved any closer to Pompeius Magnus? That need
not follow. The motives behind Caesar's marriage to Calpurnia are
worth examining. Dio Cassius (for once) has an acute and almost certainly accurate analysis: Caesar was uneasy about Pompey and the
prospect of the Pompeian Gabinius in the consulship; hence, he married
off his daughter to Pompey and took Piso's daughter as his own wife;

---

[32] Cic. *Pro Sest*. 20: *Mihi denique homines praecipue gratulabantur, quod habiturus
essem contra tribunem pl. furiosum et audacem cum amicum et adfinem, tum etiam fortem et gravem
consulem; Ad Q. Frat*. 1.2.16 (ca. early December, 59): *Tribuni pl. designati sunt nobis amici;
consules se optime ostendunt.*

[33] Cic. *Ad Att*. 2.12.2; cf. Gruen, *Phoenix* 20 (1966) 123–124.

[34] Cic. *Pro Sest*. 20, quoted above, shows just the reverse. Val. Max. 8.1.6
speaks of a prosecution of L. Piso by a certain L. Claudius Pulcher. Since "Lucius" is not a
praenomen found among the Claudii Pulchri, some have emended to "P. Clodius Pulcher" and
identified L. Piso with the consul of 58. If that is so, hostility between the two is clear. But the
identification cannot be proved and there are other possibilities; cf. Syme, *Class et Med* 17
(1956) 133. Nonetheless, the anecdote reveals friction between the Pisones and the Claudii.

[35] Cic. *Pro Sest*. 24–25; 33–34; 53–54; 64; 69; *In Pis*. 15; 28.

[36] Cic. *Pro Sest*. 26; 54; 68; *In Pis*. 12–13; *P. red in sen*. 17; cf. Ciaceri
(supra, n. 8) II, 48ff.

it was a design to cover all his flanks.[37] The implication is clear. Caesar wanted a counterweight in the consulship. The "triumvirate" in 59 was, at best, a loose coalition for immediate mutual benefits. Caesar played his hand shrewdly. While advocating Pompeian causes in the 60's, he had simultaneously cooperated with Crassus, Pompey's most formidable rival. So also in 59 Caesar insured his interests not only by a closer link with Pompey, but by wooing Piso, whose *gens* had already showed its displeasure with the Pompeians. Caesar's policy seems clear and consistent.[38] It is not to be expected that L. Piso had come to love Pompey. Nor do we find that to be the case. Cooperation with Gabinius was mutually advantageous so long as both men were beneficiaries of Clodius' bounty in 58. But when Clodius began to attack Pompey verbally and physically later in the year, the loyal Gabinius resisted on Pompey's behalf. Not so with Piso. Indeed he encouraged Clodius. Piso had no reason to regret the discomfiture of Magnus.[39]

An overt clash between Piso and the great man would not have been in the interests of Piso's son-in-law. But conflict with Pompey's agents and supporters is attested. The difference with Gabinius late in 58 is only one example. When Piso returned from Macedon in 55 he sought no triumph. That may be, as Cicero claims, because none would have been forthcoming. But in any case Piso paraded his Epicureanism and affected to scorn the honor. In justification he singled out an ex-legate and close ally of Pompey for ridicule, criticizing him for his unwarranted appetite for triumph. The object of that attack was M. Pupius Piso, of whom we shall have more to say below.[40] And Cicero was not the only man who lambasted Piso for his deeds in

---

[37] Dio 38.9.1: φοβηθεὶς δ'οὖν καὶ ὡς μή τι ὁ Πομπήιος ἐν τῇ ἀπουσίᾳ αὐτοῦ. ἐπειδὴ ὁ Γαβίνιος ὁ Αὖλος ὑπατεύσειν ἔμελλε, νεωτερίσῃ, ἐκεῖνόν τε ἅμα καὶ τὸν ἕτερον ὕπατον Λούκιον Πίσωνα συγγενείας ἀνάγκη προσηταιρίσατο. τῷ μὲν γὰρ Πομπηίῳ τὴν θυγατέρα καίπερ ἄλλῳ τινὶ ἠλλυηκὼς συνῴκισε, καὶ αὐτὸς τὴν τοῦ Πίσωνος ἔγημε. καὶ ὁ μὲν οὕτω πανταχόθεν ἐκρατύνθη.

[38] The death of C. Piso, consul 67 and *inimicus* of Caesar, probably shortly before 59, doubtless smoothed the path for the new marriage alliance.

[39] Cic. *In Pis.* 27–28: [Gabinius] *conlegit ipse se vix sed conlegit tamen, et contra suum Clodium primum simulate, deinde non libenter, ad extremum tamen pro Cn. Pompeio vere vehementerque pugnavit ... Erat ipse sceleratus, erat gladiator, cum scelerato tamen et cum pari gladiatore pugnabat. Tu scilicet homo religiosus et sanctus foedus quod meo sanguine in pactione provinciarum iceras frangere noluisti ... omnium ut suorum scelerum socium te adiutoremque praeberes;* also *De Domo* 66: *postea fregit foedus Gabinius, Piso tamen in fide mansit;* cf. *In Pis* 16; Dio 38.30.2, and see Meyer, *Caesars Monarchie* 103–104.

[40] Cic. *In Pis.* 62: *Inrisa est abs te paulo ante M. Pisonis cupiditas triumphandi, a qua te longe dixisti abhorrere.*

Macedon. The returning proconsul had a sharp exchange in the senate with L. Manlius Torquatus. It is perhaps not coincidental that Torquatus too had been a legate with Pompey during the pirate wars a decade earlier.[41] The cumulative effect of all this testimony is decisive. L. Piso Caesoninus, whatever the vagaries of his relations with Cicero, exhibits (at best) ill-disguised hostility toward Pompey and the Pompeian hangers-on.

A solitary exception disturbs the picture. M. Pupius Piso was a Pompeian if ever there was one. Selected as a legate for the pirate war, he served under Pompey for the duration, it seems, of that conflict and of the Mithridatic war that followed, in both instances executing important responsibilities.[42] With the war over and Pompey on the verge of returning in 62, Piso was sent ahead as the general's consular candidate. Pompey sought even to have the elections postponed in order to make matters easier for his legate. Piso's canvass was successful and he continued to operate in Pompey's interest in 61.[43] Of the man we are rather well informed. He was an individual of sour disposition and sardonic humor. Though not endowed with an abundance of natural gifts, he was a shrewd and effective speaker when he troubled to equip himself. On the whole, however, Piso lacked the patience to endure for long the petty activities of the forum and his irascibility made that obvious. He much preferred the delights of Greek learning and won renown as an expert in Peripatetic philosophy.[44]

Cicero's attitude toward Piso, as toward so many others, shifted radically over the years in accordance with the political circumstances. As young men the two were close. Studies and rhetorical training were shared in both Rome and Athens. Piso was a few years older and Cicero had the benefit of his learning as student and as companion. In succeeding years they seem to have drifted apart. By the time of Piso's consulship in 61, Pompey was cool and aloof on the matter so dear to Cicero's heart, the execution of the Catilinarians. And Pompey's

[41] For Torquatus' exchange with Piso, see Cic. *In Pis.* 47; 92. For his service with Pompey, see Broughton, *MRR* II, 149: 151, n. 16.

[42] Sources in Broughton, *MRR* II, 149; 151, n. 18; 171. On Pupius Piso generally, see H. Gundel, "Pupius," no. 10, *RE* 46 (1959) 1987–1993.

[43] The candidacy: Dio 37.44.3; Plut. *Pomp.* 44.1–2; *Cato* 30.1–2; cooperation with Pompey in 61: Cic. *Ad Att.* 1.14.1; 1.16.12. Cicero's remark in *Ad Att.* 1.14.6 is evidently wishful thinking.

[44] The description is culled from Cic. *Brutus* 236; *Ad Att.* 1.13.2; 1.14.6. Piso's erudition and philosophic competence: Cic. *Ad Att.* 13.19.4; *De Nat. Deor.* 1.16; *De Fin.* 4.73; 5.1f; *Brutus* 236; *De Orat.* 1.104; *In Pis.* 62; Asconius 15 (Clark).

former legate clashed openly with Cicero on another matter, Clodius' trial for sacrilege. Piso opposed the measure for a *quaestio extraordinaria* and gave Clodius the opportunity to tamper with the jurors. Cicero was furious, laced Piso publicly, and managed to deprive him of his expected province of Syria. The orator's most bitter comments on Piso derive from letters written in 61, describing him as idle, worthless, and subversive. Nothing is heard of Piso after 61; death may have come shortly after his consulship. Later Cicero could, in retrospect, describe him in the most glowing terms: a man of extreme eloquence, integrity, and nobility.[45]

The vicissitudes of Cicero notwithstanding, Piso's connection with Pompey is incontrovertible. In this he did not follow the *gens Calpurnia*. His early life may supply some explanation. It must be noted that he was a Calpurnius Piso only by birth. For reasons unknown to us, he moved from that noble house to a family of no prominence, receiving adoption from a M. Pupius when the latter was already in extreme old age.[46] Perhaps a lucrative inheritance provided attraction. He held on to the *cognomina* of his former house (M. Pupius Piso Frugi), but no political cooperation with members of that family stands on record.[47]

The decade of the 80's was a critical formative period for men who had recently come into maturity. Both Pupius Piso and Cn. Pompeius fall into that category, though the former was a few years older. Civil war and upheaval forced men into early political decisions which shaped their future careers. While Sulla was off waging war in the east, Cinna sought to assemble a viable government in Rome. Both Piso and Pompey elected to remain in Italy. Pompey had close con-

---

[45] For Piso as Cicero's mentor, see Asconius 15 (Clark); [Sallust] *Inv. in Cic.* 1.2; their closeness and companionship in studies: Cic. *Brutus* 240; 310; *De Fin.* 4.73; 5.1. On Piso and the trial of Clodius, see Cic. *Ad Att.* 13.2–3; 14.5–6; 16.1–10; cf. Ciaceri (supra, n. 8) II, 20–29. The same man whom Cicero could describe in 61 as *parvo animo et pravo* and *somni plenus, imperitus, ἀπρακτότατος, adductus studio perditarum rerum* (*Ad Att.* 1.13.2; 1.14.6) is characterized in 54 as *nobilissimus, innocentissimus, eloquentissimus* (*Pro Planc.* 12); cf. also Schol. Bob. 96 (Stangl).

[46] Cic. *De Domo* 35.

[47] It is true that, as consul in 61, he called upon C. Piso, consul 67, to deliver the first *sententia* in senatorial debate; Cic. *Ad Att.* 1.13.2. Meier, *Res Pub.* 19, takes this as proof that familial cooperation transcended the two men's contradictory attitudes toward Pompey. But this formality ought not to be taken too seriously just because Cicero expressed pique at being passed over. The crucial fact (which Meier omits) is that precisely in 61 Pupius Piso and C. Piso had an open political clash. The former was acting in support of Clodius while the latter was viciously attacked at the rostra by Clodius; Cic. *Ad Att.* 1.13.3; 1.14.5–6; 1.16.1; 1.16.8.

nections to the regime. When prosecuted in the middle of the decade, he could call upon illustrious defense counsel: L. Philippus, censor in 86, and Cn. Carbo, consul in 85, 84,and 82. And the presiding magistrate shortly became Pompey's own father-in-law. No one will have doubted the outcome of that particular prosecution.[48] Piso's connections with ruling circles in Rome were equally close. When Cinna perished in 84, Piso promptly married his widow. Profit came immediately as Piso received a quaestorship for 83; and when mobilization began against Sulla he was assigned to the anti-Sullan consul Scipio Asiagenus. But the year 83 was a crucial moment of decision for many a Roman aristocrat. Calculation of military probabilities determined the moves of numerous individuals who were not troubled by conscience. Sulla had the bigger battalions and drew most of the profits. Young Pompey recruited troops from clients in Picenum and brought them over to Sulla. Pupius Piso refused to accept his assignment under Scipio and thus prepared the way for his own defection. And when Sulla's victory was secure a striking parallel linked the fortunes of Pompey and Piso. Both men were burdened by embarrassing wives. The remedies were similar. On the dictator's insistence Pompey divorced Antistia to marry Sulla's own step-daughter, pregnant though she was by a former husband, and Piso at the same time discarded the widow of Cinna.[49] The two men evidently had much in common on which to look back. It should no longer evoke surprise that Piso's later career shows him a loyal partisan of Pompey the Great.

A conclusion can now be stated with some confidence. The Calpurnii Pisones formed no monolithic political bloc. There was no "family line" to which members were expected to adhere. Precise familial ties among the Pisones of this era are themselves incapable of reconstruction. The name held in common was no guarantee of like-mindedness. Individuals made up their own minds and association with other major figures varied and shifted. But continuity is discernible in the flux. No single issue exercised the Roman aristocracy in the 60's and early 50's more than that of Pompey's rise to extraordinary power and

---

[48] Plut. *Pomp.* 2.2; 4.1–5; Cic. *Brutus* 230; Val. Max. 5.3.5; 6.2.8.

[49] For Piso's refusal to join Scipio Asiagenus, see Cic. *Verr.* 2.1.37: *Quaestor cum L. Scipioni consuli obtigesset, non attigit pecuniam, non ad exercitum profectus est:* for the divorce of Annia, Cinna's widow, see Vell. Pat. 2.41.2: *cum M. Piso, consularis Anniam, quae Cinnae uxor fuerat, in Sullae dimisisset gratiam.* For Pompey's divorce and remarriage, see Plut. *Pomp.* 9; *Sulla* 33.3. On defections to Sulla in the late 80's, see further Badian (supra, n. 23) 206–234; Gruen, *AJP* 87 (1966) 385–399.

prestige. Was the supremacy of the traditional ruling class compatible with the existence of an individual who might, through resources and following, control the springs of power? Some of Rome's older *gentes* split over the matter. But the Pisones, whatever their predilections on other questions, show persistent opposition to Pompey and the Pompeians. The continued ascendancy of the oligarchy, of which they formed a central part, seemed to require it. The members of the *gens* who were active in this pivotal period demonstrate steady leanings in that direction. A single exception elected to tie his future to Pompeius Magnus. But those two men had at a critical time shared the same fate; the bond forged then never dissolved.

University of California
Berkeley

W. R. JOHNSON

11

Micio and the Perils of Perfection

διὸ πάντα ἄνθρωπον χρὴ φεύγειν τὸ σφόδρα φιλεῖν αὑτόν . . .

Plato, *Laws*, 732B

In the manner of fine comedy, the *Adelphoe*'s initial snarl is extremely neat: irascible and rigid, Demea has allowed his brother, the affable and marvellously sane Micio, to adopt his elder son, Aeschinus; his young son, Ctesiphon, he keeps with him and rears with the strictness which alone, he feels, will ensure for the young man a life of virtue; Ctesiphon, of course, comes to pine for a music-girl, and Aeschinus, sophisticated, high-spirited, and ingenious by virtue of the liberal upbringing his adoptive father has given him, contrives to steal the girl from the pimp who possesses her and to hand her over to his brother. Throughout four acts of the comedy Micio skates with grand finesse on very thin ice, while Demea flounders from misunderstanding to absurdity to utter humiliation. But in the fifth act, having tactfully and patiently illumined the muddle which Aeschinus' generosity had brought about, Micio, all without warning, takes a pratfall, while Demea prances, grins and chortles.

This sudden reversal, the humiliation of Micio, has made not a few readers nervous.[1] Why has this paradigm of classical humanism been subjected to wild mockery? Why is he given no final chance to

---

[1] For a skillful summary and pertinent bibliography, see W. G. Arnott, "The End of Terence's 'Adelphoe'," *Greece and Rome* 10 (1963) 140–144; see also, O. Rieth, *Die Kunst Menanders in den Adelphen des Terenz*, Nachwort, K. Gaisser (Hildesheim 1964) 11ff.

defend himself? Has Terence botched his original?[2] Or may we somehow ignore, somehow mitigate, the violence of the denouement?[3] Or does the violence itself establish a satisfying and necessary equilibrium? I join those who find the violence and the final equilibrium it creates aesthetically and psychologically sound;[4] in this paper I want to examine how the violence functions in the hope of defining the nature of this equilibrium. The *Adelphoe* is less concerned with two rival theories of education in conflict or with a confrontation between a gentleman and a boor than it is with two self-satisfied men who are made to collide in order that we may witness the universality of self-satisfaction and its inevitable frustrations. The smugness of Demea is abundantly clear from the moment he opens his mouth, but the smugness of Micio, the poised and gentle humanist, is far from evident and so requires careful probing and forceful revelation: the heart of the comedy is Micio's self-deceptions and self-contradictions.

[2] For theories of botching, see the article to which Arnott addressed himself, T. A. Dorey, "A Note on the 'Adelphoe' of Terence," *Greece and Rome* 9 (1962) 37–39; Rieth (Gaiser) (supra, n. 1) 133–134; Rieth felt that in Menander Micio was "als uneingeschränkt vorbildliche Gestalt konzipiert," which required, of course, that Demea "die Abweichung zum Fehlerhaften verkörperte." Terence, who admired Menander, was unfortunately incapable of dealing with Hellenic subtleties (107ff, 128, 131) and therefore "hat diese Beziehung so verändert, dass in seinem Stuck allerdings das Richtige etwa in der Mitte zwischen Micio und Demea zu liegen scheint." Roman national pride replaces Micio with Demea: "Aus Demeas Schlussrede spricht römischer Stolz."

[3] For Micio's unassailable virtues, see Rieth (supra, n. 1) *passim*. T. B. L. Webster (*Studies in Menander* [Manchester 1950] 67) feels that "Menander has allowed Demea a true criticism of Micio" but persists in viewing Micio as Aristotle's equitable man (206); his philosophical emphasis naturally allows him to believe that "Micio is more nearly right than Demea" (66). The same preoccupation, apparently, leads him to this scandal: "Terence is at best like a Roman copy of a Greek statue; the outlines are well preserved but the bloom of life is largely lost." ("The Comedy of Menander," *Roman Drama*, ed. T. A. Dorey and D. R. Dudley [London 1965] 19; the volume, unfortunately, contains no essay on Terence). See also, P. MacKendrick, "Demetrius of Phalerum, Cato and the Adelphi," *RivFC* (1954) 26ff.

[4] For a fine description of the closing scene, see G. Duckworth, *The Nature of Roman Comedy* (Princeton 1952) 144, where, quite reasonably, the palm goes to Demea; so, M. Neumann, *Die Poetische Gerechtigkeit in der neuen Komödie* (Diss) (Speyer 1958) 172–173. See also, G. Norwood, *The Art of Terence* (London 1923) 127 and F. Wehrli, *Motivstudien zur Griechischen Komödie* (Zürich 1936) 83. Arnott (supra, n. 1) 142, deals vigorously with Dorey's attempts to show that Terence invented the last scenes of the comedy himself, but his attempt to explain away Donatus' *heuretikôs* (on which, see Neumann, *op. cit.*, n. 903, 174) is quite uncertain. Perhaps Terence invented most of the fifth act, perhaps he simply heightened Micio's irritation at the prospect of marriage, and perhaps Menander himself decided to chasten the *eleutheriotes* (see n. 15, infra).

That Micio's opening soliloquy is marked by immense charm and agreeable wisdom none would deny, yet for all its charm and wisdom there are indications of other aspects of Micio's mind and heart which want scrutiny here at the outset. From the comparisons which he draws between wives whose husbands tend not to come home at night and himself, anxious because Aeschinus has not returned from an evening of partying, it would appear that he has a fair opinion of himself, his sensitivity and his deep concern:

> profecto hoc vere dicunt: si absis uspiam
> aut ibi si cesses, evenire ea satius est
> quae in te uxor dicit et quae in animo cogitat
> irata quam illa quae parentes propitii.
> uxor, si cesses, aut te amare cogitat
> aut tete amari aut potare atque animo obsequi,
> et tibi bene esse soli, sibi quom sit male. (28–34)

The wives, then, are concerned only for themselves, but the bachelor father is concerned only for the well-being of his son:

> ego quia non rediit filius quae cogito!
> quibus nunc sollicitor rebus! ne aut ille alserit
> aut uspiam ceciderit aut praefregerit
> aliquid. vae, quemquamne hominem in animo instituere aut
> parare quod sit carius quam ipse est sibi!
> atque ex me hic natus non est, sed ex fratre. . . . (35–40)

Though *vae, quemquamne hominem* defines the genuine concern of *quibus nunc sollicitor rebus*, it also defines the attitude which invites the bachelor father to imagine that his anxieties are unselfish, while the anxieties of real wives are not. For all his sensitivity, his real concern for and generosity to Aeschinus, Micio is rather self-centered, rather used not to having to be concerned for others (*carius quam ipse est sibi* will reappear at the climax of the play). He further reveals this predeliction which has become a lifetime's habit when he blurts out, almost as if taken by surprise, that Aeschinus is not his natural son, that his having taken on this (once) alien worry was a gratuitous (rather generous?) act.

It is this recollection of his brother which brings him composure. For a while he forgets his worries to meditate on the wide differences between his brother and himself (40ff), then passes from this comparison to his justly famous disquisition on humane child-rearing.[5] Since most of what Micio says here is, as usual, admirable, I shall remark only on such passages as suggest that he says more than he is aware of saying.[6] His initial comparison between Demea and himself is quite well-bred; only at *ego hanc clementem vitam urbanam atque otium* (42) and at *(ille) semper parce ac duriter* (45) do we hear tones of righteous superiority. There is no reason to doubt his statement of his deep love for Aeschinus (48–49), but his honest admission that he works hard to ensure that Aeschinus return his love (*ille ut item contra me habeat facio sedulo*, 50ff)[7] yields gradually to meditations on the triumph of his own handling of Aeschinus and on the failures of other fathers in general and of Demea in particular; amid self-congratulations wherein his particular *liberalitas* seems to become universal law the significance of his self-interest, and indeed any awareness of it, gets lost.

> nam qui mentiri aut fallere insuerit patrem aut
> audebit, tanto magis audebit ceteros.
> pudore et liberalitate liberos
> retinere satius esse credo quam metu.
> haec fratri mecum non conveniunt neque placent. (55–59)

There is no question, of course, of Micio's describing Demea unfairly. The crabby, sour, hectoring speech which Micio imagines for Demea at 60–63 will soon be familiar enough to us; the parody is exact, and if Micio parodies Demea out of irritation with him, we can surely allow that Demea is very irritating. But Micio's great error lies in assuming that his *liberalitas* must necessarily have the overwhelming efficacy he imagines for it:

> ille quem beneficio adiungas ex animo facit,
> studet par referre, praesens absensque idem erit. (72–73)

---

[5] Micio's mention of his brother at this point is not merely a question of necessary exposition; dramaturgical necessity and subtle characterization are carefully blended.

[6] I am not saying that Micio is a hypocrite, for in fact he practices what he preaches; rather, failing to understand his own limitations, he misunderstands Aeschinus and Demea. His failures with Aeschinus are well described by Norwood (supra, n. 4) 114 and 129.

[7] There is nice irony here if we remember what Demea will say at the play's close: *ex adsentando, indulgendo et largiendo.*

Aeschinus is soon to prove him wrong on this point, and though he will complain of the way that Aeschinus behaves,[8] he will not admit that he is wrong until the end of the play, where squeals and mutterings neatly betoken the guilt and the confession of this eloquent, unruffled spirit.

> nimium ipse est durus praeter aequomque et bonum;
> et errat longe mea quidem sententia. . . . (64–65)

The doctrine of Micio is, then, for the moment foolproof; but as he cannot see the virtues of Demea, so he cannot see the defects of his own virtues, virtues on which he preens himself, completely unaware that he is doing so:

> hoc patriumst, potius consuefacere filium
> sua sponte recte facere quam alieno metu:
> hoc pater ac dominus interest. hoc qui nequit,
> fateatur nescire imperare liberis. (74–77)

Fateatur nescire? It is a ruthless judgment and for so accomplished a humanist rather a narrow one. In a short while Micio will be wanting to recant what he has just said, and the fine irony of these verses flares just at the moment when Demea makes his entrance. Demea enters not knowing that he is about to spend hours of weariness, ridicule, and anguish, and he now blusters for all he's worth. For the moment, then, the gracious and witty Micio can give a wry smile, lift a suave eyebrow and say: *credo iam, ut solet, iurgabit* (79–80)[9]—for a little while, but not for long.

We have been prepared for Demea's entrance (and to some extent prejudiced against him) by Micio's description of him; for the first four acts we see Demea mainly through Micio's eyes, for not only do we accept Micio's initial evaluation of his brother's character, but as we watch Micio exacerbate Demea's worst traits[10] (thereby displaying

---

8 *Prodidisti et te et illam miseram et gnatum,* 692. And, not least of all, he feels himself betrayed, for Aeschinus has not confided in him about Pamphila or about Ctesiphon.

9 *Dixin hoc fore,* 83, whether to the audience or to himself, compounds his boundless self-esteem.

10 See Micio's *scio . . . scio* and *quid ni patiar,* 724ff; here the irony is in the service of egotism. It can be argued that Micio tends to take advantage of Demea's ignorance and helplessness in the second confrontation to dramatize, for his own enjoyment, Demea's folly and his own wisdom, Demea's irascibility and his own self-control.

his own best traits to their best advantage) we come to adopt Micio's attitude to his brother. Indeed, the wrath of Demea increases in proportion as his brother's patience, tolerance, and genial resourcefulness increase. The wrath is comic, of course, by virtue of Demea's wildly excessive responses to what he misunderstands, his unfailing capacity for being victimized, his strength, discipline and purpose mocked and foiled at every turn—there is in this a brilliant handling of a great comic motif: tremendous energy and determination squandered on hopeless and trivial obstacles, the fight to get out of the paper bag. Yet towards the end of the comedy, at the very climax of this comic wrath, after a quick poignant moment of grief, his rage, though remaining comic, is changed to extravagant cunning, and it is the turn of patient benevolence to be mocked:

> derides? fortunatu's qui isto animo sies.
> ego . . . (852–853)

For what I have to say about the nature of the three encounters between Micio and Demea, I had best begin with the implications of *derides*. (First Confrontation, 1.2, 82ff, where Demea, having heard of Aeschinus and the music-girl, comes to rebuke Micio; Second Confrontation, IV, 7, 719ff, where Demea returns to rebuke his brother, this time because he has heard that Aeschinus has seduced Pamphila, and is aghast to hear Micio—who is being rather naughty here, since he amuses himself by not telling all that he might at this point—blandly discussing preparations for the wedding; Third Confrontation, V.3, 787ff, where Demea vents his rage, having at last learned the truth about Ctesiphon and the music-girl.) The debonair gentleman, having got a wife for his adoptive son and a concubine for his nephew, allows himself a coarse joke at the expense of his baffled, angry brother (third confrontation). What is to be done with Ctesiphon's girl? Take her out to the farm and make her perform menial chores? Micio lends his support to these suggestions with heavy irony:

> nunc mihi videre sapere. atque equidem filium placet:
> tum etiam si nolit cogam ut cum illa una cubet. (849–851)

Never, of course, does Micio descend to the sheer crudity of Syrus,[11]

---

[11] See the lecture on cookery, 419ff, and the wild goose chases; his malice at 548, *rideo hunc: primum ait se scire: is solus nescit omnia*, defines the situation for the first four acts but will ricochet in the last.

but it is worth noticing that he can ridicule Demea rather mercilessly as well as read him lectures.[12] The lectures, like the ridicule, issue from an amour-propre, a belief in his moral and intellectual superiority over Demea which nothing in his life has shaken, which nothing in his life will shake, until Demea parodies that superiority with grand wit and so trims his younger brother down to his proper size.

It is true that Demea lectures Micio on every possible occasion, that his lectures are funny and irritating (funny because irritating) even as his rage and self-pity are funny and irritating. But the wounds he gives are clean, and for all his energy and bluster he is not merely narrow-minded and tough but rather desperate and rather lonely as well. We should expect much more of the self-assured Micio; but with a habit of patronizing and a smugness which has its roots in real arrogance he combines callousness and something very close to sophistry:

> homine imperito numquam quicquam iniustiust,
> qui nisi quod ipse fecit nil rectum putat. (98–99)

>   et tu illum tuom, si esses homo,
> sineres nunc facere, dum aetatem licet,
> potius quam, ubi te expectatum eiecesset foras,
> alienore aetate post faceret tamen. (107–110)

> natura tu illi pater es, consiliis ego. (125)

> tamen vix humane patitur; verum si augeam
> aut etiam adiutor sim eius iracundiae,
> insaniam profecto cum illo. (145–147)

> DE. quid facias? si non ipsa re tibi istuc dolet,
> simulare certe est hominis. MI. quin iam virginem
> despondi; res compositast; fiunt nuptiae;
> dempsi metum omnem: haec magis sunt hominis. (736–
> 741)

---

12 See 747ff and 831ff as well as his first speech to Demea. In this regard I call attention to the fact that Micio teases his brother when Demea least needs it; so, in his great scene with Aeschinus, the *quor non ludo hunc aliquantisper* is, for all its dramatic neatness, not without a certain cruelty. Micio's *hilarum ac lubentem fac te gnati in nuptiis*, 756, and *hodie modo hilarum fac te* would be callous if Micio knew what Demea was suffering as he speaks these words.

DE. ceterum
placet tibi factum, Micio? MI. non, si queam
mutare. nunc quom non queo, animo aequo fero.
ita vitast hominum quasi quom ludas tesseris:
si illud quod maxime opus est iactu non cadit,
illud quod cedidit forte, id arte ut corrigas. (736–741)

        multa in homine, Demea,
signa insunt ex quibus coniectura facile fit,
duo quom idem faciunt, saepe ut possis dicere
'hoc licet impune facere huic, illi non licet',
non quo dissimilis res sit sed quo is qui facit. (821–825)

In the first five of these passages (from the first and second confronta-
tions) Demea is *imperitus* and *insanus*, and Micio is the champion of
humanitas, self-assured, infallible (*si esses homo, vix humane, haec magis
sunt hominis*). In the sixth passage (second confrontation) and in the
seventh (third confrontation) Mico begins to make excuses, but there is
not the least admission of error. *Id arte ut corrigas*? Here, as always,
Micio's theory is unquestionably attractive, for we need to be reminded
of making do, easy go, muddling through, *je me débrouille*. And yet—how
much sloth and irresponsibility and self-indulgence does this wisdom
labor to excuse? So, in the final passage, the notion is beautiful, and
one of the glories of humanism is its insistence that we consider the
individual, refuse moralities that cannot allow for discriminations; but,
again, there lurks here a lazy relativism which derides (and has no
business deriding) another great moral truth: that human beings have
to work very hard merely to become decent and to stay barely decent.[13]
The virtues of Micio, then, exclude the virtues of Demea utterly, and
that is their ruin. But Micio is as graceful as Demea is clumsy, and for
the moment the ruin is not apparent, and the self-satisfaction which
ensures the ruin continues blithely as before. Micio has some genial
remarks to offer his brother on the natural goodness of some individuals
(natural gentlemen of Micio's stamp?) and on the dangers of stinginess
in old age (831ff), but his suavest barb and his crowning sophistry
come when he answers Demea's charge (799ff) that Micio has inter-

---

[13] In this scene Micio excuses Ctesiphon's behavior in order to excuse
Aeschinus' involvement; in this way he excuses himself, as he must, since he had seen to
Aeschinus' upbringing.

fered with Ctesiphon after having himself suggested that each father tend to his own son (129ff):

> nam vetus verbum hoc quidemst,
> communia esse amicorum inter se omnia. (803–804)

In listing the defects of Micio's virtues, I am aware that it is not fair to snatch them from context, but I can only hope to dispel Micio's charm by bunching his defects together in such a way that the seductiveness cannot force us to mitigate or ignore those defects. Nor would I wish to pretend that these remarks are unprovoked (it would be impossible to forget that Demea is also smug, and *rasping* in the bargain). What I am concerned to show is that Micio, for all his equability, can be provoked by Demea (even as he can provoke Demea), that what Demea succeeds in eliciting from Micio falls far short of what Micio's own notion of his *humanitas* leads us to expect from him. If the vitality of Demea and the good sense of Micio combine to center our attention on the flaws in Demea's character it is perhaps worth suggesting that our reverence for *liberalitas* and *humanitas* blinds us to the defects of Micio.

Since we have here to do with a carefully imagined representation of a human being, we ought not to be surprised if his virtues are in large measure connected with and even dependent on his vices; nor should we fail to wonder whether playrights who spend their time leafing through philosophers might be thought to have a poor understanding of what playwrighting is. Micio is really generous and really devoted to making and keeping peace?[14] Yes, but to what extent does this trait arise from a temperament which is essentially lazy and squeamish about "scenes," the easy way out? To what extent does his benevolence have its origins in hunger for approval and delight in controlling others by ensuring their gratitude and their dependence? Finally, then, to what extent is this delightful humanist ignorant of his self-contradictions?[15] I feel that it is precisely the disparity between his

[14] See the use of *corrigo* at 593 and 741. In both instances what he has to say is eminently sensible, but in the second instance, considering that it is Demea he speaks to and considering his own failures, the remark is rather pompous.

[15] Wilamowitz remarks (*Hellenistische Dichtung* [Berlin 1924] 75) that Menander alone among Greek writers understood "dass der Mensch erst mit seinem Widerspruch ein vollständiger Mensch ist . . . dass man ihn als Werdenden begreifen muss." The first statement seems to me specially important to this play; the second needs careful qualification.

ignorance and his smugness on the one hand and his wisdom and tolerance on the other that will make him at the end of the play a brilliant and significant figure, and it is precisely the unexpected reversal, the abruptness and poetic justice with which his ignorance and self-contradictions are revealed, which provide the play with its verve and intellectual sting.

The brothers' third confrontation ends with the triumph of Micio, and I now turn to Demea in total defeat. Exhausted from running fool's errands, enraged, humiliated, confused, wholly bitter, this whirlwind of bluster and scorn now sinks down (or so it might be staged) and tries to understand what has happened to him. His difficulty and his success in this regard are more interesting than they are often thought to be. He is not, on the one hand, suddenly transfigured,[16] nor is it a question of his naively supposing that, if only he can manage to ape his brother's *Lebensart*, he can trick his sons into loving him.[17] The opening verses of his soliloquy (855–861) are to be delivered neither pensively (all passion spent, his mind made up, his personality transformed) nor shrilly;[18] he is thinking, he is upset—there are pauses, changes of mood, tempo: a living voice.

[16] See Rieth (supra, n. 1) 107ff, for a lively attack on those who assert "innere Einkehr." See also P. E. Legrand, *The New Greek Comedy*, trs. J. Loeb (London 1917) 241, 442, and W. Schmid, "Menanders Dyskolos und die Timonlegende," *RhM* 102 (1959) 179. I suggest that autoanagnorisis, a sudden recognition of defects in oneself of which one was previously unaware, such recognition being caused by a sudden reversal of circumstances and not infrequently combined with the self-knower's repentance and, if circumstances permit, resolution to amend his life, is rarer in ancient and in Shakespearian drama than some critics assume. (For the theory see F. L. Lucas, *Tragedy* [London 1927 (1957)] 112; L. A. Post, *From Homer to Menander: Forces in Greek Poetic Fiction* [Berkeley, Los Angeles 1951] 47–48, 174; N. Frye, *The Anatomy of Criticism* [Princeton 1957] 212, 302, 346.) So far as I can see redemptive autoanagnorisis is foreign to ancient drama as to modern; in ancient drama even plain autoanagnorisis is rare: Admetus approaches it, perhaps; Charisius in the *Epitrepontes* satisfies the canons of Lucas and Post. For Demea, as for Knemon, we should at most speak very cautiously of a possible modification of character. If we are intent on finding Lucas' "blinding flash," we had best look in personal lyric (Herbert's "My God, I mean myself") or the modern short story (Porter's "Theft").

[17] Rieth (supra, n. 1) 111. "Früher brüstete sich Demea mit seiner überlegenen Einsicht (397, 545—he ignores the trait in Micio); jetzt glaubt er nur noch an Micios Lebensregel, so wie er sie versteht; unfähig zu Selbsterkenntnis ist er nach wie vor . . .". In pointing out what Micio had said at 737 (what I can't change, I endure), Rieth remarks: "Micio ist der echte Vertreter dieser ernsten Lebensweisheit. Demea ist seine Karikatur." The last sentence is neat enough; what Rieth did not consider is that Demea is, for his own purposes, a deliberate caricature.

[18] *Ibid.*: "Weil die irrationalen Kräfte bei ihm die Oberhand gewonnen haben, ist seine Urteilskraft getrübt." Demea's anger and confusion issue in a clear under-

> numquam ita quisquam bene subducta ratione ad vitam
>   fuit
> quin res, aetas, usus semper aliquid adportet novi,
> aliquid moneat: ut illa quae te scisse credas nescias,
> et quae tibi putaris prima, in experiundo ut repudies.
> quod nunc mi evenit; nam ego vitam duram, quam vixi
>   usque adhuc,
> prope iam excurso spatio omitto. id quam ob rem? re ipsa
>   repperi
> facilitate nil esse homini melius neque clementia.

What seems to him now the complete reversal of his beliefs, of his very existence, forces him to utter what tragic choruses had been saying for centuries, but from Demea this is not mellow gnomic wisdom; he has been shocked, and he is shocked into bitter irony: *ego vitam duram*, like *facilitate nil esse melius*, expresses terrible self-pity and savage envy. *Omitto*? Does he mean that he will change his way of life? The closing scenes of the play argue against this interpretation as does the bitter reprise of Micio's self-satisfied *ego hanc clementem vitam* (40ff). With *omitto* he does not announce the necessity for (much less the possibility of) changing his life; rather he admits that his life seems suddenly ugly and hopeless, and he himself a failure. *Omitto* is an angry cry of despair, for he sees himself now as Micio and the others see him, though he does not, as the denouement shows, in any way agree with their estimate. But what is more important, he sees Micio as *he* is:

> ille suam egit semper vitam in otio, in conviviis,
> clemens, placidus, nulli laedere os, adridere omnibus;
> sibi vixit, sibi sumptum fecit; omnes bene dicunt, amant.
> ego ille agrestis, saevos, tristis, parcus, truculentus,
>   tenax . . . (863–866)

These verses express not self-hate but indignation (what has happened is not fair) and jealousy, and from this combination comes the insight he needs: *sibi vixit!* (*carius quam ipse est sibi*, 39). He who gives himself to no one may give himself to everyone, and that without cost. Micio's secret is that he is not responsible to or for anyone or anything, he is carefree,

standing (of Micio's character and of his own predicament) and in utter self-control, nor does Rieth allow for the possibility that "die irrationalen Kräfte" gain in momentum during the course of the speech and subside at its close.

papillon de Parnasse. The butterfly, then, is adored by one and all, while *paterfamilias* and his paraphernalia are swept to oblivion (*duxi uxorem: quam ibi miseriam vidi! nati filii: | alia cura*, 867–868). A calm philosophical speech that issues in humility and repentance? Here the wrath of Demea hits its stride:

> heia autem, dum studeo illis ut quam plurimum
> facerem, contrivi in quaerundo vitam atque aetatem
>   meam:
> nunc exacta aetate hoc fructi pro labore ab eis fero,
> odium: ille alter sine labore patria potitur commoda.
> illum amant, me fugitant; illi credunt consilia omnia,
> illum diligunt, apud illum sunt ambo, ego desertus sum;
> illum ut vivat optant, meam autem mortem expectant
>   scilicet. (868–874)

Each *illum* strikes like a hatchet. He is hated and he hates. Rage begets understanding, and it is the climax of the play:

> ita eos meo labore eductos maxumo hic fecit suos
> paulo sumptu: miseriam omnem ego capio, hic potitur
>   gaudia.

He is still concerned with money, to be sure, but beyond that far he is very jealous and very angry. Why should he not be? *Paulo sumptu sibi vixit.* Then a long and fiendish pause, and then, rather slowly, smiling like an Elizabethan villain:

> age age nunciam experiamur contra, acquid ego possiem
> blande dicere aut benigne facere, quando hoc provocat . . .

It is a Revenge Comedy.

The plot, of course, seems taken care of by this point in the play, and everyone (or so it seems) but Demea is happy. But Demea surprises us by securing the happiness of Sostrata, Hegio, Syrus and his wife, and in so doing manages to secure his revenge as well. In the closing scenes of the play, as in the soliloquy which sets them in motion, reprise yields deft and stinging ironies. Demea parodies the *liberalitas* and the *humanitas* of Micio to expose their limitations and preconceptions, and by this parody he takes his revenge, altering Micio's life radically by an ingenious application of Micio's methods to Micio.

At 909–910 (*unam fac domum; | traduce et matrem et familiam omnem ad nos*) and at 925–927,

> ego vero iubeo et hac re et aliis omnibus
> quam maxume unam facere nos hanc familiam,
> colere, adiuvare, adiungere . . .,

there seems to me a witty echo of Micio's joke at 746–748:

> DE. pro divom fidem,
> meretrix et mater familias una in domo!
> MI. quor non? DE. sanum te credis esse? MI. equidem
> arbitror.

The bachelor father, who had managed to avoid the responsibilities and annoyances of total domesticity and had therefore been able to joke about large households, a prostitute, a matron and two old gentlemen keeping high holiday in a *ménage à quatre*, suddenly sees the walls that create his solitude and independence totter and fall. *Unam fac domum*: "only connect"—a lovely humanistic idea. But the wise, detached gentleman who had viewed the busy lives of others with amused tolerance is now being swept from the decorous periphery of life into its frenzied center. No sooner has his calm establishment more than tripled itself than he is urged to marry Sostrata. The poise and good humor are strained to the breaking point, break, and we may now speak of the wrath of Micio.[19] Having thus transformed the tranquil philosopher to a petulant bourgeois, Demea quite logically proceeds to tamper with his pocketbook. He who did not *have* to support anyone and could therefore use and abuse his money as he chose is now treated to an exquisite reprise of his last piece of advice. At 832ff Micio had hinted that Demea was stingy and had counselled generosity and a wise un-

---

[19] In this scene it is possible that we have another reprise. At 733–734 Demea had said, in respect of Micio's handling of Pamphila, "si non ipsa re tibi istuc dolet / simulare certe est hominis" (a decent human being). Micio had answered that he had arranged the affair with efficiency, tact and sympathy, "haec magis sunt hominis" (a humane and cultivated gentleman). I suggest that at 934 Demea's *si tu sis homo* might be addressed to Micio rather than to Aeschinus, a fine piece of malice if we look back to 733ff. This would require a slight and possible change: *hoc facias* for *hic faciat*.

concern for wealth.[20] The free spirit now sputters as he sinks from easy detachment into human bondage. Hegio, Micio's new relation by marriage, is not very well off, and Demea can quote scripture:

> postremo nunc meum illud verbum facio quod tu, Micio,
> bene et sapienter dixti dudum: 'vitium commune omniumst,
> quod nimium ad rem in senecta attenti sumus': hanc maculam nos decet
> ecfugere; et dictumst vere et reapse fieri oportet. (952–955)

Wives chattering and scolding, children shrieking, the strange sudden appearance of impecunious relations on the wife's side, china clattering, hungry mouths everywhere, money fluttering away, irritations, near despair: the abyss yawns. Where now are equability, inexhaustible patience, scrupulous impartiality? These luxuries are doomed when Micio becomes a part of humanity (at least, humanity as Demea understands it, and he understands it tolerably well), and here the irony of Demea is superb. When Micio concedes to Demea's demands for Hegio, Demea's reprise of Micio's distinction between kinship by blood and kinship by mind and spirit (126) is flawless:

> nunc tu mihi es germanus frater pariter animo et corpore.
> suo sibi gladio hunc iugulo. (957–958)

But the manumission of Syrus and his wife is Demea's finest irony. The license of Syrus represents *liberalitas* gone mad, and Syrus, even more than Aeschinus, represents the potential dangers of *liberalitas*. Thus when Demea pleads for Syrus' freedom,

> postremo hodie in psaltria ista emunda hic adiutor fuit,
> hic curavit: prodesse aequomst: alii meliores erunt,

he echoes the indiscriminate tolerance which Micio had propounded:

> ille quem beneficio adiungas ex animo facit,
> studet par referre, praesens absensque idem erit.

---

[20] The irony was noted by Norwood (supra, n. 4) 119, n. 3; but on 121 he describes Micio's speech as an "exquisite, brief sermon" and asks, "Could anything be better than these gentle, pointed and witty lines?" The description is apt enough, but it ignores the dramatic irony which Norwood has just pointed out.

Aeschinus hardly lived up to his father's hopes; Syrus overturned them. So Demea: "This man fleeced you of money for the whore; naturally when the other slaves observe how you reward industry and initiative, they'll do their damndest to improve on their model."

When the last shot has been fired, Micio cannot restrain himself:

> quid istuc? quae res tam repente mores mutavit tuos?
> quod prolubium? quae istaec subitast largitas?

Demea's answer,

> ut id ostenderem, quod te isti facilem et festivom putant,
> id non fieri ex vera vita neque adeo ex aequo et bono,
> sed ex adsentando, indulgendo et largiendo, Micio,

is not entirely honest, but Micio's question is not quite precise. Demea has not changed his habits, he has ridiculed Micio's;[21] he has done this not so much to show his sons the truth of the matter as to give Micio a taste of his own medicine, to expose his weaknesses to everyone and so humiliate him as he himself had been humiliated. Demea has not changed (nor, probably, will Micio), but he has glimpsed the essential limitations of his personality (as, probably, has Micio; as, perhaps, have we—that is the point): comedy can do no more.

Hodie modo hilarum fac te. Demea has joyfully taken this advice and so become *pater festivissimus*, and the boisterous ingenuity of his revenge, for all its origins in anger and resentment, yields to a gracious close: Micio's *istuc recte* is at once praise for his brother's virtues and a vindication of his own, for the varieties of arrogance have now been exorcised, and, after a ruthless winnowing, the great virtues of parenthood, firmness and tenderness, are reasserted as grand unity.

For all its emphasis on what is worst in us the play is not, ugly. Both heroes are arrogant, lively, and inadequate; neither knows what he is or what he is up against: that is comic enough and human enough. The play's major theme could be the paradox of liberal smugness (its major theme can hardly be the vice of conservative smugness),

---

[21] There is a possible reprise here, *neque adeo ex aequo et bono*, of Micio's *nimium ipse est durus praeter aequomque et bonum.* I should like to offer my thanks to my unsigned referee for his very kind and very useful criticism.

but the play is not so shaped. It is not a question of Demea's being (finally) right and of Micio's being (finally) wrong, nor is it really a question of both men having some right on their side or of both men having some wrong on their side: both men are victims of their illusions and of the limitations those illusions impose on them.

I would prefer to say that the play is about the illusions of fatherhood, or, more precisely, about the arrogance of adults. Experience and maturity? To be sure. But to believe in one's own seasoned infallibility and to inflict that belief on other human beings is probably never very safe, and it may be that experience and maturity are among our most dangerous illusions; add pure *liberalitas* to such fancies and the dangers are past counting. And here, I think, is the reason for the play's sudden shift in point of view and for its peculiar shape. It is easy enough to demonstrate that Demea is more smug than is good for him, and few of us would wish to be like Demea in any case; but Micio, as Webster and Norwood make all too clear, represents a persistent and somewhat treacherous cultural ideal, and to demonstrate his weakness the playwright must catch us off our guard, as pleased with ourselves (for we too are convinced that Demea is neither very bright nor very nice) as Micio is with himself. Lulled to a rapture of self-esteem by the familiar pageant of humanism's irresistible triumph, we are suddenly smacked in the face with the truth about the limitations of our favorite *paideia* and about our own chances for perfection. Whether we are Micios by temperament or Demeas by temperament, we need to be reminded that our predilections do not constitute eternal law, that few of us will be very close to the ideals we profess. Whether Micios or Demeas, we need all to be reminded how ignorant, droll, and selfish we are. In its universal chastening the *Adelphoe* is a triumph of moral dialectic and of mirth.

University of California
Berkeley

12

"Five Lines" and *IG* I², 324

Plato states in the *Republic* (II: 374c): "No man in the world could make himself a competent expert at draughts (πεττευτικός) or the dice (κυβευτικός) who did not practise that and nothing else from childhood but treated it as an occasional business." The complexities of "kubeia" and "petteia" presumably required such practice and skill as to render it unlikely that modern scholarship can recover the details of the games.[1] Of two games common in the ancient literature, "poleis" has been much clarified by W. Ridgeway[2] and R. G. Austin,[3] but "five lines" has been the despair of all commentators, including, most recently, Sir John Beazley, who wrote: "Of course we know next to nothing about the game."[4]

The most thorough study of ancient games is that of Lamer in *RE* (1927) *s.v. Lusoria Tabula.* R. G. Austin (*Antiquity* 14

---

[1] Cf. Plato *Rep.* 333b and 487b. In *Phaedr.* 274d, Plato assigns an Egyptian origin to petteia and kubeia.

[2] *JHS* 16 (1896) 288–290. In this game, the pieces were in the shape of dogs. For markers of various shape, see O. Broneer, *Hesperia* 16 (1947) 241 and pl. 61, no. 20.

[3] *Antiquity* 14 (1940) 263–266. Ridgeway's work does not seem to be known to Austin. Austin (p. 263) states that three games, the names of which are known, were popular among the Greeks. In addition to "poleis" and "pentegramma" there was "diagrammismos." Pollux (9.97) reports that this used also to be called "lines." Hesychius calls it a game of sixty pieces, white and black, moving in spaces (ἐν χώραις). This phrase suggests a game of the checkerboard variety.

[4] *Attic Vase Paintings in the Museum of Fine Arts, Boston* 3 (Boston 1963) 4. Cf. Austin (supra, n. 3) 270: "We are bound to accept the conclusion that this 'sacred line' is not only in itself an insoluble problem without further evidence, but also precludes identification of the Greek game with any other until its nature can be established."

[1940] 237–271) has written an article on Greek board-games. The standard, but out-of-date, book on games in antiquity is that of L. Becq de Fouquières, *Les Jeux des Anciens* (Paris 1873). The numerous metaphorical references to dice and games in the ancient Greek literature have recently been collected by M. N. Kokolakes, Μορφολογία τῆς Κυβευτικῆς Μεταφορᾶς (Athens 1965). In these studies the archaeological material played little part; but in 1963 Beazley brought together such evidence relating to the game of πέντε γραμμαί. The evidence includes representations on many vases, and on two Etruscan mirrors, a clay model and six stone gaming-boards.[5]

   A collection and description of the stone gaming-tables containing five or eleven lines known to me is presented here in the hope that some progress toward elucidation may be made, and that other boards for the game, whether in museums or carved on the stones of Greek buildings, may be identified and published. Our recognition of the table proceeds from the assumption that, although there were several varieties of the tables for "five lines," those having certain features in common would have been used for the same game. Photographs for only four of the gaming-tables have hitherto been published. The illustrations which accompany this article are far from ideal, since several of the tables are stored in covered areas and are much too heavy to be moved into the light; but the photographs do show the various markings on the boards.

   There are at least thirteen of these stone tables which can be recognized as such, as follows: three from Epidauros (including one which the museum guard could not find in 1965), six from the Amphiareion in Attika, one from Corinth, one from Salamis, one from Delos, and one from Cyprus. In addition, Deonna referred to eight boards which were cut on the stylobate of a temple in Delos, some of which are illustrated herein; and I have discovered one incised in the rock at Agios Andreas in the Thyrean plain of the Peloponnesos.

   My interest in the Greek game of "five lines" stems from a study of the Salamis table which had been thought by some scholars to be an abacus.[6] Indeed, the table has been used as a model on which calculations were made permitting the restoration of virtually every

---

[5] See supra, n. 4, 1–6. One of the six boards (*Delos* 18 [Paris 1938] no. 2515, p. 336 and fig. 423) listed by Beazley is not actually meant for this game. In 1965 Professor G. Daux reported to me that the French authorities had not been able to find the stone on Delos. No photograph of it has been published.

[6] *Hesperia* 34 (1965) 131–147.

lacuna in an important but very fragmentary record (*IG* I², 324) containing loans to the Athenian State from sacred treasuries during the period 426/5 to 423/2 B.C. Not only were computations offered, but, since arithmetical accuracy could not be achieved for the desired results relating to the Athenian calendar, the pattern of lines and spaces on the so-called Salaminian abacus was used to show how numerous errors could be made by an ancient operator in moving the pebbles. Rangabé's detailed study in the *editio princeps*, in which he identified the table as a gaming-board, was ignored; and Sir T. Heath's arguments against the abacus theory received only a passing reference.

After a description of the stone gaming-tables for "five lines," I wish to proceed in the second part of this article to a study of recently proposed texts of *IG* I², 324.

1. (plate 1:1) Epidauros. Publications: 'Εφ. 'Αρχ. 1883, 27; P. Kavvadias, *Fouilles d'Épidaure* 1 (Athens 1891), no. 109; C. Blinkenberg, *AthMitt.* 23 (1898) 2–3; *IG* IV, 984. Found in the hieron of Asklepios at Epidauros. Dated possibly in the fourth century B.C. (Fränkel). Inventory No. 513. In 1965, located in the covered southern portico of the museum.

On one of the shorter sides is inscribed the dedication: 'Αρκεσίλαος | Λύσανδρος | ἀνεθέταν.[7]

The table measures 1.13 m. × 0.60 m.; it stands 0.52 m. high. There is a raised rim on all four sides. In the middle a little left of center is a dedication, and on either side five lines parallel to the short ends of the board. The dedication, partly worn away, repeats that on the side of the table, except that the verb is in the plural. The height of the letters is 0.025 m. At both ends of the two longer sides of the table, and parallel to the long side, is a gaming area with five parallel lines or grooves. One of these areas is illustrated in plate 1:1. The distance from the first groove through the fifth measures 0.307 m.; each line is ca. 0.255 m. long. The space between the two lines nearest the center of the table seems to be worn in the shape of an X. Hitherto unnoticed is the fact that there is a curving line, the section of a semicircle, ca. 0.05 m. in length, which lies at its apex about 0.045 m. from the innermost line. Inscribed in the same script as the dedication are six numerals, spaced so that one is on the center line, the others between lines.

---

[7] Text agrees with Kavvadias. Blinkenberg and Fränkel read 'Αρκέσιλλος; but the horizontal hasta of the alpha becomes visible when the stone is moistened.

These numerals are as follows: $M X H - O I$. These characters are common in the Epidauros inventories and are used as monetary signs, as follows: M = 10,000 drachmai; X = 1000; H = 100; $-$ = 10; O = 1 drachma, and I = 1 obol. The height of the numerals varies between 0.015 and 0.02 m. They come about midway in the grooves. The gaming area to the left is likewise made up of five lines or grooves extending over a space of 0.315 m. There is an M 0.025 m. high cut between the first and second lines (counting from the edge). It remains to describe four other lines, each ca. 0.04 m. long, two of them centered above and below the dedication, the other two between the dedication and the gaming area at the right. That above the dedication is a short vertical line, the one below is horizontal; while of the other pair, the one at the top (that is, opposite the beginning of the dedication) is horizontal, and the lower one vertical, thus making an alternating pattern.

In all ten lines of the games proper, the grooves are worn much more deeply at the ends than in the middle; they are fairly wide, and suggest much wear from the movement of "pieces."

2. (plates 1:2 and 1:3) Epidauros. Found beside Number 1. Publication: Blinkenberg, *AthMitt.* 23 (1898) 3–4. In 1965, in the covered southern portico of the museum.

The table measures 1.27 m. × 0.585 m.; it stands 0.485 m. high. There is a bevelled rim on all four sides, rising to a height of 0.015 m. The board originally contained two large gaming areas for "five lines" on either side; four additional gaming areas were added as graffiti (pl. 1:2). The grooves of the gaming area on the right half (pl. 1:3) have been worn as deep as 0.015 m. The space between the fourth and fifth lines has been worn into the shape of an X. A semicircle extends outwards from the fifth groove, that nearest the center of the table; its diameter is 0.05 m. The area covered by five grooves is 0.33 m. wide; the grooves are 0.075–0.08 m. apart, as measured on center. The five-grooved area on the left covers a space of 0.32 m. A semicircle likewise abuts on the fifth groove, this the one nearest the edge. A straight line was incised ca. 0.055 m. from the fifth groove, parallel to, and about two-thirds the length of, the groove. There are four short lines, in the same alternating pattern as on Number 1, in the center in corresponding positions.

In the center of the table, another gaming area for "five

lines," 0.22 m. in width, was incised with very shallow lines, 0.246 m. in length. Three other five-lined areas were added in the right half of the table, two (0.063 m. and 0.11 m. in width) between the original gaming area and the front bevelled edge, one (0.065 m. wide) between the grooved area and the back bevelled edge.

3. Epidauros. Reported as found outside the Museum. Publications: Blinkenberg, *AthMitt.* 23 (1898) 4–5; *IG* IV 988 (text only). The museum guards could not locate this table in July 1965. Dimensions of the partly preserved table are given as 0.78 m. × 0.48 m. × 0.51 m.; the right part is lost. On the side, a fourth-century dedicatory inscription: ᾿Εργίλος ᾿Αθαύμαντος ἀνέθεν. Blinkenberg's drawing shows five parallel grooves or furrows, followed by three parallel lines. The furrows are represented as deeper at their ends. Whether the gaming area was originally one of eleven lines, or whether the three thin lines are part of a second gaming area, as in Number 2, cannot be determined from Blinkenberg's sketch.

4–9. Amphiareion, Oropos. The following six tables are from the Amphiareion at Oropos. Except for Number 6, they were originally published by Leonardos, ᾿Εφ. ᾿Αρχ. 1925/6, 44–45 and republished by Lang, *Hesperia* 26 (1957) 275–276 as abaci. In 1965, Number 4 was fastened to the wall of the portico surrounding the museum (hence in deep shadow) and Numbers 5 to 8 were on the ground nearby. Number 9 lies in the open in the western part of the sanctuary in the area containing pedestals of statues.

4. (plates 2:1 and 2:2) Leonardos, No. 156. Table broken into several pieces but more or less completely preserved, measuring 1.28 m. × 0.78 m. × 0.085 m. Parallel to the short sides are eleven lines 0.38 m. in length, each line ending in large dots, deeply incised. The third, sixth, and ninth lines are bisected by X's. A semicircle ca. 0.03 m. in radius extends outward from the midpoint of the first and eleventh lines. At the bottom, as it is exhibited, are eleven numerals, 0.025 m. in height, as follows:

ΧΓΗΗϜΔΓΗΙϹΤΧ

In the upper part of the board, as it is exhibited, are five lines parallel to the long sides (hence, at right angles to the eleven lines), 0.24 m. in length, likewise with pronounced dots at the ends. A semicircle extends outward from the rightmost line.

5. (plate 3:1) Leonardos, No. 157. Left half of a table, measuring 0.80 m. × 0. 64 m., with a raised edge in three bands 0.01 m. wide. Four parallel lines, each 0.32 m. long, are preserved. There are traces of a semicircle, ca. 0.033 m. in diameter, abutting from the inner line. The distance from the innermost line to the left edge of the table is 0.59 m. The surface is very worn, and of the nine numerals which Leonardos read in 1925/6, I could make out only four, the first and the last three:

ΜΤϜΧϞΗϞΔΓ

The numerals, 0.023 m. in height, begin 0.14 m. from the left edge and fall in the upper space. The series of numerals was presumably completed with the signs for a drachma, an obol, and possibly a half-obol.

6. (plate 3:2) Half of a table preserving the original surface from three sides, 0.275 m. in width and 0.32 m. in length. A smooth band 0.026 m. wide runs around the edge of the gaming area. The most interesting feature about this table is that the area within the band was carefully and, it seems, intentionally, rough-picked. Parts of six parallel lines, each 0.20 m. in length, are preserved. The distance between the first five of the lines is uniformly 0.042 m.; but that between the fifth and the partially preserved sixth line is 0.054 m. A circle ca. 0.02 m. in diameter was centered on the sixth line. In the center of the third line where some of the other tables have an X, the surface has been hollowed out more or less in the form of an X.

7. (plate 3:3) Leonardos, No. 159. Fragment of a table measuring 0.38 m. × 0.23 m. × 0.137 m. One original edge is preserved with a raised band 0.045 m. wide. Parts of two parallel lines are preserved. From the left broken edge, as illustrated, to the first line there is an uninscribed space of 0.24 m.

8. (plate 3:4) Leonardos, No. 160. Fragment of a table measuring 0.45 m. × 0.235 m. × 0.10 m. Parts of two original sides are preserved, as well as parts of seven deep-cut lines with a segment of a circle 0.023 m. in diameter apparently centered on the sixth line. The lines begin 0.032 m. from the long side, and the first line was inscribed 0.103 m. from the short side of the table.

9. (plate 3:5) Leonardos, No. 158. Completely preserved but heavily weathered table measuring 1.305 m. × 0.645 m. × 0.163

m. There is a raised edge with moulding ca. 0.05 m. wide. The main part of the table is occupied by a gaming area with eleven parallel grooves, each 0.32 m. in length. The grooves are ca. 0.06 m. apart, and are most deeply worn at either end and in the center. There is a recessed area 0.02 m. from the center of the leftmost line. At diagonally opposite corners of the table are two small gaming areas each having five parallel lines; the lines of the upper measure 0.05 m. in length, those of the lower, 0.08 m.

10. Corinth. Found in a well of one of the shops of the South Stoa in the Agora at Corinth, 1933. Photographs published by O. Broneer, *AJA* 37 (1933) 563; *Corinth* 1, Part 4 (Princeton 1954) 64 and pl. 15; and J. H. Kent, *Corinth* 8, Part 3 (Princeton 1966) 13–14 and pl. 6, No. 42.

Parts of five lines are preserved at the upper edge. In the lower left corner is inscribed the name *ΔΙΟΣ ΒΟΥΛΕΟΣ* and in the lower right corner the three letters *ΔΑΜ*, interpreted as the beginning of the genitive of Demeter in Doric. In the line below the *ΔΑΜ* – – – is preserved a nu preceded by a letter first read by Broneer as a nu or an eta, then as a mu (undotted) and finally by Kent as an eta (undotted).[8] Between the two names were incised the large numerals *X H Δ*. Directly above and in the gaming area, the three numerals were repeated in smaller form. Of the *X* and the *Δ* there can be no doubt. The *X* is to the left of the first line; the *Δ* to the right of the fifth line. For the *H*, the mason seems to have used part of the midmost of the five lines for the left vertical stroke; the lower half of the right vertical is worn away, as are the other lines in this area.[9]

11. (plate 4:1) Salamis. Marble plaque found in 1845 on the island of Salamis. The marble contains much mica and traces of piedmontite, and, therefore, is most probably from Mount Pentele.

[8] The photograph suggests a mu until we compare it with the mu in the line above, when we see that the latter has slanting strokes, the former upright.

[9] Kent, but not Broneer, regarded the gaming area as "several centuries" later than the slab itself. I would infer from Broneer's description (*Corinth* 1, Part 4 [Princeton 1954] 62–64) that the table was overthrown in the destruction of the South Stoa in 146 B.C.; and therefore if the letters of the names are second century in date, as Kent believes, the gaming area must be of this date also. However, Kent described the gaming area as "crudely scratched." With this I cannot agree. To be sure, there is a tau which is graffito and poorly cut. Moreover, the lines are not entirely straight; but the other numerals, especially those in the lower line, are of very good workmanship. I see no reason to reject Broneer's assumption that the table was originally designed as a gaming board.

Because of the many impurities in the marble, the slab must have been difficult to dress evenly. The depressions, including one from lines 2 to 7, are original, to judge by the uniform depth of the lines.

Publications include Rangabé, *RA* 3 (1846) 294–304,[10] with comments by Letronne, pp. 305–308, and A. J. H. Vincent, pp. 401–405; Rangabé, *Antiquités Helléniques* 995, pp. 590–596 and pl. 19; W. Kubitschek, *Numismatische Zeitschrift* 31 (1899) 393–398 and pl. 24 (with a description of the board by A. Wilhelm); T. Heath *History of Greek Mathematics* 1 49–51; D. E. Smith, *History of Mathematics* 2 (Boston 1925) 163 (with photograph);[11] *IG* II² 2777; Lang, *Hesperia* 26 (1957) 275; Pritchett, *Hesperia* 34 (1965) 138–140.

The table measures 1.50 m. in length, 0.75 m. in width, and 0.07 m. in thickness. It is now displayed on the outside wall of the Epigraphical Museum in Athens; I have not seen the undersurface.[12] At a distance of 0.027 m. from one short side there are five parallel lines 0.205 m. long at intervals of 0.027–0.028 m. At a distance of 0.527 m. from the innermost of the five lines there begin eleven parallel lines each 0.38 m. in length, at intervals of 0.035 m. Each of these lines ends in rather deeply-cut points. The eleventh line is 0.277 m. from the other short side. A transverse line bisects the eleven parallel lines and divides them into two equal parts. The third, the sixth, and the ninth of these lines are marked with a cross at the point of intersection with the transverse line. The arms of the crosses are 0.02 m. in length. From the innermost of the eleven horizontal lines extends a semicircle which at its apex is 0.03 m. from the base. In turn, from the innermost of the five parallel lines is a partly preserved semicircle, the apex of which is 0.017 m. from the line.[13]

---

[10] The drawings of Rangabé (p. 296), Nagl (*Zeitschrift für Mathematik und Physik*, suppl. vol. 44 [1899]), pl. 2 (opposite p. 357), and T. Heath, *History of Greek Mathematics* 1 (Oxford 1921) 50 reverse the direction of the numerals at the short end. This same error is perpetuated in the drawings of an imaginary abacus (Lang, *Hesperia* 33 [1964] pls. 25–27), for which she (p. 148) claimed as a model this Salamis plaque. On the Salamis stone, the numerals faced outwards, not towards the center of the plaque.

[11] Smith's photograph, like the one in plate 4:1, shows heavy pencilling of the numerals and of some lines. This pencilling causes a distorted effect in the appearance of the unpencilled lines. In my plate, I asked the engraver to retouch the median line and the two semi-circles.

[12] Wilhelm reported that the underside was polished and hollowed out to a thickness of only 0.045 m. in the center.

[13] Wilhelm, who had the advantage of examining this heavy slab before it was securely fastened to the wall of the museum, gave an accurate and detailed description, which has generally been overlooked in subsequent discussions.

Along two long sides and the short side nearer the eleven lines are cut three series of numerals, 0.013–0.015 m. in height. All face toward the outer rims of the table. Two sequences are of eleven numbers; the series on one long side has two more characters than the others. The numeral signs are arranged in descending order, ranging from 1,000 drachmai to 1/8 obol, the two additional characters being Ϝ (= 5,000 drachmai) and *T* (= talent or 6,000 drachmai). The lowest and highest money units are at the two ends of the scale. The system of notation is that employed regularly by the Athenians.[14]

12. (plate 5:1) Delos. Published by Deonna, *Délos* 18 (Paris 1938) 336 and pl. 831. A rectangular plaque of white marble found at Delos in the area of the theatre. It measures 0.63 m. in length, 0.25 m. in width, and 0.06 m. in thickness. It is inscribed with eleven lines parallel to the short end, covering approximately half of the surface. There is no rim; the lines extend the width of the stone. The width of the lines is as much as 0.005 m. The distance between lines is 0.02–0.025 m. In the middle of every third line is cut an X, the arms of which are 0.04 m. long.

13. (plates 5:2–5:4) Delos. Deonna described numerous gaming areas inscribed on the steps of one temple as follows: "Sur le soubassement du petit temple situé entre le monument de granit et le côté Ouest de l'Agora des Italiens. Quatre jeux de ce type sur la face N., quatre sur la face E., et d'autres encore, plus ou moins distincts. Leur largeur est de 0.21–0.22 m., leur hauteur de 0.17 à 0.20 m."[15] Later, in 1959, H. Gallet de Santerre (*Délos* 24, 38, n. 2 and pls. 4 and 19) published drawings showing the position of the various gaming areas on the steps of the "Létoon." In pl. 5:2, one of the gaming areas of the north step is illustrated. Two others to the right have been worn away. In each case, there seem to be five lines bisected by a more lightly cut central line. The ends of each of the five lines are hollowed out in the form of circles. A semicircle abuts from the first line.[16] Plates 5:3 and 5:4 show two gaming areas on the heavily-worn eastern step. In

14 See Tod, *BSA* 18 (1911/12) 100–101.
15 *Délos* 18 (Paris 1938) 337. For other games incised on the stylobate of ancient temples, see D. M. Liddell, *Chessmen* (New York 1937) plate facing p. 115 (Eleusis) and A. R. Goddard, "Nine Men's Morris," *Saga-Book of the Viking Club* 2 (1897–1900) 382 (Parthenon).
16 The semicircle was not noted by Deonna; but it appears clearly in the photograph. It is not incised as deeply as the five lines, but is of a character with the bisecting line.

these examples, there is no center line, but the ends of the lines are hollowed out, and the semicircles can be detected. Gallet de Santerre's drawings failed to reproduce the semicircles. I owe the three photographs to the kindness of Professor G. Daux, Director of the French School in Athens.

14. (plate 6:1) Cyprus. Limestone block found in 1961 in Dhekelia on Cyprus. Published by I. Michaelidou-Nicolaou, *BCH* 89 (1965) 122–127 (with photograph). The block measures 0.585 m. × 0.23 m. × 0.145 m. This *lusoria tabula* has eleven parallel lines with irregular circles in the middle of the third, sixth, and ninth lines. A semicircle abuts on the eleventh line. The workmanship is poor. The letter-forms of the graffiti inscribed on the table were said by the editor to date from the third century B.C.

15. (plates 6:2 and 6:3) Agios Andreas. Gaming area inscribed on the native rock within the circuit walls of an ancient site located at the extreme southeastern corner of the Thyrean plain in the Peloponnesos.[17] The rock was dressed down to form a relatively smooth surface measuring 1.90 × 0.70 m. The markings for the game were inscribed in the center of the dressed area. There are five parallel lines, 0.22 to 0.25 m. in length, bisected by a median line of 0.215 m. The lines are about 0.05 m. apart. Each ends in a large point or circle on either side. A rough semicircle, measuring 0.04 m. in height with a base of 0.07 m., rests on the first line. Below the fifth line, not touching it, are the letters $A\ \Theta$. The height of the alpha is 0.07 m., of the theta 0.055 m. The theta is dotted. The center of the alpha is opposite the median line.

This rock-cut game was drawn to my attention by Dr. Ronald Stroud when we visited the area in the summer of 1965. The rock on which the game was inscribed lies about forty-five yards SSE of the southern temenos wall of the church of Agios Andreas at the highest point of the hill, and only four meters inside the circuit wall of the site.

In the table below are presented eleven features shared in common by two or more of the fifteen games published above:

	Numbers
Board of eleven lines (5)	6, 8, 9, 12, 14
Board of five lines (5)	1, 2, 3, 13, 16

[17] For a convenient description of the site, see J. G. Frazer, *Pausanias* 3 (London 1897) 307–308.

Board of five and eleven lines (2)	4, 11
Numerals in areas of lines (2)	1, 10
Numerals along side of table (4)	4 (11), 5 (8+), 10, 11 (11, 11 and 13)
Bisecting line (3)	11, 13, 15
Semicircle on end of line (7)[18]	1, 2 (*bis*), 4 (*tris*), 11, 13, 14, 15
X or O on 3rd, 6th, 9th lines (6)	4, 6, 8 (6th line), 11, 12, 14
Grooves worn at ends of lines (4)	1, 2, 3, 9
Points at ends of lines (4)	4, 11, 13, 15
Names of deities on board (2)	10, 15[19]

In addition to the stone games, there are two ancient artifacts which are regarded as illustrations of the πέντε γραμμαί, as well as a third which is an obvious example. One is a small painted clay model of a gaming board (plate 7:1), originally from Athens but now in the National Museum in Copenhagen.[20] Beazley dates the model to the second quarter of the sixth century. On the surface of the board are engraved nine lines. Each end of these lines is occupied by an oval counter which J. L. Ussing, the editor of the *editio princeps*, regarded as pieces or men.[21] Two dice are preserved, and traces of a third. The upper face of the preserved dice shows 6 dots; so it has been assumed that on the third die the 6 also lay uppermost.[22] Accordingly, the conclusion has been drawn that what is represented here is the "lucky throw," the τρὶς ἕξ referred to by the watchmen in Aeschylus *Agamemnon* 33.[23]

The second artifact is the mirror illustrated by E. Gerhard, *Etruskische Spiegel* 5 (Berlin 1884) pl. 109 and pp. 144–146. Gerhard's illustration is reproduced in plate 7:2. Two warriors, Achilles and probably Ajax, are represented as holding on their knees a gaming-board on which are drawn seven parallel lines. The circles at the ends of each line are taken by Gerhard to be the men or pieces; the two rectangular

---

[18] These semicircles are suggestive of what E. Falkener (*Games Ancient and Oriental* [London 1892]) calls in other games "Entering division" or Home.

[19] After the analogy of Number 10, the letters *A Θ* on Number 15 may be restored as ʼAθ[αναίας].

[20] N. Breitenstein, *Catalogue of Terracottas* (Copenhagen 1941) pl. 19, no. 171.

[21] *Videnskab. Selsk. Skrifter*, 5th Raekke, *Hist. og philos. Afdeling*, 5th Bind, 3 (Copenhagen 1884) 149–151 and 172. Ussing's illustrations are reproduced in plate 19.

[22] Blinkenberg, *AthMitt.* 23 (1898) 8.

[23] Cf. E. Fränkel, *Aeschylus' Agamemnon* 2 (Oxford 1950) 21–22.

objects between the second and third and third and fourth lines are the dice.

Since games of seven and nine lines are not otherwise attested, editors have generally taken the miniature representations on the clay model and the mirror to be free copies of the eleven-line form of the πέντε γραμμαί.

The third example is the recently published terracotta table found at Vari in Attika and dated to the "middle protoattic" period.[24] There are five straight lines on the table, with small hollows at the end of each line.[25]

Reference may also be made to the amphora in the Boston Museum, published by Beazley, which shows on both sides of the vase Achilles and Ajax playing a board-game. On one side eleven pieces are ranged at equal intervals; the other side seems to have only eight game-pieces. Ajax extends two fingers and the thumb. On an Exekias vase in the Vatican, Ajax utters the word τρία. In both cases, Beazley believes that the gesture and the word indicate what Ajax has scored with the dice. On a black-figured lekythos in Boston, Achilles says τέτταρα φέρω, Ajax δύο φέρω.[26]

Of the literary evidence relating to "five lines" there is little to be added to what Rangabé collected over one hundred years ago in the *Antiquités Helléniques*. He maintained, on the authority of Eustathios, that on the five-line board, the middle, or third, line was the ἱερὰ γραμμή; and this remains the opinion of Lamer.[27] On the eleven-line board, he stated that the sacred line was between the five lines on each half of the board. For this arrangement he cited Pollux 9.97, and this remains the opinion of Beazley.[28] Apparently, there were variations of the game. Even the number of dice used might vary. As we have seen above, the clay model in Copenhagen shows three dice, the mirror published by Gerhard two.[29] Lamer has noted about ancient games in

[24] B. Kallipolites, *Archaiologikon Deltion* 18 (1963), Part I, 123–124. Kallipolites publishes several photographs, especially plate 54, 1.

[25] Depressions have generally been interpreted as designed to hold the pieces; cf. the commentary on the gaming table published in T. J. Dunbabin, *Perachora* 2 (Oxford 1962) 131–132.

[26] For references, see Beazley (supra, n. 4) 5.

[27] *RE s.v. Lusoria tabula* (1927) 1997.

[28] See supra, n. 4, 3. Austin (supra, n. 3, 268), however, entertained the possibility of five vertical and five horizontal lines, for which, however, there seems to be no archaeological evidence.

[29] Cf. also the phrase δύο φέρω.

general that the number of dice differed, as might the number of participants.[30]

Pollux states, "Each of the players had five pieces on five lines."[31] It is to be noted that in all of the artistic representations, there is never more than one piece at the end of a line. Furthermore, as we have seen, many of the gaming-boards share two characteristics: the wear is much heavier at the ends of the lines (in four examples)[32] and there are points at each end (four examples).[33]

A final word may be said about the provenience of the stone gaming-boards. There are several notices in the ancient literature that games were played in sanctuaries, especially in the temple of Athena Skiras. See Eustathios *ad Ody.* 1.107: καὶ ὅτι ἐσπουδάζετο ἡ κυβεία οὐ μόνον παρὰ Σικελοῖς, ἀλλὰ καὶ 'Αθηναίοις· οἳ καὶ ἐν ἱεροῖς ἀθροιζόμενοι ἐκύβευον, καὶ μάλιστα ἐν τῷ τῆς Σκιράδος 'Αθηνᾶς τῷ ἐπὶ Σκίρῳ.[34] The provenience of the Salamis board is unfortunately not expressly given; but Rangabé, publisher of the *editio princeps*, associated it with the Temple of Athena Skiras on Salamis. The tables from Epidauros were found in the hieron, and two were dedicated by two of the *hieromnemones*.[35] The six tables from the Amphiareion were excavated within the precincts of the sanctuary.[36]

Apart from the dramatic and musical part of Greek festivals, our preserved literature gives few clues as to what transpired on festival days. Since the *panegyris* often lasted several days, it has been inferred that much went on which seems to have had little connection with religion.[37] Indeed, the ancient, as the modern, *panegyris* was a

[30] See supra, n. 27, pp. 1943 and 1921–1922.

[31] 9.97. This limitation on the number of pieces makes it unlikely that the game resembled backgammon. S. G. Owen in his notes on Ovid *Tristia* 2 (Oxford 1924) 257, compares it to "Gobang" and Irish "Top Castle," games in which a player's pieces must be arranged in a row. A table for a rare game played by American Indians is illustrated by S. Culin, "Games of the North American Indians," *Annual Report of United States Bureau of American Ethnology* 24 (1907) 162, fig. 194. A slab is inscribed with an ellipse with five transverse lines. There are small circles at either end, and in the middle. Two men play, each having one piece which is entered at opposite ends of the line; see H. J. R. Murray, *A History of the Board-Game* (Oxford 1952) 148. Murray (p. 28) wrongly identified a modern Cretan game called pentalpha as pente grammai.

[32] Numbers 1, 2, 3, and 9.

[33] Numbers 4, 11, 13, and 15.

[34] Cf. the Etym. M., the Souda, Harpokration, and Steph. *s.v.* Σκίρος.

[35] See Fränkel, *IG* IV 237.

[36] Dr. Markellos Mitsos informs me that two of the longest tables from the Amphiareion published above were found with gaming-boards of the checkerboard pattern.

[37] See W. K. C. Guthrie, *The Greeks and their Gods* (London 1950) 268.

medley of religion, art, athletics, and recreation. The discovery of six gaming-boards of one type—there are known to be unpublished boards of other games—at the one sanctuary alone is clear evidence of how some of the crowd found their amusement.

To return to the question with which this investigation started, is the Salamis board (Number 11) a gaming-board or an abacus? It is now clear that it shares many features with other tables, which are admitted to be gaming-boards, and must have been *designed* for games. The first scholar to urge that it was an abacus was A. J. H. Vincent.[38] He argued that the calculator must have used the spaces between lines for computations and that the points at the ends of each line were for the purpose of attaching metal thread or strips, which would have helped to keep the counters within columns. This theory of attaching metal threads was refuted by Rangabé.[39] Hultsch[40] and Nagl,[41] who among others revived the theory of an abacus, argued that the five-line part of the Salaminian board was used for the computation of obols and their fractions.[42] All overlooked the fact that those tables that exhibit wear show that the deepest grooves were made on, and not between, the lines. Moreover, these same scholars show the line of numerals at the short end of the Salaminian table as facing inwards to be read by an operator standing at the long side;[43] whereas in fact these numerals face outwards in a position awkward for a calculator who must then read the sums upside down, so to speak.

But the chief reason for assuming that the table was an abacus seems to have been the series of monetary numerals at the edges. Our comparative study shows, however, that these same numerals could appear in the area of the lines;[44] and some method of scoring may have been used comparable to that in some modern card games where the points are kept in terms of dollars and cents, although each "point" may be equivalent to only a small fraction of a cent when the winner is paid off.

[38] *RA*, première série, 3 (1846) 401–405.
[39] *Antiquités Helléniques* 591.
[40] *RE s.v.* Abacus (1894).
[41] *Zeitschrift für Mathematik und Physik* 44 (1899), suppl. vol. 9, 337–357.
[42] In the Lang method, this final part of the operation was performed off the board.
[43] See Nagl (supra, n. 41) pl. 2, and Lang, *Hesperia* 33 (1964), pls. 25–27.
[44] Numbers 1 and 10.

My aim has been to establish the purpose for which the table was *designed*. One can of course argue that a table originally intended for games could have been used at some time for an abacus. This argument might hold for any sort of table. Indeed, we are told that a table or tablet, covered with sand in which lines and figures could be drawn, was used by the ancients in geometry and arithmetic.[45] Such was the abacus used by school-children. But before the modern scholar builds a theory of ancient calculation on the design of one particular table, he should offer some evidence other than his own system that the table was so used.

The conclusion that the Salaminian table (Number 11) was designed for a gaming board opens the door for a restudy of recently proposed texts of *IG* I² 324. These restored texts were obtained by computations simulated on a board like the Salaminian table, which was taken to be an abacus. But first, before a discussion of restorations, it may be shown that a major error has been made in some reports of readings for the preserved text.

Line 32 of *IG* I² 324.[46] A photograph of the fragment showing the letters of this line was published in plate 57 of *Hesperia* 34 (1965), and the identical photograph was reproduced in *Phoenix* 20 (1966) 215. Only a trace, if that much, of the first numeral, which corresponds to the 27th letter-space as counted from the original left edge, can be seen (the third complete line from the top of the plate). There is no palaeographical justification for reading this numeral as an *H* (undotted).[47] As Professor J. Caskey observed, "only the right-hand side of the vertical groove is preserved, the stone being broken along this groove." No one can say for certain whether the upright was joined at the left by a horizontal stroke.

The numeral in the next preserved letter-space, the 28th from the original left edge, gives rise to considerable dispute. There is good reason for this. No restoration for the sums itemized in the third year of the document can even be attempted unless one can recover this

45 Plutarch, *Cat. Min.* 70; Cicero, *N.D.*2.18.48; Sen. *Epi.* 74, 27; Apul. *Apol.* 16, p. 426; Pers. 1.131.

46 I am again indebted to Mr. Peter Solon for his generous assistance with the mathematics. Mr. Borimir Jordan kindly arranged to have the photographs taken in Athens. They were paid for by the Committee on Research of the University of California.

47 *Hesperia* 33 (1964) 166.

numeral, which gives the final figure for the principal of the third payment. Of the four payments of the year in question (424/3 B.C.), the preserved letters give us only the interest of the first and third payments complete and the principal of the second payment in part (the first five letter-spaces—unfortunately, the least significant part). For the sums for the year not one numeral is preserved, either of the principal or of the interests.

The striking fact about the commentary which accompanies plate 57 of *Hesperia* 34 (1965), as well as the commentary on the same two numerals which appeared the previous year,[48] is that the two editions offer no report of a new inspection of the stone. The photograph is out of focus in the critical area, as can be seen by comparing the right half of the plate with the left half. Moreover, a deep shadow has been cast by the lighting (from the left) into the deeply recessed area on the stone, so that quite a false impression about the condition of the surface is given. The commentary is largely historical, and shows that since the discovery of the fragment, ca. 1838, some editors have reported only the uprights of two vertical strokes; others have read in their text of letter-space 28 a numeral representing the sign for one hundred drachmai. Klaffenbach's report of what he sees today on the Berlin paper squeeze is included. Finally, a reference has been made to what Meritt reported in his publication of 1928. But the stone is in existence, and the critical question is not whether the authority of Pittakys, Kirchoff, Kirchner, Caskey (plus his distinguished conferees), and Pritchett, is greater than that of Rangabé, Ross, Boeckh, and Meritt, or vice versa. Caskey's description, made from the stone and concurred in by at least two of our most eminent living epigraphists, has been praised as a model of descriptive detail, and must take precedence over all previous reports which, in any case, with one exception lack any detailed account.

As the stone is available for examination, anyone who disagrees with Caskey's 1949 report has only to look at it. Since 1949 I have examined the critical letter-space both alone and in the presence of other epigraphists. Moreover, I hold communications from scholars who have examined the stone when I was not present. Of these, none has been prepared to say that the reading *must* be an *H*; nor has there been anyone who does not agree that the uprights may perfectly well stand for obols. In plate 8:1 I offer one photograph which shows the

---

[48] *Hesperia* 33 (1964) 152.

general area. The critical letter-space appears at the beginning of the fifth line. In addition, because of the lengthy discussion of the numeral in the recent literature, and in order to afford some control over further speculation, I offer three close-up views (pls. 8:2–8:4) of the letter-space in question.[49] These photographs, taken by Emile Serafis, Athens, show the numeral under different types of lighting. Slightly more than half of the lower part of the letter-space has been eroded away.[50] The erosion begins far to the right of the disputed numeral and follows the outline of at least seven discolored dots or scars, and carries down into the line below. Similar scars appear in other parts of the fragment, and can be seen in plate 8:1 and, in particular, in plate 8:2 at the top of the photograph. The statement that the weathering follows the outline of a Greek numeral is incorrect; rather, it is in the form of a shallow arc, as can be seen in plate 8:2. Three of the dots which helped to shape the outline of the eroded area appear to the right of the numeral in plate 8:3. Apparently water or acids dissolved the calcite along the outline of the dots. There is no trace of a horizontal hasta.[51] A paper squeeze gives an entirely false impression because three of the dots are in roughly horizontal alignment in the center of the space. Furthermore, a satisfactory paper squeeze of the fragment cannot be made because of the depth of the dissolved area. Hard pounding would only cause a hole in the paper. The photographs show, as well as can be, the great depth of the erosion and establish quite clearly that the outline of the eroded area does not conform to the shape of any Greek numeral.

It has been stated that the eroded area contains an "island."[52] However, the erosion is as deep within the lower part of

[49] These photographs are enlarged approximately three times.

[50] The outline of the erosion is brought out even more clearly on the photograph of a latex squeeze published in my *Ancient Athenian Calendars on Stone* (Berkeley 1963) pl. 20a.

[51] Cf. Meritt in 1928 (*The Athenian Calendar* [Cambridge, Mass., 1928] p. 27): "all trace of the central bar of the *H* is missing." Less clear is Meritt's statement in 1965 (*Hesperia* 34, 236): "all the strokes of the final *H* are preserved, or where not preserved unblemished preserved in the depths of the erosion." The first statement is accurate, the second is not.

[52] The introduction of this word into the account was unfortunate, for it was not based on an inspection of the stone. Miss Lang first used the word, writing in 1964 (*Hesperia* 33, 152, n. 7): "Pritchett's new photograph shows the less eroded island between the lower uprights which confirms Meritt's reading." The photograph in question (Pritchett, *Ancient Athenian Calendars*, supra, n. 50, 397, pl. 20a) is of a latex squeeze, not of the stone. In 1965 (*Hesperia* 34, 238) Meritt repeated the word, but the significant fact is that in his 1928 description (*The Athenian Calendar*, p. 127) when he was working from the stone, the word was

the hole (the south position, so to speak) as within the upper (the north position); and no Greek numeral was shaped with a horizontal stroke at the base; so the eroded area cannot outline an ancient numeral. An "island" therefore, could not affect the reading one way or another.[53] But in any case, there is no "island."[54] The calcite may have dissolved a little more along the edges of the hole, but if so, it is not perceptible to the naked eye.

The above observations are based on an inspection of the stone itself. They accord in all essentials with the description made by Caskey and his associates at the American School and the Epigraphical Museum in Athens, and my comments are intended to be merely supplementary. The continued reading of the two numerals as if they were clear (undotted) is wholly unjustified. Fresh observations may indeed be made, but only starting from the stone itself.

According to Lang and Meritt, the numerals are hundred-drachmai signs, and they are read without dots beneath.[55] But if the original text contained obol signs, this text would be quite erroneous; and, epigraphically, obol signs are as possible as hundred-drachmai signs. The following three readings are possible:

$$\mathsf{H\overset{.}{I}\overset{.}{I}, \quad [I]\overset{.}{I}\overset{.}{I}\overset{.}{I}, \quad H\overset{.}{H}}$$

All must be read with dots.

The only honest conclusion is that, since the stone does not permit certainty, the recovery of the sums of the third year is impossible. But of one thing I am certain. By using the methods of Lang and Meritt, one can produce a text which will exhibit a regular prytany calendar. This means that one may assume: (1) errors by the stonemasons; (2) errors in the additions; and (3) errors in the manipulation of the pebbles by the abacus operator, and one may at the same time (1) introduce a formula which cannot be found in the many entries which appear on

---

not used. Finally, in 1966, M. F. McGregor (*Phoenix* 20, 214) again referred to "an island of less eroded surface." Clearly McGregor in this inscription, as in the others he discusses, was not working from the stone.

[53] The "island" clearly cannot be on the same plane as that of the face of the stone; see Pritchett, *Hesperia* 34 (1965) 132.

[54] Although there is no island in this particular spot on line 32, there is an island, as I indicated in *Hesperia* 34 (1964) 132, in the interspace between lines 32 and 33, where no ancient text was inscribed.

[55] *Hesperia* 33 (1964) 166.

the stone,[56] and (2) distribute the obol signs in restorations in a way that the stonemason did not do in the preserved text.[57]

In 1965 I observed that the Lang-Merritt theory of a stone "damaged" on the right side, the "damage" extending over 11 lines and removing the surface for 16 letter-spaces, was without parallel and to my mind completely unacceptable. Lang-Meritt assume that this damage took place when the stone was being transported,[58] and, hence, it must have occurred prior to the time the mason began to dress the stone and to inscribe the letters.[59] Meritt has rejoined: "The theory of the damaged edge does not really require the citation of a parallel, but there are numerous instances in Attic inscriptions, overlooked by Pritchett in his search, where a *blemish or damage* to the stone has caused omission or misplacement of the letters" (italics supplied).[60] (The reader will observe that Meritt has now introduced a new factor, *blemish*, and then charged me with overlooking it.) Meritt continues by referring to Dow for examples, but he does not quote Dow. The omission is significant. Dow has written in summation of his study of gaps in inscribed texts: "Two facts may impress the reader. One is the brevity of such gaps: longer ones may well exist, but the flaws listed above are all of one space only, except for one gap which is of two spaces. The other impressive fact is the rarity of such flaws. The foregoing lists, for instance, include all the instances encountered in one search through *I.G.* II i I² with its 831 inscriptions. I suggest that the two facts, brevity and rarity, are related to each other: themselves subject to condemnation, ordinarily the state officials would refuse to accept from a mason a stele with a flaw. Actually a few defective inscribed stelai escaped condemnation, the flaws in these instances being very small."[61]

[56] The accounts of Athena exhibit the interest formulas τόκος τούτον or τόκος τούτοις ἐγένετο. But Lang-Meritt in 1965 restore in lines 33, 39, and 46, a formula which does not occur on the stone: τόκος τούτοι ἐγένετο. The difference is only one letter-space, but it is fatal for their restorations. This matter was discussed in Pritchett, *Ancient Athenian Calendars* (supra, n. 50) 296 and, in particular, 311, with reference to M. N. Tod.

[57] This latter may seem a small point, but in restorations the difference of one letter-space is often critical. Lang-Meritt read [⌊ | | | ⌋] for line 40 and [⌊ | | ⌋] for line 31. But in the nine cases where the signs for 5 obols and 4 obols are found on the stone, five obols were cut in three letter-spaces, not four as Lang-Meritt would have it, and four obols in two, not three (5 obols = lines 29, 66, and 88; 4 obols = lines 65, 72, 80, 82, 83, 84). Lang-Meritt discuss this matter in no way.

[58] *Hesperia* 33 (1964) 163.

[59] Lang-Meritt cited no parallels for such extreme damage.

[60] *Hesperia* 34 (1965) 241.

[61] *HSCP* 67 (1963) 65. Meritt adds one example to Dow's brief list, *IG* I², 19.

In all of this there is no word of "damage." Indeed, the point of Dow's commentary is that the ancient workmen and officials would never have accepted a stele with a large and obvious flaw. With regard to *IG* I² 324, there is even less reason to conjecture that they would have accepted a "damaged" stele. It is misleading to confuse "damage" and "flaw," and to claim examples of what are really imperfections in the crystallization of the marble as parallels for a hole in the stele, made before inscribing and equal in linear surface to the size of a man's two fists. A text which must be bolstered up by such an unparalleled theory of "damage" deserves no serious consideration.

Since it is now demonstrated that not enough of the accounts of the third year are preserved to permit a convincing attempt at restoration, any recovery of the ancient system of computation is rendered highly unlikely. My opinion is that the ancient computor used some rule of thumb, for we *know* that such a method was used a decade later at Athens in the accounts of the poletai. This opinion is shared by mathematicians with whom I have discussed the subject. It may be recalled that in 1928, Meritt attributed to the ancient auditors a system of reckoning in which the fractions $\frac{1}{2}$, $\frac{1}{3}$, $\frac{1}{4}$, $\frac{1}{6}$, etc., were amenable to their processes of computation, but not the fractions $\frac{1}{5}$, $\frac{1}{7}$, $\frac{1}{10}$, $\frac{1}{11}$, etc.[62] In 1961, Meritt reaffirmed the system of fractional approximation to the extent of using the words "fact," "knowledge," "demonstrated" for deductions based on the text restored on the basis of this system.[63] Some reviewers concurred in language which endorsed this system as inevitable.[64] There was proposed in 1964 an entirely different system,

[62] *The Athenian Calendar*, 33.

[63] *The Athenian Year* (Berkeley) ch. IV, "The Logistai Inscription," 60–71.

[64] Members of what Huxley (*AJP* 86 [1965] 303) refers to as the "Princeton school of epigraphy and its dependencies" (M. McGregor, *AHR* 67 [1961/62] 463; A. E. Raubitschek, *Phoenix* 17 [1963] 137; and A. G. Woodhead, *Gnomon* 35 [1963] 80) at once rallied to the support of the 1961 text, which their leader, however, quickly threw out. Some claimed epigraphical advantages, which were left undefined. Epigraphically speaking, the Pritchett-Neugebauer text of 1947 (*Calendars of Athens* [Cambridge, Mass.] 99–102) or the alternate text of 1963 (*Ancient Athenian Calendars*, 304) is far sounder than a text which has to depend among other anomalies on the introduction of a new siglum, the "inverted slug," to indicate damage. Moreover, the range of my error falls within that permitted by Meritt or by Lang-Meritt. (Cf. Lang, *Hesperia* 34 [1965] 246: "within the comparatively small range of inaccuracy: three drachmas.") All that my text lacks is an explanation for the error; but that can be remedied by anyone who cares to play with pebbles long enough. I may add that none of the three reviewers pointed out that Meritt had omitted from his book a body of epigraphic evidence containing virtually no restorations, which had been a cornerstone of the Pritchett-Neugebauer theories; see, for this evidence, *Ancient Athenian Calendars*, ch. V.

one of long division performed on an abacus containing a median line,[65] with the final step requiring a conversion table. It was assumed that the operator was "muddled"—the term is Miss Lang's[66]—and that numerous errors were made in the computations of the better preserved portions.[67] Again, such words as "inevitable," "proof," "establish" are applied to the results. Meritt was cited as a collaborator in the preparation of the article, and in 1965 he wrote very strongly in support of the restorations in the new system. What Meritt does not tell us is how the "facts" of his 1928 and 1961 texts became non-facts, and his "proved" system unproved.[68] However, in spite of the claims of certainty for the results, the 1964 text was patently wrong. Whether because of a mistake

[65] As discussed in the first part of this study, the Salamis stone and other marble tables containing a median line, which formed the models for Lang's original abacus studies, have been shown to have been designed as gaming tables, not abaci. In 1965 (p. 244) Lang writes, "Neither the decimal nor the duodecimal system of abacus calculation hinges on the median line of the Salamis stone." But some of Lang's "errors" require the configuration of pebbles which the presence of the median line induces, viz. the first "error" of payment 3, Year 1 (of the 1964 text, repeated for the 1965 text) and the "error" of payment 4, Year 1 (1965 text). The reader would do well to look at the drawings on plates 25–27 of *Hesperia* 33 (1964).

[66] *Hesperia* 33 (1964) 156.

[67] Lang refers (p. 244) to the computations as the work of "plain 5th century citizens holding office." Clearly, the abacus operators were either experts or not, and the auditors who reviewed the accounts were competent or not. If they were experts, the errors which Lang conjures up could never have been made in such numbers. If they were not experts, they may be expected to have made errors for those sections of the text which are lost, the recreation of which would be impossible. It has not been demonstrated that the fifth-century mathematician was as inept as Lang's system would lead us to believe. Indeed, in problems of division, Sir Thomas Heath (supra, n. 10, 88) has shown on the evidence of the earliest preserved solutions in the history of Greek mathematics that the Greeks performed the operation much in the same way as we perform it today, by the use of alphabetical numerals. If the fifth-century Athenian did not compute simple problems of division, such as we have in *IG* I² 324, on an abacus, it behooves us not to attribute to him a system he did not use. The problem is one in the history of mathematics, and the burden of proof rests on Lang to establish her system in a broader context, especially since it finds no corroboration in Heath (cf. *op. cit.*, p. 51: "The Greeks in fact had little need of the abacus for calculations.") Lang's dismissal of the subject (1965, p. 244, n. 1) does not do it justice.

[68] In 1961 (*Athenian Year*, p. 66), Meritt wrote with respect to a deviation of 2 drachmai 1.5 obols assumed by Pritchett and Neugebauer as follows: "The fact that even so the amount of interest must be fully two drachmai (or more) higher than the calendar demands merely shows that the preferred text cannot be correct, and that the calendar dates based upon it are of no value. . . . This error in the amount of interest is intolerable." But in the 1964 text of Lang, which Meritt subsequently endorsed, there is, among others, an error, not of 2, but of 122½ drachmai; but Meritt is silent about this.

of one obol,[69] or because the most unlikely "error" could be eliminated and the number of errors reduced by one, Lang in 1965 offered a new text, the corrections in her 1964 work requiring a *full* page.[70] Restorations of *IG* I² 324, resemble the nine-headed Hydra, each head of which, cut off, is immediately replaced by a new one. What was accepted as mathematically true in 1964 and made the source of "an auditor's mistake" becomes "practically unbelievable" in 1965.[71] Whereas for the 1964 text it was assumed that the operator had made an error in one payment and attempted to correct it in the next, but that he added the amount of the error instead of subtracting,[72] in 1965 an equally implausible explanation is proposed: that the operator arose from his position, moved around the board, and then not only confused pebbles in one column with those in another, but confused units with fractions at a stage prior to the conversion of the fractions.[73]

Lang nowhere proves that the interest in *IG* I² 324, was calculated on an abacus.[74] She changes her method of calculation as to

[69] According to the computation on page 156 of *Hesperia* 33 (1964), Lang made a mistake of one obol. I now note that the figure for the interest is different from that in line 10 or her text on page 165; so the former may involve only a typographical error. In the third line from the bottom of my note 17, *Hesperia* 34 (1965) 136, the word "equal" should be corrected to "do not equal."

[70] *Hesperia* 34 (1965) 235.

[71] *Hesperia* 34 (1965) 228: "The coincidence of a principal ending in the same eight figures as its interest is practically unbelievable." But in 1964, Lang's restored text (see her p. 157) for both the principal and the interest of the fifth payment (122/2¼) was made to end in the same eight figures. Again, in 1965 (p. 246), we are told: "Again the year's total and the spacing combine to make any principal other than 18 T impossible." But in 1964 it had in fact been something else.

[72] See *Hesperia* 34 (1965) 136, n. 17.

[73] There is no reason to assume that the operator would treat 1.8 dr. as a unit.

[74] Lang originally suggested (*Hesperia* 26 [1957] 271ff) that her system of abacus computation (*sans* any system requiring a conversion table, however) could account for errors in computations which she believes Herodotos made. Lang fails to state that according to the text which Enoch Powell attributes to Herodotos in 7.187, there is no error. To be sure, emendation is involved; but at least it is on the authority of one of our most eminent Herodotean scholars, and hence, deserving of mention. The scholar who will read Book 7 from chapter 187 to the end will discover that regardless of which text is used, Powell, Legrand, van Groningen, or others, the preserved recension is in poor condition and that lacunae and emendations are posited by all. Similarly, with regard to the passage in Herodotos 3.89–95, there are modern editors whose text would have it that Herodotos was correct. The problem is a familiar one of the transmission of numerals, a subject deserving of much further study. We have no work for Herodotos comparable to that of Hemmerdinger for the numerals of the Thucydidean manuscripts.

conversions arbitrarily,[75] and in 1965 she changes all but two of her restorations arbitrarily[76]—arbitrarily in that they are not caused by changes in the system of computation.[77] But the chief interest in the inscription lies not in the system of computation but in the information which *IG* I² 324, may afford for the fifth-century Athenian calendar. Unwilling to accept the fact that where restoration is not a factor, the text of *IG* I² 324 accords with the theory of a regular prytany calendar, a few scholars are prepared to support now one text, now another,[78] so long as the restorations are made to accord with the theory of an irregular prytany calendar, a theory for which they have failed to produce any support *sans* restorations.

The subject of the Athenian calendar brings us to line 79.

Line 79. Whereas for line 32, neither the historical approach, that is, the weighing of the conflicting reports of early epi-

[75] In 1964, Miss Lang justified her conversion table on the principle (p. 164) that "the goddess must not be scanted of any interest and must be overpaid rather than underpaid." In 1965, for her new table, which she labels as "crude" (p. 226), she adduces a general principle of "rounding off to the nearest" number. The goddess has been abandoned.

[76] Lang's riposte to my article in her Appendix II (pp. 243–247) begins with the misquotation of "his opponents" for "their opponents," an error which changes the meaning entirely; proceeds on the same page to an attack on the use of the law of averages for this inscription, a law which she had just invoked in the second paragraph of her article to justify her conversion table for the records of Athena Polias; couples Nos. 5 and 6 and thereby replies only to No. 5; in No. 7, leaves quite unexplained the markings on the Salaminian board; and in Nos. 8ff misses the point that the Salaminian board was a gaming table. Nothing is gained by simply repeating that it was an abacus, without offering one bit of supporting evidence.

[77] Lang claims that the changes in her 1964 system of calculating interest are brought about by the "new insight into the ancient practice of rounding-off and obol-equivalence gained from the accounts of the Other Gods" (p. 246, No. 17) and that these changes require revisions in the errors (pp. 246, 226/7, 230: "Thus by this revised method all calculations are completely consistent and the necessary errors not only arise naturally from the methods of calculations . . .," and p. 243: "five errors, all of which are required by the surviving text"). To the contrary, if one studies the 1965 calculations not in the order of presentation, but in logical sequence, one sees that since Lang wished to remove error 2 from Payment 4 of Year 1, as explained above, she apparently realized that by raising the principal of Payment 3 she could eliminate this error. The elevation of principal, in turn, affected Payment 5 of Year 4. She made the changes in her text that these observations stimulated. These "changes" have nothing to do with any new "insight" gained from the accounts of the Other Gods on the lower half of the stone, accounts which, in any case, she believes were kept by an entirely different method of bookkeeping.

[78] One writer (Clement, *AJA* 69 [1965] 192 and 193) manages to endorse both systems simultaneously. Fortunately, strong and sane voices are now being heard condemning the excessive claims made in Attic epigraphy on the basis of restorations; see G. Huxley, *AJP* 86 (1965) 303 ("It is high time that the expression 'inevitable restoration' and the attitude of mind it presupposes were dropped from epigraphical practice").

graphists, nor the evidence of paper squeezes can be decisive since the stone is in existence, the problem of line 79 is quite different. Here a fragment was broken off after the discovery of a piece and never recovered. The preserved part of the line in question appears in the third line of plate 8:5. The photograph (taken by a non-professional) affords a control of the four letters of the line as they appear today. The most critical letter is the rightmost in the photograph. The following observations may be made:

1. All who saw the stone intact read the letter as an omicron. This includes Rangabé, Pittakys, and Velsen.

2. The evidence of the excellent nineteenth-century squeeze, as attested by Klaffenbach, is as follows: "Der 2. runde Buchstabe ist ohne Zweifel ein Omikron (nicht phi!)."[79]

3. On the stone today there is no trace of an upright stroke, as for a phi.

In face of this overpowering evidence, what is the basis for the repeated claim by Meritt that this letter is to be read as an *undotted* phi?

In 1928, Meritt wrote in part as follows: "The stroke of the rounding stops short of the upper centre, so that if the letter were really an omicron there must have been a space of perhaps a millimeter at the top where the circle did not close. . . . I think a stonemason would be more apt to leave unfinished a phi than an omicron, because of the greater danger of splitting away the surface of the stone when the vertical bar of the phi should be added, if the stone at that point happened to be especially friable."[80]

About this commentary three observations may be made:

1. There is no evidence on the stone that an upright stroke was ever carved.

2. There is no flaw in the marble, no blemish in the area of this circle. As I reported in *AJP* 85 (1964) 43, the stone was removed

[79] Quoted in *AJP* 85 (1964) 142. Where in line 79 the stone is broken but Klaffenbach possesses in Berlin a squeeze made on very fine bond paper, Meritt writes "his quoting of Klaffenbach that the letter is omikron (nicht phi!) proves nothing." On the other hand, in line 32, where the stone is preserved and where no paper squeeze could be conclusive, Meritt quotes with approval Klaffenbach's communication to him about what he saw on the Berlin paper squeeze.

[80] *Athenian Calendar*, p. 10.

and carefully inspected by Prof. C. G. Higgins, a geologist, under magnification. There was no evidence of faulty crystallization.

3. As can be seen in the photograph (pl. 8:5), there is no interruption on the preserved segment of the circle. The stroke runs from the upper edge of the fracture to the lower edge.[81]

It is noteworthy that in 1964 Meritt bases his renewed claim of a broken circle not on a fresh inspection of the stone, either by himself or by others, but on his mistaken interpretation of my photograph of a latex squeeze.[82]

The epigraphist who respects the evidence must report this line as reading *OEIO*. If a modern scholar wishes to believe that at this critical point in the text the mason was in error, he must indicate the error by proper sigla and read for his text, for example, *OEI(Φ)*.[83]

If the stonemason made no mistake, the preserved four letters cannot be recognized as part of any calendar date and must be part of a word or words which elude us. Restorations, especially if they require the assumption of error, should be offered with great caution, and the historian who builds any theory on the basis of them should be warned that it is a very rare event when the discovery of a new fragment confirms a restoration not based on formula.[84] But let us suppose that the mason did make an error and inscribed an omicron when he meant a phi, and that a calendar date, of which we have four letters, may be restored. Let us suppose, too, that a festival date was inscribed in line 58, as Meritt believes, where there are only five letters of the entire line preserved. Two of the letters are *oγ*, which could be completed as for

[81] Actually, whether the circular letter was or was not completed is not germane to the problem, since the circular letters of *IG* I² 324, were made freehand and vary in circumference. Many of them are quite irregular. These points are discussed at length in *AJP* 85 (1964) 43, and it is not necessary to repeat them.

[82] *AJP* 85 (1964) 413. The mistakes are not confined to the interpretation of the squeeze. Meritt writes: "He [Pritchett] does not remember that the upright of the phi did not cross the center of the oval in 'Αφροδίτες of line 66." The better part of a paragraph was devoted by me to this phi, and it was proved that the letter was malformed because of faulty crystallization and was not characteristic of the script of this particular stonemason. Furthermore, a photograph of the phi was published as figure 2.

[83] Meritt's insistence that the letter before the first omicron is a delta (undotted) cannot stand. No other scholar has ever reported the delta, and it cannot be seen on the stone as a certain letter.

[84] After 1928, one new, though small, fragment of *IG* I² 324, was discovered and published by O. Broneer (*Hesperia* 4 [1935] 158–159). It proved that Meritt's 1928 readings were incorrect.

the 8th, 18th, or 23rd of a month.[85] But what months are to be restored in the two lines? Meritt by giving 75 letter-spaces to line 58 and 74 to line 79 restores the names of Hekatombaion, spelled with an aspirate sign, and Skirophorion, respectively. But what are the other possibilities?

In answering the question with any precision, we must not fall into the trap of using the word stoichedon, a definition of which word has not been agreed upon, for it is applied sometimes to the number of letter-spaces, sometimes to the number of letters; and there are other uses. What is critical in an Athenian fifth-century record is what the mason did at the right edge, for the normal pattern in this type of document is to inscribe the text line by line with the same number of letters up to two or three spaces of the right margin. Then, there are great and inexplicable variations which any fair-minded scholar must agree are unpredictable, at times having nothing to do with syllabic division or word-ending.[86]

Neither the left nor the right edge of *IG* I² 324 is preserved in any of its 120-odd lines. The right edge is lost for never less than six letter-spaces; and in some places considerably more. If the names of months are to be restored in the left half of lines 58 and 79, the critical determination obviously is how did the mason end lines 57 and 78.

For the sake of argument, and on the debatable assumption that dates were inscribed in the two lines, I have taken the Meritt-Lang text of 1964 which goes as far as line 53 (*Hesperia* 33, 165–167) and the Meritt text of 1928 (pl. 1 of *The Athenian Calendar*) for lines 54–110 inclusive, and I present in the table below the text as restored at their right edge.[87]

Number of lines flush to right edge (75)   = 40[88]
Number of lines having one uninscribed space at right edge (74) = 22[89]

---

[85] Numerous possibilities were indicated by me in *AJP* 85 (1964) 47. In the eighth line from the bottom of the page, the word "twelfth" should be corrected to "tenth."

[86] I have treated this subject at some length in *AJP* 85 (1964) 46–47; *BCH* 88 (1964) 457–459; *Ancient Athenian Calendars* (supra, n. 50) 310; and *AJA* 70 (1966) 174–175.

[87] Restorations were not attempted for many lines, and others again are ambiguous. Substitution of their numerous 1965 emendations would not materially affect the results.

[88] Lines 1, 3, 4, 5, 6, 7, 8, 9, 11, 12, 13, 14, 15, 16, 18, 19, 20, 21, 23, 25, 26, 30, 31, 32, 33, 34, 35, 36, 43, 45, 46, 52, 54, 55, 56, 57, 58, 66, 67, 69.

[89] Lines 10, 17, 37, 41, 42, 47, 48, 49, 50, 75, 77, 78, 79, 80, 93, 95, 98, 99, 103, 104, 109, 110.

Number of lines having two uninscribed spaces at right edge
$$(73) \;=\; 7^{90}$$
Number of lines having three uninscribed spaces at right edge
$$(72) \;=\; 3^{91}$$
Number of lines having five uninscribed spaces at right edge
$$(70) \;=\; 2^{92}$$

Of the 120-odd lines, the length of 74 lines can be estimated according to their text. Of the 74 lines, only 40 are inscribed flush to the right edge. The ratio of lines with 75 letter-spaces to those with 74 is less than 2:1.

Applying the table to the end of lines 57 and 78, we find that if one gives these lines 75 letters, we may restore in the line below the names of the months Hekatombaion (spelled with an aspirate), Metageitnion, or Maimakterion. If we allow one uninscribed space, we may restore Hekatombaion (without an aspirate), Anthersterion, Elaphebolion, or Skirophorion. If we give two uninscribed spaces, we may restore Boedromion. Whereas Meritt restores Hekatombaion in line 58 (with 75 letter-spaces in line 57) and Skirophorion in line 79 (with 74 letter-spaces in line 78), one may restore the reverse.[93] Or we may restore Hekatombaion in both places, both with the aspirate, or both without, or one with and one without; for we have observed elsewhere the folly of attempting to predict what masons of this period did with regard to the *spiritus asper*.[94] And so with other possibilities. And we can make the year ordinary or intercalary according to what we assume about the festival calendar.

We must take into consideration one clue which the text provides in its opening two lines, where it states that the accounting

[90] Lines 22, 38, 39, 40, 96, 100, 102.

[91] Lines 51, 106, 107.

[92] Lines 24, 44.

[93] In 1964 (*AJP* 85 414), Meritt writes: "The fact of the stoichedon order is clear, and Σκιροφοριõνος meets the requirements. As nearly as sound epigraphic method can determine it, this is the unique restoration for this line; it is indeed more than just one of several possibilities. It is the only possibility, and, in my judgment, it may be accepted as a 'fact.'" All this has a very familiar ring. It is the sort of writing which accompanies every successive restoration. Similar sentences were written about the 1928–1961 texts, based on a system of computation which Meritt himself has now abandoned. Interestingly, in one of the very lines under discussion, line 58, Meritt-Lang in 1965 changed their restoration for the prytany date (*Hesperia* 34 236).

[94] *AJA* 70 (1966) 174–175.

runs from Greater Panathenaia to Greater Panathenaia. One may assume that the last date in the document should fall as close to the festival as possible. This fact of the reference to the Panathenaia might seem, therefore, to favor the restoration of Hekatombaion in line 79, always assuming that there was a month; but I hasten to add that the possibilities are so numerous that the only honest course is to recognize that we cannot be certain.

Various arguments may be advanced for favoring one text over another. In the above table, the last line which is carried flush to the margin (i.e., 75) is line 69; below that there are many lines with one uninscribed space (i.e., 74). One may say that this arrangement would favor our assigning to line 78 seventy-four spaces.[95] To this one may reply that by consulting Meritt's plate 1 of *The Athenian Calendar*, one sees that in the stretch of 14 lines from lines 38 to 51 inclusive, twelve are given one uninscribed space, but two are carried to the right edge. The same may apply below line 69, and line 78 may have been one in which the mason carved to the margin. Or we may assign 74 letter-spaces, but give two letters to the final letter-space (or, for that matter, any other), as W. E. Thompson does twice in similar documents in a recent study of another inventory.[96] Furthermore, the entire statistique is based on Meritt's text, which has no probative value, but only serves to illustrate the fact that in all restorations thus far attempted, the treatment at the right edge is highly unpredictable. The stonemason may have treated the lines quite differently, and probably did. All that we can be sure of is that many inscribed lines ended some distance from the right edge in an uneven pattern.

We are confronted with the fact, however frustrating it may seem, that *IG* I[2] 324 is too fragmentarily preserved to permit positive conclusions about restorations. Face to face with the deep erosion in the area of the alleged *H* only the scholar desperately bent on restoration could print any letter here as certain. In any case scholars, who are

---

[95] Cf. Meritt, *Athenian Calendar*, p. 29.

[96] *Hesperia* 34 (1965) 303, line 1 of the lower text, and p. 306, line 4 of the middle text. Both are labelled by Thompson as stoichedon, and he writes on his p. 308 about inventories with the same number of *letter-spaces*. If we examine the Greek text on his pp. 306–307, which he labels as stoichedon 85, we find that of the 10 completely restored lines of Thompson's text, only 5 (50%) run flush to the margin. The others have uninscribed spaces (1 to 3) at the right edge. Divisions of words include σ^v|τέφανοι and στέφανο^v|ς. Here we see that a scholar who has made a speciality of the formulae of this type of financial document has no hesitation in assuming a diversity of line endings on the part of the mason at the right edge.

themselves periodically visiting Athens, should have recourse to the actual stone if they wish to debate these conclusions.

To sum up our thoughts: a long trail of complicated arguments has led us to the conviction that the Salamis tablet was designed as a gaming-board; that there is no evidence that the logistai calculated their accounts on an abacus; and that restorations of *IG* I² 324 based on computations simulated on a board like the Salamian table are inevitably unproven.

University of California
Berkeley

ADDENDUM

The sixth of the Meritt-approved series of texts for *IG* II², 324 appeared while this article was in press: *CQ* 62 (1968) 84–94. Epigraphically, this is the weakest of the lot and can be dismissed from consideration by the scientific worker. The printer's "inverted slugs," used as sigla for alleged damaged surface, have risen to the number of nineteen and are now introduced, not only at the end, but in the middle, of lines. The best antidote to Meritt's epigraphical legerdemain is to stand before the stele and look at the highly polished surface and then to ask oneself whether it is likely that the mason failed to dress the lost surface as he did the preserved part.

Meritt claims (p. 84, n. 2) that the stone was damaged by "vandalism" in 1965. When I inspected the area in question in 1968, I saw no change. It may not be entirely coincidental that I submitted to Meritt's journal an article, summarily rejected, which included photographs taken, as I had stated, in 1965. The present article includes photographs taken before 1965, and I shall publish others elsewhere. Meritt attempts to get away from the evidence of the stone by this feeble stratagem. The important fact remains that the stone was examined in 1949 by a group of able scholars whose testimony about the debated numeral in line 32 was published in the *Ancient Athenian Calendars* 270–273, with drawings. Significantly, Meritt omits this item from his bibliography on page 84, n. 1.

1. Epidauros: right half of *IG* IV 984.

2. Epidauros: center and right half of Number 2.

3. Epidauros: gaming area on right half of Number 2.

Plate 2   Pritchett

1. Amphiareion: Number 4.

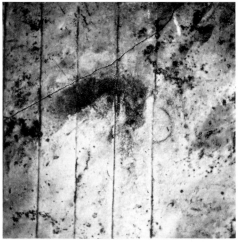

2. Amphiareion (detail of Number 4).

1. Amphiareion: Number 5.

2. Amphiareion: Number 6.

3. Amphiareion: Number 7.

4. Amphiareion: Number 8.

5. Amphiareion: Number 9.

Plate 4   Pritchett

1. Salamis: Number 11 (*IG* II² 2777).

1. Delos: Number 12.

2. Delos: Number 13. Letoon, north side.

3. Delos: Number 13. Letoon, east side.

4. Delos: Number 13. Letoon, east side (to the south).

Plate 6   Pritchett

2. Agios Andreas: Number 15.

3. Agios Andreas: Number 15.

1. Cyprus (Dhekelia): Number 14.

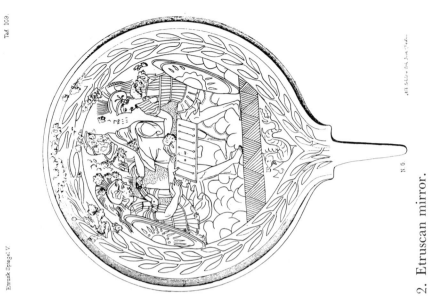

2. Etruscan mirror.

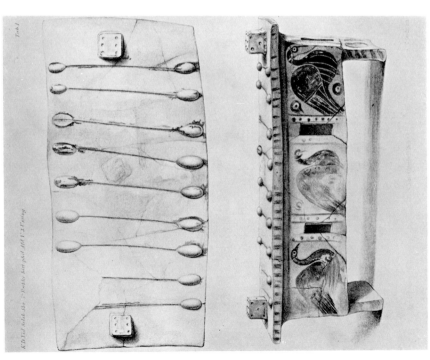

1. Clay model of gaming board.

Plate 8   Pritchett

1. *IG* I² 324, lines 28–40.

2. Eroded surface of line 32 (enlarged).

3. Another view of plate 8:2.

5. Line 79 of *IG* I² 324 (third line).

4. A third view of plate 8:2.

13

Elegiac and Elegos

Aristotle (*Poetics* ch. 1) mentions the ἐλεγειοποιοί, with the writers of epic, as poets who write verse without music.[1] This sets them off against others, such as the dithyrambic, nomic, tragic, and comic poets who use μέλος along with ῥυθμός and μέτρον in their production. The whole discussion is part of Aristotle's introductory section in which he states, with an air of delighted surprise, that the Greeks have no word for literature. He does not *argue* that elegiac poetry is non-musical; he simply assumes it, as an obvious truth. The casualness of the passage

[1] Aristotle's classification of elegiac as non-musical continues to be operative later; see Dionysius Thrax *ars gramm.*, περὶ γραμ. §2: we should read (=deliver) tragedy ἡρωικῶς, comedy βιωτικῶς, τὰ ἐλεγεῖα λιγυρῶς, epic εὐτόνως, lyric ἐμμελῶς, τοὺς δὲ οἴκτους ὑφειμένως καὶ γοερῶς. The position of elegiac, between comedy and epic, speaks for itself. λιγυρῶς means "clear", but not necessarily (or usually) "plaintive," *pace* Harvey (cf. infra, this note) 170–171. Cf. also Photius's report of Proclus's *Chrestomathy* sections 24–27 Severyns, where elegiac appears between epic and iambic (A. Severyns, *Recherches sur la Chrestomathie de Proclos* 1.2 [1938] 98 conjectures that this must have been the original order in section 12 also), thus implicitly casting doubt on the connection with elegos and lament which Proclus accepts.

The following abbreviated references will be used: Bowra: C. M. Bowra, *Early Greek Elegists* (Harvard 1938); Campbell: D. A. Campbell, "Flutes and Elegiac Couplets," *JHS* 84 (1964) 63–68; Dover: K. J. Dover, "The Poetry of Archilochus," *Entretiens Fond. Hardt* 10 (1963) 181–212; Garzya: A. Garzya, *Studi sulla lirica greca* (Messina 1963); Harvey: A. E. Harvey, "The Classification of Greek Lyric Poetry," *CQ* (1955) 157–175; Huchzermeyer: H. Huchzermeyer, *Aulos und Kithara in der griechischen Musik* (Emsdetten 1931); Lasserre: F. Lasserre, ed. tr. comm., *Plutarque: De la musique* (Lausanne 1954); Page: D. L. Page, "The Elegiacs in Euripides' *Andromache*," in *Greek Poetry and Life* (Oxford 1936) 206–230; Peek: W. Peek, *Griechische Grabgedichte* (Darmstadt 1960); Wilamowitz 1913: U. von Wilamowitz-Moellendorff, *Sappho und Simonides* (Berlin 1913); Wilamowitz 1921: U. von Wilamowitz-Moellendorff, *Griechische Verskunst* (Berlin 1921).

9—C.S.C.A.

does not lessen its importance; it is our earliest explicit testimony about the mode of performance of elegiac.[2]

In the light of this, it is surprising that most moderns have taken it for granted that the elegiac was sung, and accompanied by the aulos, well into the fifth century and beyond. Bowra's assertion may stand for many: "The elegiac, then, came into existence as a flute song, and such it remained for some three or four centuries."[3] Wilamowitz and Felix Jacoby attempted to do justice to Aristotle's testimony by suggesting that elegiac was ranked as recited rather than lyric verse because the performer spoke rather than sang his lines to the aulos accompaniment.[4] But Rhode undertook to demolish Wilamowitz' arguments, and Jacoby found few followers.[5] The habit of thinking of elegiac as aulodic is so strong that in a recent translation of Aristotle's *Poetics*, his words on elegiac are glossed: "A plaintive song accompanied by the aulos."[6] Other scholars continue to feel the difficulty. W. Peek: elegiac "was sung to the flute, or at least delivered by means of a dynamic, modulated speech-song; it was and remained, for a while, a lyric genre."[7] H. Koller ventures to find his own intriguing solution: from the start, he feels, elegiac was embellished, "umspielt," by the aulos, that is, the reciter took turns chanting and playing his instrument.[8]

In 1964, D. A. Campbell went beyond the hesitations of Wilamowitz and Jacoby and showed, in a well-argued and fully documented article, that the case for an originally and essentially musical elegiac is even weaker than they thought.[9] He did this by methodically reviewing the evidence, both from within the corpus of elegiac poetry

---

[2] By "elegiac" I mean a poem, or collection of poetry, written in elegiac couplets. The term "elegy" is better restricted to the Hellenistic and Roman uses of the verse form.

[3] Bowra 7. Cf. also G. Luck, *Die roemische Liebeselegie* (Heidelberg 1961) 18–21.

[4] For the references, see E. Curtius in *RE* 5 (1905) 2262–2263. See also Wilamowitz 1921.101–102. Wilamowitz's middle position derives in part from his interest in ancient notices concerning παρακαταλογή; cf., e.g., his *Die Textgeschichte der griechischen Lyriker* (Berlin 1900) 53 and n. 2. For a similar hesitation in antiquity, see Demetrius *On Style* 167; he complains that some of Sappho's poetry is not really "poetic," and that it does not go with dance or lyre, "unless there is such a thing as conversational lyric": εἰ μή τις εἴη χόρος διαλεκτικός.

[5] E. Rohde, *Der griechische Roman*[3] (Leipzig 1914) 149f n. 1.

[6] K. A. Telford, tr. comm., *Aristotle's Poetics* (Chicago 1961) 3.

[7] Peek 13.

[8] H. Koller, *Musik und Dichtung im alten Griechenland* (Bern 1963) 126–131.

[9] Campbell passim.

and from ancient remarks about elegiac, and concluding that it is insufficient to support a claim which would fly in the face of Aristotle. We may now abandon a fiction which never was very plausible in the first place, and which has had the unfortunate effect of suggesting to some that other types of spoken poetry, such as iambic, was also as a rule delivered to aulos accompaniment.[10] If in what follows I propose to review some of Campbell's evidence once again, it is because I feel that his argument, excellent as it is, may be supplemented in two ways. We may show that other internal references, if taken as narrowly as the references to auloi in elegiac, would lead to preposterous results; and second, it may be possible to say more about the relation between elegiac and elegos, a putative kinship which had much to do with the rise of the aulos myth.

*   *   *

In the pastoral lyric, the characters claim to be singing lines which are in fact not sung but recited. This should remind us that it will not do to confuse the poetic reality with the circumstances of production. Let us distinguish between two kinds of references to music, which we may term, awkwardly I fear, (1) referential, and (2) circumstantial. The latter use is of course extremely common; such nods to the accompanist(s)—usually in the present tense, less commonly in the future, more rarely in the past[11]—are pervasive in drama and in choral poetry.[12] There are examples in the three tragedians, in Aristophanes, in Alcman, Pindar, and Bacchylides.[13] Other passages are less conclusive. Pindar's *Pythian* 12, written to celebrate a victory on the aulos, presents a dactylo-epitritic treatment of Athena's invention of the instrument. In spite of the weight put on the aulos, there is no way of saying whether this particular song was accompanied by an aulete. Similarly, when Bacchylides talks about the music now being played in the city of the victor,[14] or when Pindar describes spring celebrations of

[10] Huchzermeyer 29ff.

[11] This is my general impression, from a rough tally of the tenses. The subject merits a more exact investigation.

[12] For the dramatists, see esp. Aeschylus *Suppl.* 69 and *Prom.* 574–575; also Pratinas 708.6–7 PMG. In the latter, I do not think that the force of ὕστερον has been explained to everyone's satisfaction.

[13] The following examples, out of many, may serve: "Stesichorus" 947 PMG; Pindar *Ol.* 5.19–20; *Nem.* 3.76–79; *Parth.* 2.11–16; *Paean* 7.11; Bacchylides 2.11–12; "Sophocles" 737b.2–4 PMG.

[14] Bacchylides 9.68, with Blass's supplements.

the gods,[15] there is no assurance that the references to auloi tell us anything about the production of the hymn in question. Nor, obviously, does Pindar's song about the Locrian invention of music for voice and auloi permit us to make inferences about the accompanist.[16] Sappho's words, in the Hector and Andromache poem,[17] about the music in the bridal procession in Troy should not be taken to mean that Sappho accompanied herself with a mixture of aulos and another instrument (castagnets?). Or is the poem choral after all?

In none of these selective examples does the narrator, or one of his characters, talk about himself as playing the aulos.[18] It is more difficult to demonstrate that what is true of the pastoral piper may be true also of the persona of an elegiac or an iambic poem. But once we acknowledge that a musical instrument may be part of a poetic reality precisely as any other object in the life of an imagined character is, the case should not be so very difficult after all. When Theognis, or the speaker of a Theognidean poem, tells us that he is silent (420), what are we to make of it, except to conclude that the silence is not part of the auditory texture of the line, but part of his poetic role? The same with his statement (313–314) that he is a madman surrounded by madmen. Real madmen do not, as a rule, talk in elegiacs (nor, to avoid petitio, do they sing, except καταχρηστικῶς). His μανία, here, is referential, not circumstantial. When Archilochus (56A D.) gets ready to lower sail, are we to imagine him going through his nautical maneuver while reciting, or singing, his poem to the (boatswain's?) pipe?[19]

Campbell has shown that none of the internal evidence necessarily documents aulos accompaniment. I think we can go further, in the light of the considerations just introduced, and argue that by and large the evidence is referential, hence *cannot* indicate performance. As in pastoral poetry the term ἀείδειν is not uncommon; but it is generally agreed that when Solon (2.2) uses the term ᾠδή,[20] and Aristophanes *Pax*

---

[15] Pindar *Dithyr.* 75.18–19.

[16] Pindar fr. 140b.2–4.

[17] Sappho 44.24–25 LP; cf. Bacchylides 10.54.

[18] But see Archilochus 76 D. Can we be sure, in spite of *Monum. Par.* (fr. 51 I A 47 and IV A 52 D.), that Archilochus is talking about himself? At any rate, the meter makes it less than likely that the speaker is conducting a paean, unless "Lesbian paean" is a nickname for quite another type of composition.

[19] See also Archilochus 77 D., which is obviously *not* from a dithyramb. For references to aulos in elegiac, besides Campbell 64ff, cf. also Huchzermeyer 38ff.

[20] Cf. Plutarch *Solon* 8: there is no mention of an aulete, and Pisistratus is made to refer to Solon as τῷ λέγοντι. Cf. Campbell 65–66.

1267–1268 has ᾄδειν, both in a circumstantial sense, the reference is to the reciting of epic rather than to a musical setting.[21] Theognis 533–534 is the model passage to show the irrelevance, to the mode of performance, of the mention of musical instruments: "I rejoice drinking, and singing to the accompaniment of an aulete;[22] I also rejoice holding the tuneful lyre."

> χαίρω δ' εὖ πίνων καὶ ὑπ' αὐλητῆρος ἀείδων,
> χαίρω δ' εὔφθογγον χερσὶ λύρην ὀχέων.

Which is it to be, aulodic, or lyric? At 1065 we learn that it is proper, while engaged in a κῶμος, to sing to aulos accompaniment, ὑπ' αὐλητῆρος ἀείδων. This is one of the pleasures that men and women may have; but it is not what the speaker is doing at the moment; κωμάζειν is not conducted in elegiacs. The typical Theognidean utterance is not descriptive, but imaginative, or expressive of his desires, and often prescriptive; and when the "thou shalt" includes mention of an aulos, we learn nothing about the delivery of the poem.[23]

[21] At Aristophanes *Pax* 1279, a Homeric hexameter like the preceding ones, singing is out of the question. Stanford's vauable reminder (W. B. Stanford, *The Sound of Greek* [Berkeley, Los Angeles 1967] 28ff) that Aristoxenus and Aristides Quintilianus allowed for types of delivery intermediate between conversational speech and lyric song (cf. also similar warnings by Th. Zielinski, *Die Gliederung der altattischen Komoedie* [Leipzig 1885] part 2, ch. 2) should not cause us to drop the distinction between unaccompanied recitation, however elevated and resonant, and accompanied chanting or singing; cf. the remarks of Aristoxenus *Elements of Harmony* 1.8ff, cited by Stanford. Another question related to our set of problems is whether skolia were sung to the accompaniment of an aulos or a lyre. Huchzermeyer 57 decides in favor of the lyre, on such evidence as Aristophanes *Nub.* 1354ff and Cicero *Tusc.* 1.4. The decision, though based on little evidence, is not inherently unlikely, seeing that many Attic skolia are composed in Aeolic meters. But when H. adds that "der Aulos begleitete beim Mahle wohl nur . . . die Lieder im elegischen Masse," and refers to Aristophanes *Ves.* 1217ff, he fails to convince: (1) the meal is over; (2) the auletris has played a prelude, prior to the beginning of the skolia; and (3) the skolia themselves are, at this point at least, iambic.

[22] ἀείδων is Pierson's correction for the ms ἀκούων which Young accepts into the text; cf. however, most recently B. A. van Groningen, *Theognis* (Amsterdam 1966) 211–212. In any case, the disjunctive χαίρω δέ—χαίρω δέ shows that we are to think of separate occasions, neither of which needs to be identified with the present one.

[23] For passages in which the speaker expresses a desire for music, see Theognis 1041; 1055–1058; 761; 791. Desire implies want; hence the passages cannot tell us anything about performance. Theognis 239ff poses an interesting question. Campbell 64 thinks that the αὐλῳδία which, according to the speaker, will celebrate Cyrnus in the future, must be Theognis's own elegiacs, but that Theognis has in mind, not his own performance, but a more formal or elaborate occasion. To this the answer must be that we have no legitimate reason for the assumption that a poem can be performed in two different ways. Hence,

The external evidence is equally inadequate. Most of it derives from a tradition which crops up most alarmingly in the ps.-Plutarchean *De musica*, especially ch. 8, which is a mine of ill-considered and jumbled information.[24] It records a notice, also given by Strabo,[25] that Mimnermus played a tune called Kradias on the aulos. This piece of information is supposed to go back to Hipponax (96 B.). *De musica* 8 continues: "In the early period the αὐλῳδοί sang ἐλεγεῖα μεμελοποιημένα, elegiacs put to music; this is clear from the Panathenaic inscription concerning the musical contest."[26] If Hipponax really said that Mimnermus played the Kradias on the aulos (we do not have his own words), then the piece was not aulodic but auletic, hence the further comment of *De musica* that early elegiac was aulodic is not pertinent. The reasoning seems to be something like this: (1) Mimnermus performed a nomos on the aulos; (2) (but wasn't Mimnermus an elegist?); (3) (Yes, but) in the old days elegiac involved aulos playing; compare the inscription.[27]

It is clear from the discussion in *De musica* ch. 8 (cf. also chs. 4, 9, 19, 28) that ἐλεγεῖον and ἔλεγος are, in the author's mind, associated with the nomos and choral poetry. Actually there is some doubt that nomoi were usually choral. W. Vetter, while stressing that nomos is not a technical term but a name that can be applied to many

either Theognis's elegiacs are sung, or Theognis is *not* referring to his own lines. I think the latter is correct; Theognis envisages a time when his own verses about Cyrnus will have made the youth a celebrity, to be further eulogized in musical encomia. Finally, Theognis 825–830 and 939–942 (or 939–944, as Young arranges the lines) are two rather mysterious passages which have not yet been sufficiently explicated by the commentators. But on any interpretation they cannot be pressed to support the theory of sung elegiacs; one refers to the past, with disapproval, the other to the future. The latter, in particular, appears to me to be a griphos.

24 I assume that in many cases the confusions of *De musica* go back to its sources, among them Heraclides Ponticus; cf. the corrections recommended by H. Weil and Th. Reinach in their treatment of chs. 8 and 9, in their *Plutarque: De la musique* (Paris 1900) 23ff. F. Wehrli, *Die Schule des Aristoteles* 7 (Basel 1953) 112–115 has nothing on the relative merits of this section of Heraclides's work on music. Cf. also U. von Wilamowitz-Moellendorff, *Timotheos: Die Perser* (Leipzig 1903) 89.

25 Strabo 14.1.28.

26 For μεμελητοποιημένα cf. infra, p. 224. I do not understand Lasserre's comment, p. 158, that the Panathenaic inscription is cited to explain why the elegiac writer Mimnermus appears in Hipponax in the capacity of aulete.

27 The logic is faulty; the inscription we do not know. As regards the unreliability of much that is said about music and poetry in the later accounts, see Campbell's showing, 67–68, that Athenaeus 14.620C (the poetry of Homer, Hesiod, Archilochus, Mimnermus, and Phocylides was composed to be sung) and 14.632D (Xenophanes, Solon, Theognis, Phocylides, and Periander did not compose their verses to be sung) cancel each other out.

different things, finds that songs called nomoi are usually astrophic, "durchkomponiert," and often monodic, or purely instrumental.[28] When *De Musica* 4 and 5 informs us that Clonas of Tegea created his nomoi for aulos in the wake of Terpander's nomoi for kitharis, it is not clear whether his nomoi were aulodic or auletic, a distinction which is occasionally obscured in the tradition of which *De musica*, Pollux, Strabo, and Pausanias are representatives.[29] For some of the nomoi whose invention is ascribed to Clonas, including the elegos which is featured in the series, Sacadas is claimed as the creator. The best account of the tradition about Sacadas is still that of E. Hiller,[30] although Hiller himself, perhaps unavoidably, fell a victim to the harmonizing tendencies of which he accuses his predecessors. Hiller showed that Sacadas was mainly known for his work as an aulete; his most famous composition, the νόμος Πυθικός with which he won at the Pythian games in 582, 578, and 574 B.C.,[31] appears to have been a variety of Programmmusik for solo aulos, representing the struggle of Apollo with the serpent. Hiller allows for the production of aulodic and choral pieces by Sacadas; though some of the evidence on which he bases this, especially *De musica* 8 and 9, is unreliable, there is no reason why we should deny Sacadas some measure of versatility. But his reputation was built on his accomplishments as an aulete.[32]

It is against this background that we must take stock of the information (*De musica* 3; 5; 8) that Clonas, Polymnestus, and Sacadas

[28] W. Vetter, s.v. νόμος in *RE* 33. Halbband (1936) 840–843. U. von Wilamowitz-Moellendorff, *Timotheos: Die Perser* (Leipzig 1903) 93–94 was the first to put the study of νόμος on a sound footing; cf. H. Grieser, *Nomos* (Heidelberg 1937) 27. Recent literature on the subject is summarized by R. P. Winnington-Ingram in *Lustrum* 3 (1958) 37–41. Grieser 71 suggests, probably correctly, that after Sacadas aulodic νόμος became rare; from then on, νόμος was usually citharodic. But see Telestes 810 PMG who distinguishes between a Phrygian νόμος (ἐν αὐλοῖς) and a Lydian ὕμνος (ὀξυφώνοις πηκτίδων ψαλμοῖς); contrast 806 PMG.

[29] See the apparatus and commentary of Weil and Reinach (supra, n. 24) 20–21. Even the great August Boeckh allowed the ancient confusions to trick him into writing a brief paragraph defining νόμος in which just about every point is questionable: *de metris Pindaricis* iii. 6.201.8: Nomi quidem, qui aut αὐλῳδικοὶ aut κιθαρῳδικοὶ antiquitus simplicis erant metri, citharoedici ex hexametris heroicis, quamquam et τροχαῖος νόμος laudatur, auloedici ex distichis elegiacis; paulatim vero priscae simplicitati successit complicatior structura, adeo ut ne antistrophas quidem haberent.

[30] E. Hiller, "Sakadas der Aulet", *RhM* 31 (1876) 76–88. Cf. also J. G. Frazer, ed., *Pausanias' Description of Greece* V (1913) 245–246.

[31] Paus. 2.22.9; 4.27.7; Strabo 9.421; Pollux 4.74; 78.

[32] Cf. also Pollux 4.81: Pythian auloi played τὸ ἄχορον αὔλημα, τὸ Πυθικόν, οἱ δὲ χορικοὶ διθυράμβοις προσηύλουν. May we infer that typically the fluting in Delphi, in honor of Apollo, was solo work?

were composers of ἐλεγεῖα and μέλη. On the one hand, Clonas and Sacadas were responsible for a kind of music for (voice and?) aulos called elegos; on the other we learn (Pausanias 10.7.4) that αὐλῳδία had an extremely short life at the Pythian games, being in fact presented only once, in 582 B.C. Thereafter, according to Pausanias, the Amphictyons decided that αὐλῳδία was not appropriate to the sanctity of the occasion; ἡ γὰρ αὐλῳδία μέλη τε ἦν αὐλῶν τὰ σκυθρωπότατα καὶ ἐλεγεῖα [θρῆνοι] προσᾳδόμενα τοῖς αὐλοῖς.[33] If there is anything we can make of this garbled text, it is that αὐλῳδία consists of dismal (or: disfiguring?)[34] tunes on the aulos and dirges sung along with the aulos. Note the unusual order; the aulos appears to be the lead, and the voice the accompaniment. And as if this was not bad enough, Pausanias proceeds to cite a dedication in which an Echembrotus of Arcadia was hailed for winning a victory at Delphi

"Ελλησι δ᾽ ἀείδων μέλεα καὶ ἐλέγους.

What are we to make of the distinction between μέλη and ἔλεγοι, which also underlies the association of μέλη and ἐλεγεῖα μεμελοποιημένα in De musica 8?[35] It may well be that μέλη, as in Pausanias's report of the decision of the Amphictyons concerning αὐλῳδία, refers to the playing

---

[33] μέλη τε is Dindorf's plausible emendation for codd. μελέτη. Wilamowitz 1913.298 notes: "Die Inschrift ist so seltsam, dass es schwer faellt, ihr in allem zu trauen." We cannot be sure that it was not θρῆνοι rather than ἐλεγεῖα which originally stood in the text, but it is unlikely. The association of μέλη with ἐλεγεῖα or ἔλεγοι is common enough; cf. the Suda's note on Olympus. Cf. De musica 3, from Heraclides, where Terpander, and after him Clonas, is said to have taken his own and Homer's ἔπη and to have added tunes, μέλη περιτιθέντα. Here ἔπη stands in the position elsewhere occupied by ἐλεγεῖα or ἔλεγοι. I am inclined to interpret this to mean that both poets used dactylic rhythms. Cf. also Alcman 39.1 PMG.

[34] σκυθρωπότατα can hardly refer to facial expression, or only to facial expression, since auletic performance, which continued after the vetoing of aulodic, has an even larger share of facial distortion. It is true that in classical writers, from Aeschylus to Plato and Xenophon, σκυθρωπός always means "scowling" or "frowning." But in some of the later writers, particularly in Plutarch, a figurative use of the word is found: De curios. 518B, De def. orac. 417C, etc. In such cases the item to which σκυθρωπός is applied is treated as if it had a face, or the ascription involves the idea of consequences which will be a frowning matter. On balance I suggest that in the Pausanias passage the adjective is used figuratively, and goes with both μέλη and ἐλεγεῖα.

[35] The verbal participle suggests that Plutarch thinks of ἐλεγεῖα as nonmusical. μελοποιέω originally simply meant "to make music" = "to sing"; see Aristoph. Thesm. 42, 67; Ran. 1328; like μελοποιία and μελοποιός it was used without an object. But in Longinus ch. 28.2 and Athenaeus 14.632D, as in our Plutarch passage, it takes an object, and means: to set to music a piece which is originally non-musical. This is particularly clear from the Longinus passage: Plato used tropes and periphrasis to add music to his speech: ψιλὴν λαβὼν τὴν λέξιν ἐμελοποίησε.

of the aulos, while ἔλεγος points to a vocal performance. But as we saw in connection with Sacadas, this is by no means certain, and Euripides's later use of the term ἔλεγος to refer to Orpheus playing his lyre (*Hypsipyle* 62 Page) serves to confuse the picture further.

The really significant issue in this snarled tissue of terms and claims is the nature of the relation between ἔλεγος and ἐλεγεῖον.[36] An explicit statement that elegoi were sung and consisted of elegiac distichs, goes back to Didymus, who takes it from Demoleon.[37] At the same time Strabo (14.64.7) and Horace (*AP* 77) indicate that even in antiquity the beginnings of elegiac were no longer known or understood.[38] The combination of these two positions, viz., that we know nothing about the origins of elegiac, but that early elegoi were composed of elegiac couplets, has haunted scholarship for centuries.[39] The first scholar poet, Euripides, acted upon the combination, and in the *Andromache* wrote a piece in elegiac couplets which was designed to invoke the shades of the early elegos of whose form he himself had no inkling.[40] The passage is in the nature of an experiment, although we may regard the sung couplets as in some way analogous to sung hexameters; cf. the difficulties of, say, Sophocles *Trach.* 1010–1022, and *Philoct.* 839–842; in both passages the distribution of singing, chanting, and speaking is not at all clear. The Alexandrian poets, among them

[36] Dover 188.ff has a good appraisal of the evidence. The only drawback of his reconstruction is its success. Any reconstruction that manages to arrive at a tidy picture by accommodating all the data is likely to arouse both admiration and suspicion.

[37] See Severyns (supra, n. 1) 101 who refers to *Et. Gudianum* 180.19–21.

[38] Cf. also L. Alfonsi, "Sul περὶ Ποιητῶν di Aristotele," *RivFC* 21 (1942) 193–200. Alfonsi, and Rostagni whose writings he cites, are perhaps a little too certain that they know what was in the second book of Περὶ ποιητῶν.

[39] Cf. Bowra 5: "Hellenistic and Roman writers regarded the elegiac as a mournful measure—Ovid's 'flebilis Elegeia'." Bowra notes that our earliest Greek elegiacs are military and convivial; he sees the contradiction, but does not explain it. Actually, "mournful measure" is not quite correct; when the Augustans, and particularly Horace, use the term *elegi* (always in the plural), the reference is either to the metrical form (*AP* 77; Ovid *Fasti* 2.3), or to complaints, especially lovers' complaints (*Carm.* 1.33.3). Disappointment and frustration, rather than death, provide the occasion for most elegi. The term "mournful," then, is yet another symptom of the muddle resulting from the combination of the data concerning elegos and elegiac.

[40] For Euripides's assumption that elegos = lament, cf. *Helen* 184ff. Page analyzes the metrics of Andromache's lament; the scarcity of dissyllabic metra, and the regularity of the caesura after the third longum, seem to him to point to a lyric (choral) model, as does the "Doric" dialect. He further speculates, less convincingly, that the uniqueness of the lament may be due to the performance of the *Andromache* in another city (cf. schol. 445 and 734); Page guesses Argos, ca. 421 B.C. Garzya 175–179 finds, against Bergk and Page, that the sequence is not threnodic, but an attempt to recapture the old νόμος αὐλῳδικός.

Callimachus (fr. 7.13 Pf.) and Apollonidas (*A.P.* 10.19.5) drew on
Euripides's experiment and put the equation on its head; the very
obscurity of the term ἔλεγος made it an attractive substitute for the
more humdrum (in their days, not earlier, as we shall see) ἐλεγεῖον.
This comes to be imitated by the Roman elegists. Hence there is nothing surprising about Pausanias (10.7.5) and *De musica* (8) confusing
the terms in reverse and writing ἐλεγεῖα where we should have expected
ἔλεγοι.[41]

One thing on which most sources seem to agree is that the
old elegos was a mournful tune.[42] This, in turn, may have encouraged
the close association of elegos with flute playing, because according to
one tradition the aulos was at first used exclusively for songs of mourning.[43] The consequences of this combination, along with the muddling
of the history of elegos and elegiac, have been disastrous. "Elegos meant
lament, . . . and the elegy was recited to the accompaniment of a flute
. . .".[44] Scholars have been hard put to it to square this dogma with the
fact that so much of early elegy is not lament, and so much aulos playing
is connected with occasions of a joyous or playful nature.[45] To cope
with this difficulty, some speak of "threnodic elegy" whenever they
wish to talk about that elegiac tradition which, they think, sprang
directly from the old elegos-lament.[46] But the qualification merely

[41] See Campbell 67.

[42] Cf. the evidence collected by Page. He also shows that the sources indicate
a readiness to think of elegos as accompanied by a string instrument. The assumption that
elegos was a kind of lament was held to be corroborated by various etymologies; cf. schol.
Aristoph. *Aves* 217 (p. 215 Duebner) who, apparently following Didymus, derives ἔλεγος from
ἒ ἒ λέγειν; and the modern discussions cited by H. Frisk, *Griechisches Etymologisches Woerterbuch*
fasc. 6 (1957) 486, *s.v.* ἔλεγος. For the ancient etymologies, see also Severyns (supra, n. 1)
99–101.

[43] Plutarch, *De E apud Delph.* ch. 21. Cf. also the passages cited by E. Reiner,
Die Rituelle Totenklage der Griechen (1938) 67–70, with notes. Reiner's distinction between
γόος (private, informal) and θρῆνος (public, stylized) does not concern us here.

[44] P. Friedlaender and H. B. Hoffleit, *Epigrammata* (1948) 66.

[45] See the evidence compiled by Huchzermeyer, and his conclusion p. 27.
For ἄναυλος in the sense of "sad," cf. Euripides *Phoen.* 791, and Campbell 66, who refers to
Miss Dale's note on Euripides *Alcestis* 447. "Unmusical" or "unfestive" are other possible
translations; but whatever the exact meaning of the negative adjective, it argues against a
necessary tie-up between the aulos and grief.

[46] Friedlaender (supra, n. 44) 68–69 speculates that Anacreon 100 and 102
D., and perhaps 101 D., were "specimens of that very genus of poetry which we sense in the
background of the elegiac epitaphs," i.e., poems "sung before the tomb." But surely ἐγόησε
in 100 D. makes that quite impossible. (Their authenticity is not here at issue). Cf. also Page
214, n. 2, on Archilochus 10 D.; he refers to Plutarch, *quom. adulesc. poet. aud.* 23B, who quotes
the poem.

serves to make the case for an original identity of elegos and elegiac even more precarious. Add to this that it is now generally becoming recognized that the earliest writers of elegiac couplets were Ionians, and that the genre itself, and its language, bear the marks of Ionian origin.[47] If Tyrtaeus was a Spartan who composed his elegiacs in (digamma-less) Ionic because elegiac was at that time an Ionian property, one may well wonder what is left of the connection between elegiac and the Peloponnesian elegos of Clonas, Sacadas, Echembrotus and their peers.

Nor does the use of elegiac couplets as funerary verse help to associate elegiac with the elegos-lament. There were funerary hexameters as well as elegiacs, and even some funerary iambics.[48] It is true that it was the elegiac couplet rather than hexameters which soon achieved a virtual monopoly on tomb markers and votive tablets. The reason for this is that the couplet is a closed system, better suited to the needs of a self-contained avowal than the open-ended hexameter or other stichic patterns. There is very little doubt, however, that funerary elegiac is a specialized adaptation of the heroic hexameter for lapidary use. Note the occasional difficulties encountered by epigraphers in their decipherment of early dedicatory inscriptions whose fragmentary state makes it difficult to determine whether they are written in hexameters or in elegiacs.[49]

Kenneth Dover has recently reminded us that the term ἐλεγεῖον for an elegiac couplet does not crop up before the fifth century.[50] Earlier writers usually prefer to use the same term, ἔπη, to desig-

---

[47] See Dover 193; also Bowra 43.

[48] See Peek 12; Friedlaender (supra, n. 44) 157–158. It is difficult to see a difference in kind between public elegiacs and public iambics; the iambs from Ptoion, *IG* I² 472 (Friedlaender no. 167), could equally well have been composed in elegiacs. I am doubtful, however, about Dover's suggestion, p. 189, that Archilochus did not regard his (personal) poems in elegiacs and in iambs as belonging to different genres, and that perhaps he used the word iamboi "with reference to all the forms of poem which he composed, their common characteristic being not their metre or language but the type of occasion for which they were composed—their social context, in fact."

[49] Perhaps the most interesting case is that of the spit-holders from Perachora with their fragments of writing which Wade-Gery attempted to reconstruct as an elegiac (H. Payne, *Perachora* I (1940) 262, 266; cf. also T. B. L. Webster, "Notes on the Writing of Early Greek Poetry," *Glotta* 38 (1960) 263, n. 1; while Miss L. H. Jeffery, *The Local Scripts of Archaic Greece* (1961) 124 arranges the remains so that they turn out to be two hexameters. There is little doubt that Miss Jeffery's reading is the more likely one.

[50] Dover 187ff.

nate either epic or elegiac verse,[51] and this usage continues to be found in Hellenistic and Graeco-Roman discussions.[52] In later treatments of material from the sixth and fifth centuries B.C., especially in Hephaestion and the metrical scholia, we sometimes come across the term ἐλεγεία in the place of the more usual ἐλεγεῖον. Whether Anacreon's ἐλεγεῖαι[53] were any different from the elegiacs he is known to have written may be doubted. Aristotle is the first to use the feminine form, but we cannot be sure that this form of the word in the text of the papyrus is not due to the fact that by the second century A.D. ἐλεγεῖον and ἐλεγεία had come to be used interchangeably.[54] One notice in Hephaestion deserves special attention (4.1–3 Consbr.): he remarks that Sophocles in his ἐλεγεῖαι could not accommodate the name "Archelaus" either in the ἔπος or in the ἐλεγεῖον, and so he wrote Ἀρχέλεως. There are two points here: (1) Sophocles wrote ἐλεγεῖαι; and (2) ἐλεγεῖον may mean the last line of an elegiac couplet.[55] It is, I think, a reasonable supposition that the term ἐλεγεία was introduced when an effort was made to distinguish between an elegiac poem as a whole, and the second line of an elegiac couplet, with its characteristic rhythm. For all we know this happened in the time of Aristotle, or perhaps even earlier. In any case we may assume that Sophocles's ἐλεγεῖαι were, simply, elegiac couplets, whether of the ordinary kind, or akin to those in the *Andromache*.[56]

The foregoing discussion will, I hope, have established the

---

[51] See Solon 2.2; Theognis 20; 22; Herodotus 5.113.

[52] Theocritus epigr. 21 calls Archilochus's elegiacs ἔπεα; I assume that he does so on the basis of an old terminology. In Hephaestion, who uses the term ἔπος to designate the hexameter, ἔπη may also refer to the combination of hexameter and pentameter; example: 65.11 Consbr. Hermesianax and Callimachus used the term πεντάμετρον to distinguish elegiacs from straight hexameters; cf. Wilamowitz 1913.298 note. Perhaps it was an awareness of the confusion between ἐλεγεῖον and ἔλεγος which prompted some to avoid using the term ἐλεγεῖον to refer to elegiacs. Conversely ἐλεγεῖον may be applied to a hexametric couplet; see *Vita Homeri* 36 (λς'); and Pherecrates *Cheiron* fr. 3.7–9 Meineke (153.7–9 Kock, Edmonds) features ἐλεγεῖον in the sense of "hexameter line."

[53] Hephaestion 5.2 Consbr. What he quotes is a hexameter, fr. 95 Bergk (55 Gentili). Hephaestion 9.10ff Consbr. also speaks of an ἐλεγεία εἰς Ἀλκιβιάδην, and cites two couplets from it.

[54] Aristotle, Ἀθ.πολ. 5.2. Severyns (supra, n. 1) 1.1 (1938) 209–211 provides specimens of variation in Photius, between ἐλεγεία and ἐλεγεῖον or ἐλεγεῖα. Clearly the scribes did not know any difference between the words, but tended to replace the feminine with the neuter.

[55] Cf. Hephaestion 51.21 Consbr., and Appendix Dionysiaca ch. 4 (= Hephaestion pp. 315–316 Consbr.). On the other hand, at 63.4–6 Consbr. ἐλεγεῖον clearly means elegiac couplet. ἔλεγος does not occur in Hephaestion.

[56] Cf. my remarks supra, p. 225.

following points, or at least made them probable. There is no hard evidence for a family tie between elegos and elegiac. Elegiac derives from epic verse, as early references to it prove.[57] There is no evidence that it was sung, and some evidence that it was not. There is no reason to assume any necessary connection between elegiac and the aulos.

That leaves us with one last question: how did the kind of poetry introduced by Tyrtaeus and Callinus and Mimnermus come, in a subsequent age, to be called by the name ἐλεγεῖα, a name which could not but remind people of the old elegos performed by Clonas and Sacadas and their fellow producers of nomoi and sung verse? In default of reliable information, we can only guess. Wilamowitz warns us[58] that it is not always warranted to think of the unit $-\smile\smile-\smile\smile-$ (Maas's D) as a hemiepes, i.e., as half of an epic period; he points to such passages as Aeschylus *Suppl.* 843–846 = 853–856,[59] where the unit appears serially; elsewhere it appears along with other metrical units. In another context Wilamowitz comments[60] that Pindar and Bacchylides (and, we may add, the playwrights) avoid the doubling of the unit within the period, while Stesichorus (219 PMG 2) and Simonidies (581 PMG 2) have it.[61] Actually Wilamowitz's distinction is hard to maintain; one occurrence each in Stesichorus and Simonides is no better than what we find in Pindar.[62] Wilamowitz, again, is inclined to believe that certain ancient hymns employed refrains of the metrical type $-\smile\smile-\smile\smile-$; and Page speculates that formulas of that type in Andromache's lament, such as ὤμοι ἐγὼ μελέα and καὶ τὸν ἐμὸν μελέας may be in imitation of

---

[57] See Wilamowitz 1913.291: "Von einem elegischen Stile der Griechen zu reden, ist ein Unding." "Euphorion, der Nachtreter des Kallimachos, macht nur Hexameter." It would take a bold man to show that the sentiments expressed, or the mood, of Theocritus 8.33–60, a sequence of elegiacs, differ appreciably from what is found in comparable hexameter passages.

[58] Wilamowitz 1921.101; his remarks assume his own text of Aeschylus, which posits brevis in longo, hence disqualifies the sequence from consideration as double hemiepes.

[59] Cf. also Euripides *Troad.* 1094–1098 = 1112–1116; Alcestis 590–591 = 599–600 where, however, the rhythm of the strophe obscures the pattern.

[60] Wilamowitz 1921.432.

[61] Cf. also Alcman 39.2–3 PMG.

[62] Note such prominent exceptions as *Ol.* 13.17 = 40 = 63 etc.; also *Paean* 5.41–42 = 47–48; cf. Snell[6] II 166. It should be noted that Simonides does not use DD in 531 PMG, the encomium on the victims of Thermopylae, where we might have expected it to occur. In fact none of the texts cited by Reiner (supra, n. 43), i.e., laments attributed to lyric writers, exhibit the pattern.

refrains in traditional dirges.[63] Could it be that fifth-century choral composers disdained the doubling of this unit because they felt that the ascendancy of non-musical elegiac had disqualified the sequence for use in song?[64] Be that as it may, the process of displacement and labeling may be pictured as follows. To begin with, there was the elegos, at home in the Peloponnesus, probably a species of nomos, that is, astrophic and either for solo instrument or for voice and accompaniment. At the time when the elegos was receding in prominence, that is, in the course of the sixth century, elegiac verse from Ionia, at first merely an extention of epic and called ἔπη, happened to emerge into prominence; and when it had become entrenched as one of the principal varieties of spoken verse, somebody applied to it the name ἐλεγεία or ἐλεγεῖον, perhaps because the clash of longa in the middle of the second line of the couplet reminded the nomenclator of similar things in lyrics with which he was familiar, and which he took to represent the ancient elegos. On this admittedly hypothetical assumption—though we should not forget that the coining of metrical terms such as *Asclepiadean* and *Adonic* and *lecythion* is a notoriously willful business—the connection between elegiac and elegos would be one of nomenclature, of lexical transfer, rather than of natural affinity or even filiation. There are parallels in the history of modern poetry. The humanist sonnet, to take one instance, has little to do with the folk tune whose name was put under obligation to label the highly sophisticated, *and* recited, poems of the Italian masters.[65] The precise details of the appropriation of the Provencal term are no longer discoverable. But no one claims that the sonnets of Giacomo de Lentino, or Guittone di Arezzo, were written

[63] Wilamowitz 1921.95; Page 219.

[64] E. Fraenkel, "Lyrische Daktylen" (*Kleine Beitraege zur klassischen Philologie* 1 [1964] 165–233; reprint of his 1918 article in *RhM*) has nothing on double hemiepes. Heliodorus 3.2 has a hymn to Thetis which consists of fifteen consecutive pentameters. I assume that this is merely a prose writer's attempt to write, and rival, heroic lyric.

[65] Modern scholars have generally returned to Du Bellay's view that the sonnet is a learned Italian invention, rather than of Provencal, Northern French, or even Arabic ancestry. See W. Moench, *Das Sonett: Gestalt und Geschichte* (1955) 267–268; also E. H. Wilkins, "The Invention of the Sonnet," *Modern Philology* 13 (1915) 463–494, reprinted in a revised form in W.'s *The Invention of the Sonnet and other Studies in Italian Literature* (1959) 11–39. The section disproving the nineteenth-century notion of a popular origin of the sonnet is omitted from the revised version, for the reason that nobody believes it any more. "It is now agreed that the sonnet was an artistic invention, not a popular growth." The theory of a popular growth had been based almost exclusively on the circumstance that the term 'sonet' (diminutive of 'so') derives from Provencal folk culture; it means "sound," "lay," "song."

to be sung, to the accompaniment of rustic fiddles or bagpipes, or even to that of more courtly instruments.[66] And we may be sure that Shakespeare's "Why is my verse so barren of new pride" is not the product of a continuous tradition which has its roots in country medleys. Terms have a way of being stolen, or misapplied, as Theognis knew to his sorrow.

University of California
Berkeley

---

[66] Moench (supra, n. 65) 41 considers it a paradox that sonnets came to be set to music, particularly by the Dutch and Italian polyphonists. In the Renaissance we distinguish between songs composed to be sung (ballads, madrigals, etc.), and poems which were set to music after first having been published without music, i.e., poems to be recited. In antiquity, as far as we can tell, poems were composed for singing or for recitation. The idea of singing a poem that was not originally written for singing voice seems to be foreign to the ancient tradition.

14

Tribal Boundary Markers From Corinth

The scarcity of stone inscriptions from the Archaic, Classical, and Hellenistic periods at Corinth is notorious. Monumental inscriptions of a sacred or official nature seem very seldom to have been erected in the city before the destruction of 146 B.C.,[1] and even private inscribed grave markers are rare.[2] Extensive excavation in the central area of the Greek city has shown that this vacuum is not a product of chance; and attempts to postulate the widespread use of bronze, clay, or wood for state documents are not convincing.[3] On the other hand painted and incised texts occur with considerable frequency on archaic Corinthian vases[4] and show that a low level of literacy need not be assumed.

In view of this situation, all the more importance is attached to the recent discovery of two poros blocks inscribed with

---

[1] For the statistics see S. Dow, *HSCP* 53 (1942) 113–119; J. H. Kent, *Corinth* VIII, Part 3, *The Inscriptions* 1926–1950 (Princeton 1966) 1–2. Since 1950 twenty-six additional inscriptions from the Greek period have been found at Corinth, including the pieces published here.

[2] From Corinth itself only nine inscribed grave markers have been published which antedate the Roman destruction. No inscribed stelai were found with the 375 graves of the period 625–200 B.C. in the large North Cemetery; see *Corinth* XIII (Princeton 1964) 66, 71, n. 1. For a series of uninscribed boundary markers from the Anaploga area see H. S. Robinson, 'Αρχ. Δελτίον 19 (1964) Χρονικά, p. 101.

[3] For these see Kent, *loc. cit.* (supra, n. 1); L. Robert, *REG* 79 (1966) 735–736.

[4] See the collections in *IG* IV 210–353; H. Payne, *Necrocorinthia* (Oxford 1931) 158–169; T. J. Dunbabin, *Perachora* II (Oxford 1962) 393–400.

classical Corinthian texts of an official nature.[5] Moreover, both monuments preserve a complete text, which is another rarity among the
inscriptions *ante* 146 B.C.[6] In both cases the letters are large, carefully cut,
and perfectly legible, but the initial excitement of this discovery was
quickly tempered by the fact that at first reading neither of the new
texts made sense. Further study has shown, however, that not only are
these inscriptions among the earliest state documents from Corinth,
but they also provide important new evidence for the tribal structure
and the constitution of the city in the Classical period. Furthermore,
these texts now enable us to explain another published inscription
which had, understandably, baffled its first editor.

Corinth Inventory I 2562 (plate 1:1). Found in November 1960 lying
on the surface of a ploughed field northeast of the Amphitheatre, within
the circuit of the city wall. The block was ca. 42 m. west of the city
wall. Grid reference: T15/d8 on the Corinth Topographical Survey
Map.[7]

        Soft, light brown poros. Broken at left and at bottom; all
other sides preserved. The top surface is dressed but is slightly concave.
Back smoothly dressed. Wide chisel marks are visible on all preserved
surfaces. The left side of the inscribed face has been damaged by a long,
deep cut (from a plough?) extending from below line 2 to the top of the
block.

Height, 0.44 m.	Height of letters, 0.08–0.105 m.
Width, 0.315 m.	Depth of letters, 0.01–0.015 m.
Thickness, 0.237 m.	*ΣTOIX*

$$\Lambda \: B \: \overset{.}{\Pi} \quad \leftarrow$$
$$H \: B \: N \quad \leftarrow$$

Line 1: *Λεπ*. Of the last letter there remains only part of a
vertical stroke, 0.07 m. in height, which falls a little to the right of

[5] We owe the discovery of these inscriptions to the alertness of the Guards
at the Corinth Museum, Evangelos Papapsomas and Spyridon Marinos. I am grateful to both
for visiting the finding-places of the stones with me and for their assistance while I was
studying the stones in the museum.

[6] Only seven complete Greek texts antedating 146 B.C. are published in
Corinth VIII, Parts 1 and 3. I cannot understand Kent's statement (*loc. cit.*, supra, n. 1) that
in his publication "only two texts (Nos. 10 and 17), both of them too brief to yield any
information, . . . survive complete." Actually four Greek texts in his publication are completely preserved (Nos. 1, 8, 14, and 16), whereas both 10 and 17 are fragmentary.

[7] For a description of this new map see J. R. Wiseman, *Hesperia* 36 (1967)
14, n. 9.

center when lined up with the nu directly below it. There is no trace of a joining stroke; the bottom of the vertical is not sufficiently preserved to preclude a joining stroke at this point. Pi is, of course, only one of several possible readings; see infra, p. 237.

Line 2: *heν*. Within the area above the horizontal and between the two vertical strokes of *H* there are two deep, circular holes, the upper one larger and deeper than the lower. Other similar pockmarks on the stone show that these two holes were not intentionally cut in this position. Although the cut has removed part of its left vertical, there is no doubt that the final letter is nu.

Corinth Inventory I 2624 (plate 1:2). Found on January 26, 1965, reused upside down as a boundary marker at the north edge of the same field as I 2562. Postion ca. 200 m. north of I 2562 at grid reference T14/e7. The block was ca. 20 m. west of the city wall.

Soft, light brown poros. Preserved on all sides and top; bottom broken away. There are a few cuts and gashes on the left side and the inscribed face. The surface is more smoothly dressed than I 2562 but the same wide chisel marks are present. Top flat.

Height, 0.445 m.	Height of letters, 0.07–0.105 m.
Width, 0.295 m.	Depth of letters, ca. 0.01 m.
Thickness, 0.225 m.	*ΣTOIX*

$$\Sigma \mid \Pi \quad \leftarrow$$

$$H \, B \, N \quad \leftarrow$$

Line 1: The ends of both the central strokes of sigma are preserved, and they do not join each other.

Line 2: The two loops of the epsilon join the central portion of the vertical at two different places. As in the sigma of line 1, this may have been a precaution against the chipping away of the stone at the point where these deeply cut strokes would have met. On the left lateral face, at the level of line 2 and near the right edge, is a delta, ca. 0.065 m. in height (plate 2:1). The bottom stroke is not horizontal. This letter is less deeply inscribed than the others and its relation to the text on the inscribed face is not clear.

The disposition of the texts into two retrograde lines of three letters each, plus the size and the depth of the letters, make virtually certain a connection between our two new inscriptions and another block first published by J. H. Kent in *Corinth* VIII, Part 3, no. 8. For convenience I repeat the physical description of the stone.

Corinth Inventory I 2184 (plate 2:2). Found in February 1934 in an area called Pigadhakia, which lies high up on the eastern slope of Acrocorinth above the chapel of St. George and within the circuit of the east city wall.[8] The block was found resting on top of the city wall.

Soft, light brown poros similar to I 2562 and I 2624 but a little lighter in color.[9] All sides preserved, including the bottom, where wide chisel marks make it clear that this is an original surface. These strokes are also conspicuous on the two lateral surfaces. The space occupied by the inscription is fairly smooth but below line 2 the surface is rough and projects above the level of the inscribed portion. Kent's description of the back as "smooth" is rather misleading; it is badly weathered and eroded with perhaps little of the original surface still intact.

Height, 0.353 m.	Height of letters, 0.063–0.083 m.
Width, 0.318 m.	Diameter of omicron, 0.05 m.
Thickness, 0.167 m. (left)	Depth of letters, 0.01 m.
0.176 m. (right)	*ΣΤΟΙΧ*

ΣΥϜ ←

ΔΥΟ ←

Line 1: On the analogy of line 1 of I 2624 I would read the first letter as sigma, not Corinthian epichoric iota. Kent correctly observed that the round, shallow hole between the first two letters antedates the lettering. There are no traces of strokes anywhere on the circumference of this hollow, nor does it cut into any of the preserved letters on the stone. Moreover, the first letter in line 1 was clearly squeezed into the space between the hollow and the left edge of the stone.

These three inscriptions have enough features in common to be considered contemporary documents erected to serve similar, if not identical purposes. This much can be established from the physical

---

[8] Kent gives this as the provenance of the stone on p. 4 but on p. 17, n. 1, he says that it comes from Krommyon. The provenance given on p. 4 agrees with that in the Corinth inventory book and it has been verified for me by D. Papaioannou, who found the stone, and by G. Kachros who was Head Guard in the Corinth Museum when the block was brought in.

[9] Not "sandstone" as it is described by Kent.

facts alone: the size and material of the blocks; the similar tooling on the finished surfaces; the character, size, and depth of the lettering; the direction of the lines and the same number of letters arranged in identical manner. Even the finding-places all share a close proximity to the eastern line of the classical fortification wall.

By themselves, however, the unpromising, cryptic texts do not help to determine with any precision how they are related to one another. The meaning of the texts can only be deciphered if we find the proper key; without it, the discovery of more stones of this type might not lead us any closer to a solution.

Luckily the key exists in an inscription on marble found on August 3, 1915, near the southern side of the agora[10] (plate 2:3). The text, which the editors have dated by letter forms to ca. 350–300 B.C., is a list of names, with patronymics, arranged in groups of irregular lengths under abbreviated rubrics. The rubrics, which consist of two letters followed by a short horizontal bar or "dash" with a single letter after it, are as follows: $ΣΙ–Π$, $ΛΕ–Ε$, $ΛΕ–Π$, $ΚΥ–F$. We owe the identification of these rubrics as abbreviations of the Corinthian tribe names to an acute observation of Hiller von Gärtringen,[11] which was fully worked out by S. Dow.[12] The latter's improved text and epigraphical commentary have been the starting point for subsequent discussion of this inscription, and his suggestion that the list records the dead in battle is undoubtedly correct.[13] The connection between these rubrics and the first line on each of the three poros blocks is evident. Like the rubrics, line 1 in each case contains three letters. In two of the poros inscriptions the tribal abbreviations are paralleled on I 734, viz. $ΣΙ$ and $ΛΕ$. In all of the poros inscriptions the letters following these abbreviations correspond, or can be restored as corresponding, to the single letters which follow the dash in the casualty list, i.e. E, F, and $Π$. So far nothing new. But it would be too coincidental to expect perfect correspondence between the incomplete list of tribes on I 734 and the three newly discovered texts; hence, the occurrence of $ΣΥ$ on I 2184. Abbrevia-

[10] Corinth Inventory I 734. See *Corinth* VIII, Part 1, no. 11, superseded by S. Dow, *HSCP* 53 (1942) 90–106.

[11] *Philologische Wochenschriften*, 52 (1932) 362.

[12] *Loc. cit.* (supra, n. 10).

[13] For other suggestions see R. G. Kent, *AJA* 36 (1932) 369; W. P. Wallace, *Hesperia* 16 (1947) 119, n. 14; L. Robert, *Hellenica* 5 (1948) 12–13. The latter publishes a decree of Phlius in which the abbreviation $ΑΣ$ F appears to designate one of the small groups of ἡμιόγδοοι into which the citizens of this state were enrolled.

tions of only three tribes appear in the fragmentary casualty list, although we know that there were eight tribes in the Greek city.[14] New abbreviations, like ΣY, are, therefore, to be expected and welcomed. Accordingly, we now know the abbreviated titles of half of the Corinthian tribes, ΣI, ΛE, KY, and ΣY, but we are no closer to recovering the full names of these groups. Only one name is known: that of the $KY[\nu\acute{o}\phi\alpha\lambda\omicron\iota]$, Hesychius, s.v.[15]

Hiller and Dow made the plausible suggestion that the third letter in the rubrics of I 734 represented a division of each tribe. Again, it is not known what these divisions were, since we have only the initial letter of the word in each case. We do not even know how many such divisions there were in each tribe, but on the basis of our four documents it is certain that there were at least three, i.e. E, F, and Π groups. The appearance of digamma as a tribal division in I 2184 confirms the reading of $KY\text{-}F$ on I 734. This had been emended to $KY\text{-}E$ by Dow in order to conform to a bipartite division of each rubric into an E and a Π group. It now seems more likely that each tribe was divided into an E group, an F group, and a Π group at least. The eight tribes at Corinth are not to be reconstructed by dividing each of four tribes into two sections.

For the interpretation of the second line of the three poros inscriptions no independent key exists. It is conceivable that each letter is an abbreviation of a word, or that, following the pattern of the first lines, the first two letters form one abbreviation and the last letters another. This seems far fetched in the light of the fact that in all cases the second line contains a complete word: $\H{\epsilon}\nu$ in I 2562 and I 2624 and $\delta\acute{\upsilon}o$ in I 2184. We are still not informed what "one" and "two" mean and it is perhaps surprising, if they denote objects in a numbered series, that the terms $\pi\rho\hat{\omega}\tau\omicron\varsigma$ and $\delta\epsilon\acute{\upsilon}\tau\epsilon\rho\omicron\varsigma$ were not used. Whatever is designated by "one," it is clear that two tribes, or two divisions of two tribes, may be said to share it in some way. This interpretation is perhaps strengthened by the proximity of the finding-places of these two monuments. We might even suppose that together with $\Sigma Y\text{-}F$ another division of a fourth tribe shared term "two," and that this

---

14 Suda Lexicon, Photios, s.v. $\pi\acute{\alpha}\nu\tau\alpha$ $\dot{o}\kappa\tau\acute{\omega}$, see infra, p. 241.

15 For speculation on the meaning of this title see H. Lewy, *Zeitschrift für Vergleichende Sprachforschung* 59 (1932) 182; C. Lecrivain, *Daremberg-Saglio* 3.873, s.v. Kynophaloi; J. Öhler, *RE*, s.v. $Kυν\acute{o}φαλοι$; L. Whibley, *Greek Oligarchies* (Cambridge 1913) 182, n. 6; J. G. O'Neill, *Ancient Corinth* (Baltimore 1930) 95; S. Dow, *loc. cit.* (supra, n. 10) the best discussion; E. Will, *Korinthiaka* (Paris 1955) 293.

fact was recorded on a monument similar to and placed near I 2184. The fact that the object represented by the numbers in line 2 was shared by two divisions of two tribes suggests that the stones served as boundary markers. This theory finds further support in the large, deeply cut letters, which can be read at a considerable distance. The low projection of I 2184 above the ground is also best explained on this basis.[16] In the absence of a satisfactory restoration to explain line 2, we can only hope for some suggestion as to the purpose of these boundary markers from the date and from the finding-places of the three stones.

The only dating criteria for the three poros inscriptions are the letter forms, which show a curious mixture of epichoric Corinthian and later letters. Epsilon is represented on the same stone by both ϐ and B, and the context makes it clear, if we read the line as Λε and cite the parallel of the rubric ΛE on the fourth-century casualty list, that both signs are used to designate short e. Sigma has already replaced san and iota has the single vertical stroke. The aspirate, of open form, and digamma are both used. Taken together, these characteristics of the script, when examined in the light of L. H. Jeffery's study of the Corinthian epichoric inscriptions,[17] point to a date about the middle of the fifth century. The retrograde direction of the lines does not afford any chronological evidence; it may, however, have been closely related to the function and position of the stones. These are apparently the earliest examples of the stoichedon style on stone at Corinth, but in the absence of a large body of comparative material it is difficult to assign significance to this fact.

Arguments based upon the finding-places of ancient inscriptions are often misleading. It is a striking fact, however, that all three of the poros boundary markers turned up in close proximity to the line of the eastern city wall. It could be that some of the contiguous districts of the ancient city extended up as far as the wall and that the dividing lines between them were marked at the point where they met the wall.[18] It might also be suggested that the stones are to be tied more closely to the function of the fortification walls themselves, and this

[16] Only about 0.23 m. of this block would have projected above the surface of the ground.

[17] *The Local Scripts of Archaic Greece* (Oxford 1961) 114–132.

[18] If I 2184, however, was found anywhere near its original position, we should have to suppose a boundary line which falls in a very precipitous and sparsely inhabited section of the city. The line might have followed the crest of the long ridge which slopes down into the plain below the chapel of St. George, but the territory to the west of this line would

suggestion gains some support from the coincidence in date between the construction of the walls and the inscribing of the boundary markers.[19] With the acquisition of the mighty circuit wall in the first half of the fifth century, Corinth was also faced with the task of manning the new line. In the fourth century, for purposes of casualty lists, the Corinthian army was divided into tribes, each of which seems to have been sub-divided further into E, F, and Π groups.[20] It is not unreasonable to suggest that the defense of the city walls in the previous century was originally assigned to the army on the basis of the same tribal divisions and subdivisions. The numbers in line 2 of the boundary markers could perhaps have represented sections of the wall which were to be guarded by the several tribal contingents, or it may be that they mark distances along the wall for which the tribal divisions were responsible, viz. ἐν στάδιον, δύο στάδια.[21]

As we have seen, the four documents under discussion provide evidence of a subdivision of the Corinthian tribes into at least three component groups. It may be mere chance that only three such subdivisions are as yet known; a fourth and a fifth group could be dis-covered tomorrow. Until such a discovery, however, it is legitimate to speculate on the significance of a tripartite division of the Corinthian tribes. The subdivisions are designated by a single letter only; the Corinthians knew without additional letters what each abbreviation meant. It is very unlikely that the single letters stood for demes, since the abbreviation is too short to prevent ambiguity[22] and it is clear that the group designated for example by E was present in at least two, and

fall in the very narrow space between the Pigadhakia ridge and the steep eastern slopes of Acrocorinth.

[19] For the date of the original construction of the city walls of Corinth see R. Carpenter, *Corinth* III, Part 2 (Cambridge, Mass. 1936) 82–83, 115–126. A date in the fourth century is conjectured for most sections of the walls by R. Scranton, *Greek Walls* (Cambridge, Mass. 1941) 56–57, 85–88, 132–133, but the west wall, through the Potters' Quarter, must be at least as early as the last quarter of the fifth century and possibly earlier. See A. N. Stillwell, *Corinth* XV, Part 1 (Princeton 1948) 53–62.

[20] That no tribe on the casualty list shows all three divisions is probably due to the fragmentary state of the text and the fact that no casualties from ΛE–F were reported on this particular occasion.

[21] I am indebted to O. Broneer for this suggestion. There is also the possi-bility—though it seems to me remote—that ἔν and δύο mark a lower level of organization within the tribal subdivision. Cf. the numbered divisions of the Chian tribes, W. G. Forrest *BSA* 55 (1960) 174–175.

[22] For instance between $\Pi[ε\rhoα\hat{\iota}ον]$ and $\Pi[έ\tau\rhoα]$. Deme abbreviations are always long enough to avoid ambiguity; cf. the Athenian bouleutic lists and the lists from Eretria discussed by W. P. Wallace, *loc. cit.* (supra, n. 13). The same argument would apply

probably in all eight of the Corinthian tribes. W. P. Wallace,[23] following Dow's emended division of each tribe into E and Π groups, suggested that these letters might designate military divisions such as 'E[πίλεκτοι] and Π[ελτασταί]. To accommodate this theory to the new texts we should have to postulate a third military division which could be abbreviated by F.

It is also possible to see in the E, F, and Π designations a tripartite division more closely related to the civic organization of Corinth and the Corinthia, viz. a trittys arrangement. On the basis of our four documents we could suggest that each Corinthian tribe contained three trittyes; that the trittyes were themselves divided into three classes, E, F, and Π categories; and that each tribe contained one trittys from each category. Such an arrangement, which echoes the Athenian Kleisthenic constitution, is not contradicted by the meager evidence we have for the constitution of the city before 146 b.c.[24] In the organization of the Corinthian government the number eight was so important that a saying "πάντα ὀκτώ" grew up about it.[25] In the period after the fall of the Kypselids there were eight chief magistrates, who were called Probouloi, and the Boule itself consisted of eighty members.[26] If, as is reasonable, each tribe elected one Proboulos, and these officials were themselves members of the Boule, the remaining seventy-two Bouleutai could have been selected on the basis of nine from each tribe, which is exactly the number given by Nikolaos Damaskenos in the only passage we have about the selection of the Boule. Equal representation in the

to phratry or gene abbreviations. Perhaps relevant here are the abbreviations—too numerous to be tribes—in the archives of the temple of Zeus at Lokroi Epizephyrioi; A. De Franciscis, *Klearchos* 1 (1961) 17–41; 2 (1962) 66–93; 4 (1964) 73–95.

23 See supra, n. 13.

24 For a parallel series of boundary markers in which trittyes were distinguished, see the inscriptions from Peiraieus and Athens in *IG* I2 883–885, 897–901; *SEG* 21.108–113.

25 See supra, n. 14.

26 Nikolaos Damaskenos, Fr. 60 (Jacoby): αὐτὸς (sc. ὁ δῆμος) δὲ παραχρῆμα κατεστήσατο πολιτείαν τοιάνδε· μίαν μὲν ὀκτάδα προβούλων ἐποίησεν, ἐκ δὲ τῶν λοιπῶν βουλὴν κατέλεξεν ἀνδρῶν θ̄. The most frequently cited emendation for the numeral θ̄ is ō but E. Will, *op. cit.* (supra, n. 15) p. 614, has demonstrated that this contradicts the first part of the sentence, which shows that there were eight Probouloi. Following a suggestion of G. Busolt, *Griechische Geschichte* I2 (Gotha 1893) 658, n. 1, Will suggests: Βουλὴν κατέλεξεν ἀνδρῶν θ̄ ⟨ἐκ φυλῆς ἑκάστης⟩, which has the advantage of retaining the numeral and making sense of it. For other discussions see E. Wilisch, *Beiträge zur Inneren Geschichte des Alten Korinth* (Zittau 1887) 9–18; H. Lutz, *CR* 10 (1896) 418–419; E. Szanto, "Die Griechischen Phylen," *SB Wien*, 1901, no. 5, 16–17; G. Busolt, *Griechische Staatskunde* I (Munich 1920) 131, n. 5; 363, n. 4; Whibley (supra, n. 15) 164, n. 2.

242   Ronald S. Stroud

Boule could have been obtained by having each of the twenty-four trittyes elect three members. Speculation about the terms represented by *E*, *F*, and *Π* is risky and until more evidence is secured, the exact designations may not be known, but if the trittyes were grouped, as in Attica, with regional representation as one of the controlling factors, the entire Corinthia may have been divided geographically into twenty-four trittyes which were equally distributed among the eight tribes. Of the three groups of trittyes, one would surely have contained those from the area of the city itself. There may be an echo of this division of the city into eight trittyes in the statement preserved in the Suda Lexicon, *s.v. πάντα ὀκτώ: Ἀλήτης κατὰ χρησμὸν τοὺς Κορινθίους συνοικίζων ὀκτὼ φυλὰς ἐποίησε τοὺς πολίτας καὶ ὀκτὼ μέρη τὴν πόλιν.* The ascription of the synoikismos to the legendary Aletes is not to be taken seriously, but the details of the tribal organization are compatible with the account of Nikolaos Damaskenos. A convenient dividing line between the other two groups of trittyes might perhaps have been the Isthmos. Each tribe might then have contained one trittys from the city, one from north of the Isthmos, and a third from the territory south of the Isthmos. Each trittys may have been formed by a number of demes or villages, or perhaps in some cases by a single large town, but it is futile to speculate further. The names of only a few of the Corinthian towns are known, and in the absence of a thorough topographical survey of the entire Corinthia,[27] we do not know how many potential deme or village sites there are within the ancient province, in addition to familiar sites such as Krommyon, Tenea, Perachora, etc.

As to the validity of these constitutional speculations we can make no solid claims. The evidence is still too slight and theorizing of this sort only points up how little we know about the organization of the Corinthian state in the Classical period. It is encouraging, however, to find that new evidence of an official nature can turn up even at a site where inscriptions of this type are so rare.[28]

University of California
Berkeley

[27] The brief treatment of this subject in *Corinth* I, Part 1 (Cambridge, Mass. 1932) 18–114 is greatly in need of revision and amplification.

[28] For permission to publish these inscriptions I am grateful to the former Director of the Corinth Excavations, H. S. Robinson. For helpful discussions I wish also to thank O. Broneer, S. Dow, C. N. Edmonson, L. H. Jeffery, H. von Raits, and C. K. Williams. The Publications Committee of the American School of Classical Studies has kindly permitted me to present this new material here.

Plate 2   Stroud

2. I 2184.

1. Left side, I 2624.

3. I 734.